AN INVITATION TO

CRITICAL SOCIOLOGY

Involvement, Criticism, Exploration

Donald A. Hansen

THE FREE PRESS
A Division of Macmillan Publishing Co., Inc.
NEW YORK

Collier Macmillan Publishers
LONDON

The Free Press
A Division of Macmillan Publishing Co., Inc.
866 Third Avenue, New York, N.Y. 10022

Collier Macmillan Canada, Ltd.

Library of Congress Catalog Card Number: 75-5234

Printed in the United States of America

printing number

   3 4 5 6 7 8 9 10

Library of Congress Cataloging in Publication Data

Hansen, Donald A
  An invitation to critical sociology.

  Bibliography: p.
  Includes index.
  1. Sociology. 2. Social psychology.
3. Mead, Herbert, 1863-1931. 4. Marx, Karl, 1818-
1883. 5. Weber, Max, 1864-1920. I. Title.
HM24.H38   301   75-5234
ISBN 0-02-913750-0

FOR GEORGE AND NA
—Who Care

Contents

Preface

Some time ago, exploring the passageways of a Norwegian steamer as it set sail for Oslo, I ran across a young Scotsman, a farmer from near Edinburgh. We soon found enough in common to make our differences compelling. What did I do for a living, he wanted to know. I told him I was a sociologist; he nodded, "Ah, you're a professor then." He seemed about to say more, but just then the ship cleared its quiet harbor and our conversation turned to matters of wind and wave, matters that soon took us to the railings of the leeward deck. It was not until much later that he came back to what he had wanted to say: "I wouldn't want you to think I'm dumb, but would you mind telling me—what is sociology?"

I did not think he was dumb. In fact, after a few years in Berkeley I was not sure I knew the answer. But it felt good to be asked, for as far as I could remember I hadn't heard the question from anyone over fifteen and under forty in over five years. In America today, most of us seem to reach voting age with a fairly clear image of what sociologists do. They are seen running around taking polls, asking blacks about problems of living in "the ghetto," probing teenagers about their sex lives and drugs and ideals, discussing the problems of the failing American family. Some sit around bars to see how sex is sold; some worry and write about the Mafia, political campaigns, and other criminal things. Others are at work exposing the evils of prisons and mental hospitals. A few write of more global themes of alienation, ideologies, and identity crises; and another few launch massive studies on massive social problems such as economic inequality and educational opportunities—studies that quickly generate debate and more studies.

Sociologists, in fact, fit such images. They do such things, and for the most part such things are useful, at times highly valuable things to do. But the images do not fit sociology—or, more accurately, they do not exhaust the practices and potentials of sociology. There is far more to the enterprise and its current promise than is suggested by these popular views.

The inadequacies of popular images of sociology may be in part the fault of sociologists themselves. For in America sociologists specialize, and it is their specialities that generate the reports that find their ways into the newspapers and other popular media. Most departments of sociology in major universities offer local and even cosmopolitan specialists in a sociology of deviance, of crime and delinquency, of social stratification, of the family, of education, along with urban sociology, social theory, social change, and political sociology. Some departments boast even other specialties: medical sociology, economic sociology, a sociology of literature, a sociology of art, a sociology of knowledge, and even a sociology of music. On the horizon appears to be a sociology of just about everything: of revolution, of dentistry, of mass communication, and, of course, a sociology of sociology.

Just as the boundary lines between related disciplines—sociology, economics, psychology, political science, anthropology, social ecology, geography—are in some ways useful, so the specializations of sociology have been useful. They allow researchers to narrow and sharpen their foci and thereby develop more effective research tools. But the boundaries have also partially blinded the specialists and, even more unfortunately, have frustrated the interchange of ideas across the specializations.

When specialists enter the classroom, they often bring with them unspoken understandings of how their special topics relate to other topics and to "the big picture." Almost as often, they leave the same way—with their understanding unspoken. Their students, bored and frustrated, might charge that the research subject has taken control, that their instructors are blind to what they are doing and saying, that they have become Frankensteins of social research.

That charge often is unfair. The scholar may recognize the larger implications and relevancies that make even remote subjects valuable as well as compelling. Indeed, he or she may recognize them too well, to the point that they have become self-obvious. There is no need to justify the subject, the specialist feels, for it justifies itself. Pressed to identify its pertinence to the larger world, the instructor may have to hesitate, to recapture ideas now implicit in the specialization, to retramp paths traveled long ago to current concerns.

Students who come to that sociologist's classroom—unlike their counterparts a few decades ago—usually bring their own unspoken understanding of sociology. Their knowledge may not be faulty, but often it is fragmented and incomplete. They are little aided by most textbooks, for even introductory texts closely reflect the specializations of American sociology. It is hardly surprising that many students come away from their first course, and many even from a major in sociology, with much the same basic incomplete perspective on sociology that they brought with them from high school.

To be sure, their images of sociology may be elaborated with all sorts of facts, ideas, and methodological paraphernalia. But lacking the informing perspectives held by their instructors and the writers of their textbooks, the students "know" a sociology that is fragmented and lifeless. Worst of all, it may even be a sociology that blinds them to one of the most fundamental lessons their instructors may have learned long ago from sociology: that in the effort to understand ourselves and our times, things seemingly remote and long past can be as important as things immediate and close at hand.

Hence the title of this book. It is meant to invite not a discovery of sociology—for that has probably already been made—but a rediscovery. In the invitation, I claim no god-sent message or special knowledge that is not available to other sociologists. If I have done anything unusual, perhaps it is simply to offer an alternative to the traditional ways of telling others how sociology might be a useful and compelling enterprise.

STILL, it is tempting to read more into the title, suggesting that it also carries a challenge to sociology itself. It is no accident that I chose Marx, Weber, and Mead to display some of the sweep and depth that might be found in social inquiry. It seems to me that these social theorists point a way to images of the individual and society that might in many ways be appropriate to the sort of inquiry needed in our rapidly transforming society. I do not see such images as replacements for the methods and theories of contemporary sociology, but as complements, as informing perspectives, perhaps as correctives to the consensual, normative images of the individual and society that dominate and restrict American social thought today.

The challenges of recent radicalism and the continuing search for communal alternatives in recent years have displayed a fundamental rift in the images of the individual and society that inform our political and economic actions and which support and challenge our social order. That rift is also seen in the images of the individual and society that inform our sociology and social inquiries. The dominant "schools" of American sociology continue to embrace "normative" images, emphasizing consensus, cohesion, and the social bond—to the comparative neglect of questions of conflict, coercion, negotiation, and change.

This does not mean that the work of those who embrace or assume normative images is necessarily dangerous or even useless. An indictment could be made on these points, of course, but I believe that it would be misplaced. To be sure, many examples of triviality and costly misguidance can be pulled from the literature of and about recent sociology. But so too can examples of more positive contributions, both to a growing awareness of the individual and society and also to social and political programs that would combat the injustice and other troubles of our times.

It would be a costly error to turn our backs on the accumulated knowledge or even on the established perspectives of contemporary sociology. Such knowledge and perspectives are hard won, and the help they might offer is vitally needed in the efforts to meet the challenges of life in our transforming society. But in using these fruits of modern sociology, we must take care that they do not limit our vision and hobble our imaginations or blind us to the political effects of what we say and do.

What is needed is not the rejection of established tools of contemporary sociology. Rather, what may be needed is a "retooling," above all in a recognition of the organizational and existential dialectics of human life. To be sure, efforts have been made to develop models of social order and change that build from such dialectic awareness— notably in the theories of "institutionalization" pursued by George

Zollschan[1] and in Walter Buckley's efforts to identify the innovative thrusts of individual action in systems theory.[2] These represent, I believe, the beginnings of a search for less quantitative, less mechanistic, less normative approaches to social inquiry, that go beyond analyses based in the extensional logic of Western traditions. But they also represent only a beginning.

The retooling demands a far more intense grappling with the meaning of meaning, the thrusts of human actions, the consequences of human suffering, striving, doing. It demands going beyond such concerns to consider the varieties of human motivation, attending not only to rational choice but also to the arational, the emotional, even the mystical. This book, linking the "classical" theories of Marx, Weber, and Mead, attempts to suggest at least some directions such an effort might take.

A CAUTION IS IN ORDER. Attempting to identify general issues, I have not hesitated to use broad and interpretive perspectives. Both in substance and in method, this is not popular among my colleagues who "write sociology." Yet there are those in academic disciplines who in recent years have not hesitated to take such an approach to their subjects: Harvey Wheeler and Christopher Lasch in political science, Lewis Mumford in history, John Kenneth Galbraith and Martin Carnoy in economics. Sociology, too, has had its exceptions to the rule, most clearly in C. Wright Mills, Irving Louis Horowitz, Alvin Gouldner, and Norman Birnbaum, Seymour Lipset, Daniel Bell, and Robert Nisbet, as well as a raft of younger men and women. I do not pretend affinity with this array of individuals—indeed, as a group they cluster uneasily, ranging politically from radical to liberal-conservative. My perspectives on the individual and society differ strikingly from some of them, and I must caution against ascribing to my work any virtues found in their writings.

[1] See "Working Papers in the Theory of Institutionalization," by George K. Zollschan, in collaboration with Robert Perrucci, David Willer, and Philip Gibeau, Section Two, in Zollschan and W. Hirsch, *Explorations in Social Change* (Boston: Houghton Mifflin, 1964), pp. 89–212; see also Zollschan and D. A. Hansen, "On Motivation: Toward Socially Pertinent Foundations," in D. A. Hansen, ed., *Explorations in Sociology and Counseling* (Boston: Houghton Mifflin, 1969), pp. 30–63.

[2] Walter Buckley, *Sociology and Modern Systems Theory* (Englewood Cliffs: Prentice-Hall, 1967).

Still, this book shares one quality with theirs: much of what I have written is arguable. I have attempted to represent at least contradictions to my arguments, while avoiding the manipulative techniques of the propagandist, who purports to present both sides of the story, knowing that his readers will thereby think he is being fair and objective. Unlike the propagandist, I have attempted to be fair; but the reader should be mindful that every social statement is a profoundly personal statement. I have given the heaviest weight and closest treatment to those sides of arguments that seemed most reasonable to me, at this time in my life. Perhaps next year, or five years from now, I myself will disagree with much of what I have written here.

My intent, then, is not to win converts to a particular point of view. Rather, it is to introduce the reader to a few of the issues that I see as crucial in our contemporary society and to present those issues in ways that might stimulate thought, raise questions and arguments, and suggest the need to search for less constricting images of the individual and society.

＊   ＊   ＊

A surprising array of individuals has contributed to this book in one way or another—from the Scottish farmer, who at its inception precipitated my return to the question of "what is sociology," to the person who sits beside me now, at the close of our final proofreading. To thank each of them adequately would require an additional chapter, a chapter that must remain unwritten, for in any event it would remain unpublished. Other, less impersonal, appreciations must be found.

Not all debts can be acknowledged personally, however, for almost inevitably an author is involved in corporate relations. My thanks, then, to the University of California at Berkeley for granting me a brief leave to lay the foundations for this book, and to the Institute for Social Research in Oslo for providing the sanctuary necessary to the task. Thanks, too, to the University of Santa Clara, where at times I enjoyed a writing retreat, and to the "Wendover Foundation," for invaluable support in a time of publication stress.

DONALD A. HANSEN

Chapter One

A Prelude to Critical Sociology

HISTORY TELLS US that freedom cannot exist without responsibility. But history also shows us that responsibility can grow habitual, turning into unthinking conformity, even slavery; that freedom withers, as calls for responsible citizenship give way to demands for unquestioning loyalty. In modern societies, plagued by internal disruption and external challenge, it is especially difficult to find the delicate balance between freedom and responsibility, between the requirements of individual expression and the necessities of social order. In a society such as ours, how free can individuals be to live as they alone think best; how responsible must they be?

The question plays through the running debates of our political and social lives. To some of us, responsibility must come before all else, for without it society grows unstable. Only a stable society can have a healthy economy; only a stable society can meet the threats of competition and hostile enemies; only a stable society allows the individual child to develop fully and grow to responsible maturity. Seen in this way, law and order are the hope of modern man.

To others of us, freedom of individual thought, choice, and action must come before all else. Only in freedom can individual humanness truly develop and express itself in justice, equality, and social harmony. In this view, the processes of law have changed too little and remain hopelessly outdated. They are repressive, racist, sexist; in the service of profit and growth they help exploit human life; they carry misery and death to foreign lands and remain criminally indifferent to our suffering ecology. Law and order, as they exist today, are not man's hope; they are his repressors.

To most of us, things are not so clear. The questions nag, but when we put them into words, they seem stilted and foreign to our lives. Which is more important: individual expression or the social good? Are laws and traditions needlessly repressive, or are they necessary to a coherent, satisfying life? Are conflict and violence always destructive; can they be creative in a society such as ours? Should we struggle for a better society, or should we fight against the disruptive forces of change that would rush us headlong toward the unknown?

Posed in these ways, such questions are hard to answer. But in our everyday lives, where the questions are rarely so explicit, we live our answers. We all conform at least most of the time; some resist authorities and traditions more often than others; a few even seek out challenges to innovate or to defend our social order. But rarely do we examine our lives to find out what kinds of answers are evidenced by our actions, hesitations, and indifferences and what ideas and mute beliefs we express about the individual and society, about our own lives, about our own freedom and responsibility. Even when we do think about the answers we live, we rarely consider how adequate those answers are to the limitations and problems, to the demands and potentials of life in our times.

That is what critical sociology invites you to do: to ask disturbing questions about what you know and don't know, what you feel and don't feel, what you hope and fear; to pursue irreverent criticism of the social, economic, and political processes of the society you live in, and about its myths, ideals, and accepted wisdoms; to explore in the lives of distant others and in history for possibilities as well as problems in the ways you view yourself and the world you live in. And when you begin to feel satisfied with your answers, it asks you to start over, again and again, questioning your answers, questioning even your own questions.

That, in a nutshell, is the invitation to critical sociology. The invitation will be offered more fully throughout this book, but for now let me put it even more briefly, in a single sentence: The invitation to critical sociology is an invitation to become an involved, critical explorer of human and societal possibilities.

TO ACCEPT THE INVITATION IS to take profound risks. In the best of times, it is difficult to ask critical questions about yourself and your society; in the worst of times it is also dangerous. Some of the difficulties and dangers come from "the outside"; they involve social and political risks, for the critical explorer is often a nuisance to others, and at times a threat.

The greatest dangers and difficulties may not come from the outside, however. For to ask such questions is to risk destroying the coherence of the world you know, even your sense of who you are. In these terms, these may be especially dangerous times. For history also tells us that few societies have been as marked as ours by personal confusion and doubt.

That confusion is suffered by the individual, but it is not the individual's personal trouble alone. It is also a profound public problem, a general confusion and discontent, that rests at the heart of the problem of freedom and responsibility. For in the modern world, we seem to be losing our faith not only in gods, but in ourselves.

The Confusion: Reason and Relativity

The confusion goes under various names: a loss of community, an impoverishment of values and ideals, a failure of utopian vision, a crisis of culture. Symbolically it is called the death of God, less poetically the loss of belief in something beyond the individual as the master of human fate, the judge of human actions. Without such a belief we are condemned to freedom; we have lost the reference points from which our actions and experiences can be evaluated and worked into coherent forms.

To some, the confusion goes even deeper: In the twentieth century, not only have we lost the old beliefs, we have lost the ability to believe. It is a crisis not only of faith, but of hope. As a people, we seem to lack the capacity to transcend the idea of god, to seize a utopian vision in such a way that we breathe life into it. We seem unable to create lives that are meaningful; we lack even the capacity to recognize that we can create. We disbelieve even in belief.

After God died, Man, who was supposed to replace Him, grew sick of himself. This resulted in a crisis of belief and disbelief which made the twentieth century spiritually empty.

God died in the nineteenth century. Nietzsche announced the event as a fact, not as an argument, and his report has been taken as the starting point of most serious theology ever since. . . .

But since God did not have any heir, the funeral has been going on for over a hundred years.

Michael Harrington, *The Accidental Century*

In the modern world, the human was to replace God, and reason would show the way. But as the world grew more rational, life grew more confusing. Somehow, human reason seemed to work on everything except humans.

By the middle of the twentieth century that lesson had been made brutally clear. In little more than thirty years, the Western world had suffered in two barbarous wars waged with science and technology—the inventions of human rationality.

The lesson of the Second World War was especially dispiriting, for it showed how the new abilities to create large-scale organizations—another invention of rationality—could be turned to inhuman purposes, even to the systematic extermination of millions of persons in gas chambers and concentration camps, on the grounds that they were "racially inferior." The lesson was numbing: Inhumanity and technical rationality can thrive side by side. How, then, could people hold to a hope in the human powers of human rationality?

In the wake of the Second World War, disenchantment with life in modern societies spread, slowly at first, then more quickly in the late fifties, through the sixties and into the seventies. As all things social and cultural, it did not spread evenly through the society. Not surprisingly, it concentrated among the young, especially among those who were the most free from worry and responsibilities, the most privileged members of the most privileged generations in the history of American society: those who were students in colleges and universities. It concentrated among those who could have been students for the asking, but who chose instead to move to the edges of their society—not necessarily the geographic peripheries, but the social, political, and economic edges, away from the organizational centers of the "system," where they could find release from societal constraint and responsibility.

Freedom from the immediate and compelling demands of society also carries a high price, especially for those still unsettled in their knowledge of who they are: It isolates them from the assurances that societal demands offer their more complacent fellows.

IF THERE WERE any laws of human and social behavior, this would probably be one: When a social role is vague or ambiguous, the person who is expected to play it will suffer discomfort, even to the point of disorientation or estrangement from those who expect him to play the role.[1] The significance of this role incoherence is neglected by those who see in the youthful dissent of recent years only a generational conflict of self-indulgent children. For when youth rebel, mock, and disrupt, they carry the energies of social disorder; but their dissent is rarely the author of the disorder. Rather, it is a response to

[1] Bernard Rosenberg and Norris Fliegel, *The Vanguard Artist* (Chicago: Quadrangle, 1965), p. 146.

the disorder and uncertainty of their society, to which they are among the most vulnerable.

As the second half of the twentieth century progressed, ever more persons were denied the one certainty that had remained for earlier generations—the certainty of the past, of "what has been." In earlier decades, the relativity of human experience had been a problem only for philosophers like George Herbert Mead and for dissident artists like Picasso and the Cubists. Now, a half century later, that awareness has become familiar, even to many who could scarcely put it into words. It is their living experience, and its message is profound: Contrary to conventional wisdom, human experience is not just a series of events; it is not a simple progression of cause and effect, of this leading to that, of that leading to the next thing, and on and on. We do not live from event to event, but rather, "events" cluster and merge in our minds, with little regard for "time" and "place." The clustering is our own living art. Involved in the immediacy of our moment, we continually redefine, rewrite, and reorder our experiences, both those remembered and those anticipated.

This means there is no single world that all persons share. Indeed, each of us lives in our own unique world, and that world is ever changing. We do not all experience things in the same ways, and each of us experiences differently from moment to moment. But then, without a god of mystery or power, in a culture that fails to offer believable meaning and direction, how is it possible to know what is of value? How is it possible even to know that what seems to have happened really did happen?

EVEN IN THE UNIVERSITIES, the citadels of rationality, the aged belief in reason has eroded. Rational men and women, through their science and technology, have brought abundance and vitality. But even in abundance, life remains painful and uncertain. Reason allows only one certainty, the certainty of one's own death. Once again, a tragic vision, for centuries kept under control in Western thought, has emerged: Human life, whatever its joys and satisfactions, is also filled with pain, irrationality, and triviality.[2] Since the eighteenth century the tragic vision had played through literature and art like a muted countertheme; but in human affairs of government, business, and social life the theme was all but hidden by the heroic vision of "Rational Man" as the savior of humanity.

Through the twentieth century, however, that dissonant, tragic theme grew ever more insistent. In the early decades, it was found most dramatically in art and literature. "One can only speak of what is in front of him, and that is the mess," insisted playwright Samuel Beckett. "The mess is not my invention. We cannot listen to a conversation for five minutes without being acutely aware of the confusion. It is all around us and our only chance now is to let it in. The only chance of renovation is to open our eyes and see the mess."[3]

In the fifties, the confusion was expressed not only by the lonely artist and intellectual. Now it found new and varied voices, even among those who sought neither spiritual nor intellectual knowledge but simply coherence in their daily lives. In the second half of the century, even reason seemed to support the lessons of relativity; nothing being given, all is possible. But if all is possible, is anything possible? How can men and women believe in anything, even in themselves?

Reason and relativity had joined forces and seemed to agree with the lessons of war: to place our hopes in rationality is irrational.

The Invitation Begins: Camus' Existential Vision

Through the fifties the confusion spread rapidly. The youth of that decade have been labeled "the silent generation." Pas-

---

[2] For a stimulating discussion of the themes of rationality and tragedy in modern Western traditions, see H. Stuart Hughes, *Consciousness and Society* (New York: Vintage, 1958).

[3] Quoted by Tom F. Driver, 1961. "Beckett by the Madeleine," *Columbia University Forum* (Summer). Reprinted in Samuel A. Weiss, ed., *Drama in the Modern World* (New York: Heath, 1964), pp. 505–506 (p. 280).

sive and indifferent to the politics and problems of their times, they seem to have lacked the passion of the sixties and the doubting sophistication of the seventies, even the spirit of earlier decades. As a generation, they seemed interested only in finding their places in the world of work.

We had no sense that anything that happened in the world touched us . . . the Korean War, the blacklists, purges in government and colleges, all these stupidities happened to other people, and though we disapproved of them, we did not quite see how they mattered, very much.

Peter S. Prescott, *A Darkening Green:*
Notes from the Silent Generation

Yet in the fifties, I suspect, we can find basic clues about the meanings of the confusion we feel today. For beneath the surfaces all was not so quiet among the silent generation. Silence may cloak discontent that is yet too frail to break through the constraints that hold it in; it may also mask powerful energies that, lacking a vision of hope or injustice, have not yet found coherent expression.

Even in the fifties, issues of concern and confusion fermented on campuses, mixed with anxious discontent. Campaigns were mounted now and then against compulsory ROTC; more frequently, discussions and meetings considered problems of racial injustice, nuclear annihilation, the meaning of life in a mass society, the crises of values and identity. True, all but a few were politically apathetic; but for many the apathy stemmed not from indifference but from preoccupations with things more compelling.

The young of the fifties were not the first generation to discover that, at least for them, God had died. But now there seemed to be little or nothing to take the god's place. Even reason was failing; old worlds were dying, and with them died the points of security they had offered, the positive reference points that told a person what was right, what was wrong, good and bad, nourishing and debilitating.

Nor were there even clear points of negative reference: in the fifties, the idea of nuclear devastation was distressing, but not yet clearly accepted as an enemy in itself; nor had the sense of injustice clearly formed around the massive civil rights movement that would help inform the youth of the coming decade.

SHORT OF A BLIND HOWL, if discontent is to be expressed, even clearly identified, it must be linked to a goal—even if only an idealistic goal that only blindly promises to end the discontent. To most youth, the fifties offered neither faith nor foe, no clear goals that might turn mute anxiety to compelling action. Yet in their quiet unrest, new images were shaping. Seeds of rebellion and dissent that would sprout in the following decade were taking root.

The discontent, the quiet sense that something was missing, that much was wrong, was the legacy of their society. But in the fifties, it found its most resonant expression not in the images offered by their own society but in the tragic visions of postwar Europe. Later, in the sixties, it would be popular to trace those visions back to the young Karl Marx, but even in the fifties it took the label he had applied: "Alienation." That word—which we will look at more closely in Chapter Five— seemed to mean many things to many people, but somehow it pointed to the inability to feel one's self a "whole person" in the modern world.

From Europe also came messages of bitter hope; images of individuals who could struggle against their own alienation, accepting a tragic awareness without falling into despair. In those messages, too, the young Marx could be discovered. Even those existentialists who continued to hold a belief in the existence of something beyond human life no longer looked to the idea of god as a working assumption for life in the modern world. They agreed with the atheistic Jean-Paul Sartre and Albert Camus: Each of us, individually and alone, is responsible for our own life and for our society.

Camus' vision was exciting in its heroic refusal to either surrender to or deny the tragic futility of life.[4] If a god exists, Camus decided, he cannot be known, so we might as well forget about him. We are all strangers in a strange land; life is meaningless and absurd; we can only strive, with full knowledge that the effort is doomed.

Our only options are to give up in suicide or to escape into indifference or into an uncomfortable belief in something beyond ourselves, in a god, in mystical visions, in the supremacy of a social system. Given that choice, Camus suggested, perhaps suicide would be best. For blind faith and indifference are escapes from life, insulating us from our essential being, leading us to act in "bad faith," heightening our alienation, even contributing to barbarism and brutal inhumanity.

Peer Gynt, at the end of his pilgrimage of pretence, recognizes himself in the image of an onion: leaf after leaf of self-dramatization is peeled off, leaving nothing at the core . . . a totally unreflecting man like the "Stranger" of Camus is equally cut off from reality, imprisoned in his private world. The destruction of all meaning . . . is the ultimate point of this progression.

We can then no longer say anything in good faith, and all rational action becomes lifeless banality. . . . Having arrived at this stage, the modern intellectual will include himself in his nauseated contempt for the moral and cultural futility of his time. Having rendered the universe utterly meaningless, he himself dissolves in a universal wasteland.

Michael Polanyi, *Personal Knowledge*

But how do we know what is "good faith"? How can we know what we should do? What justifies our actions? What justifies our ends? Again, Camus sounded like a modern form of the young Marx: Our actions are justified by our goals— and our goals are justified by our actions. There is no difference between ends and means; there is only the individual acting; and when we act in "good faith," ends and means become one.

---

[4] See, for example, Albert Camus, *The Myth of Sisyphus* (New York: Random House, 1955 [1942]).

All else is falsity, alienating and destructive. Our only hope is truth, and truth is experienced only in living. That means every new moment demands a new truth; that each person's life can be true only for him or for her, and for no one else; that in every act and every failure to act we affirm our life or we deny it.

But Camus—like the discontented youth of the fifties who grasped at his images—was unable to complete his vision. He had found a way to quell rising despair in a world that had lost its bearings. But he could find no new direction to go, no new points to help him discover where he was. His existential vision, tragic and heroic, could only help him endure as old worlds crumbled.

At times, perhaps, that is the most that can be done. The roiling dust of destruction is blinding, and it is impossible to see new forms that even then may be rising to replace the old. Those who are caught in the transformations of our society —rooted in a world that no longer works, unable to foresee the world that future generations will be asked to embrace or oppose—have but few choices. They can give way, allowing themselves to be swept up by the currents of their times, little heeding where those currents are taking them. Or they can, like Camus, search dangerously for vision and coherence.

That is what critical sociology would have you do: to creatively grapple with questions of freedom, responsibility, and creativity, acknowledging the confusions of relativity and the limitations of reason, while resisting a tempting surrender to despair, to blind faith, or to comfortable uninvolvement.

But that is only the beginning of the invitation.

Summary and Direction

In the following book, as the invitation to critical sociology unfolds, you will recognize that I only deliver it; critical sociology is not my invention or my discovery. It emerged slowly, surfacing in Europe nearly two centuries ago, in an anxious concern over the fate of the individual in industrializing societies.

It is seen most powerfully, I believe, in two Europeans: Karl Marx, whose ideas exploded in the middle of the nineteenth century, and Max Weber, whose explorations spanned into the twentieth. In their incessant efforts to understand the problems and potentials of human life in Western societies, these two critical explorers pointed a way to a sociology that might be both individually creative and socially constructive. It is also seen in an American, George Herbert Mead, who grounded his critical exploration in the individual, free and responsible, existentially involved and socially aware.

It is really these three—Mead, Marx, and Weber—who offer the invitation to critical sociology. Basic threads of ideas link these three, weaving through their continuing efforts to identify the relation of individual consciousness to society, to answer the question of modern times: How can I live?

Each elaborates on that theme in different ways, but in all is seen an emphasis on individuals, conforming and innovating, as they cope with the demands, opportunities, and restrictions of the situations they find themselves in. In the works of these three critical sociologists are found the beginnings of a view of individual and society that might in many ways inform thought and action in our age of relativity and massive transformation.

I HAVE EARLIER PUT the argument that follows in a single sentence: The invitation to critical sociology is an invitation to become an involved, critical explorer of human and societal possibilities. Mead, Marx, and Weber together offer the invitation, yet each emphasized a different part of the invitation in his own life's work.

In Mead we find an invitation to self-and-other awareness. That awareness is seen as the groundwork of our personal freedom and creativity and of our personal responsibility, for neither our freedom nor our responsibility to ourselves can be untangled from the freedom of others and our responsibility to them. In Marx, we see this self-and-other involvement turn to social criticism, to a questioning of the human meanings of the ways our society is organized, and the ways it operates. And in Weber, we see critical involvement and social criticism join in a compelling exploration of the possibilities and limitations of human and societal life.

In the following three sections of this book, we turn to the invitations that can be found in each of these three social theorists, to better understand the full invitation they together extend.

Part One

INVOLVEMENT
The Invitation in Mead

You can't buy concepts in wholesale lots. You have to work them out for yourself, one to suit every occasion. And they have to be good ones, or when fate takes you violently unawares, they'll blow up in your face.

LUIGI PIRANDELLO, "The Rules of the Game"

Chapter Two

The Invitation in Mead: I

To THOSE WHO ARE restless for social change, it is a bitter irony: the more involved most of us become in our society, the more conservative we seem to grow. Even in oppressive or meaningless situations, most of us strive to maintain the given social order. For some reason, we value stability; when the community is disturbed, we take part in bringing it back to the "fixed" order. Even those whose lives seem heavy with frustration join in the battle: from all sides the dissident is told that the law must be obeyed, the constitution must be honored, the family, school, and courts must be respected.

There is no need to dwell on the human outrages of this human tendency to conserve the existing order. Clearly, it has supported injustice and exploitation throughout human history. It has also contributed, tragically, to violent riots and revolutions, for it helps preserve institutions long after they have grown intolerable. And in recent times, as we grow aware of how our lives entwine with our ecologies and biologies, we see how the conservative bias strengthens organizations and practices that may actually destroy human sensibilities and even human life.

The social conservatism of human communities bothered George Herbert Mead. When the energies of discontent are repressed, when men and women hold to ways of life grown frustrating or empty, their freedom and creative growth are thwarted. Yet Mead believed that such conservatism could not be glibly condemned: Freedom and growth are possible only in a social order that is coherent. Whatever its excesses and inhumanities, the tendency to conserve is a safeguard against social chaos. An image of the individual and society that ignores the human need for order and coherence is naive, and if it preaches violence and destruction at any cost it is blindly dangerous.

Yet, unless we accept the idea that this is the "best of all possible worlds," we must recognize that an image of the individual and society based only on maintaining our given institutions is equally wretched. If we believe that we must preserve the existing order at any cost, we might as well believe that society is beyond human control. Either way we are imprisoned in the traditions of our past and constrained and buffeted by our present surroundings.

Somehow, Mead saw, we must discover how to intentionally change ourselves and our society without destroying those things that are valuable.

_____

That is the problem of society, is it not? How can you present order and structure in society and yet bring about the changes that need to take place. . . . To bring about change is seemingly to destroy the given order, and yet society does and must change. That is the problem, to incorporate the methods of change into the order of society itself.

George Herbert Mead, _Movements of Thought in_
the Nineteenth Century

_____

The question weaves persistently through Mead's lifework: Can we identify an image of the individual and society that preserves the qualities of individual experience and creativity and yet explains social order and change? We have seen this question in Chapter One; now, in Mead, we find a solution, sensitizing and profound, that is basic to critical sociology.

Mead's solution addresses the confusions of reason and relativity. In his critical sociology, we again see an existential vision,
but it is an existentialism grown socially aware. In it, we see
relativity give way to involvement, and we see the possibility
that involvement can grow critical, as the individual turns from
questions of how to maintain the social order to questions of
how to realize his or her own individual possibilities and the
possibilities of others.

Mead insisted that each individual's consciousness is unique.
Even in an ordered society we must recognize that each of us
lives in his own special world: "It is our thought, our perception, which determines the world in which we live, so that the
world of each is in some sense different from that of the
other. . . ."[1]

Still, in some ways we also live in the same world. If we did
not, we would not know what to expect of one another, "There
would be no meaning to our conversation, no coherence in our
own thought in regard to the world. . . ."[2] Somehow each of
us lives in a different world, and yet it is organized in such a
way that we share a world in common.

But how does this happen?

Mead's answer rests on a simple insight: that we are able to
see the world as others see it. This insight led to the compelling
argument that a social order of free men and women, whether
of two persons or two million persons, is possible only if each
individual is able to "take the role of the other," is able to recognize how other individuals see the situations they are in and
the possibilities open to them. This ability—to see the world as
others see it—allows us to recognize what others make of even
new situations; it helps us predict how others will define their
possibilities and choose their actions. Thus, "taking the role of
the other" helps us define our own situations and choose our
own actions.

---

[1] George Herbert Mead, *Movements of Thought in the Nineteenth Century*
(Chicago: University of Chicago Press, 1936), pp. 141–142.
[2] *Ibid.*

The ability to see the world through the eyes of the other, then, helps us recognize our selves. As we come to know the ways others see their lives and their possibilities, we come to recognize how they see us and our possibilities. In others, we discover ourselves.

This line of argument led Mead to a tantalizing idea: that we can be unique only by being part of our community. That idea —a basic idea in critical sociology, leading us from relativity to involvement—deserves a closer look.

Self-and-Other Awareness

The infant's consciousness, Mead noted, is in ways similar to the animal's. But important differences quickly appear. Take a toddler and a dog, both greedily eyeing the same object: a plate of warm chocolate-chip cookies on the kitchen table. Mother lurks nearby, and "man's best friend" knows as well as the child that to take the cookie is to risk punishment. Not long ago, things were different. Then the child would have headed straight for the cookies. She would have been surprised at the spanking that followed; unpleasantly surprised. Just recently she realized that the cookies and the spanking are somehow related. She learned a lesson the old dog has known since puppyhood: seductive cookies hold danger.

Yesterday, however, the child learned something more, something even Lassie will never learn. If she takes the cookies, she foresees not only a spanking, but also upsetting her mother, disturbing their relationship, making herself "feel bad." Now the cookies set off dreams in her mind, involving the eternal triangle: mother, child, and cookies. The key to the new lesson is this: The child can imagine what those cookies mean to her mother. They are for later, when Daddy comes home. Now they are taboo.

In this discovery, the child has taken a pivotal step toward social consciousness. She has taken her mother's attitude into herself; as Mead put it, she has "taken the role of the other." She still wants the cookies, but she now sees them in another way as well—in the way her mother sees them.

Something even more important happens when the child learns to see the cookies as her mother sees them: She begins to see herself as Mother sees her. She learns that Mother thinks a cookie stealer is "bad" and that the guardian of cookies is a "good girl." Seeing herself as Mother sees her, she grows aware of herself as a special object in the world.

Thus the pivotal step to social consciousness is linked to the pivotal step to self-consciousness.

THAT STEP—the step toward self-consciousness—may be the most important yet made by humans. Somehow we are able to do what other animals cannot: to view ourselves as objects. Dogs recognize other objects in the "outside" world; they also know that they have a certain relationship to those objects. To a rhesus monkey, a banana is something to eat, a tree is something to swing in, a leopard is something to flee. But the human —even the toddler—is also conscious that she herself is a "thing" in the "outside" world.

As no other animals, we become objects to ourselves. We are able to step outside our subjective lives, to release ourselves from our consciousness, and to look back at our own subjective "inner" lives. Doing this, we recognize that we—our subjective beings—are also objects in the world. As we recognize that we are also objects, we become conscious of our "selfs."

One becomes conscious of himself when there is some strain, opposition, or struggle. . . . A man becomes aware of himself as a distinct object, then, when . . . his success requires the assistance of others and . . . there is a possibility that such cooperation may not be forthcoming.

Tamotsu Shibutani, *Society and Personality*

To be self-conscious is to be conscious of one's self as an object. It is this ability that allows us to talk to ourselves and to make excuses. "Sure, I did that stupid thing," we say, "but I'm really not like that." This ability allows us to contemplate our future possibilities, even our own death. No other animal, as far as we know, is burdened with this gift of self-consciousness. More than anything else, this capacity to think of ourselves as objects is the genius of human complexity and civilization. It is also the genius of our individuality, for we are not born with individuality—we create it.

This is another thing about "taking the role of the other": Seeing the world as another sees it gives new meanings to your life. You see your "experience" in a new context, "through new eyes." New possibilities appear; old ones no longer seem feasible. The "future" is somehow different, and so is the "past"; that means that the present moment, the living moment, is different. Seeing the world through the eyes of another brings novelty to your own world. In dealing with the novelty, self-awareness changes.

Take an example close to home, an example that could happen to any of us. The kid next door, as far as you are concerned, has always been just one of the neighborhood fixtures. Now and then you meet on the street, say a thing or two, and move on. Then, one day you catch an unguarded glance; you wonder what it means, and then you realize that the "neighborhood fixture" is in love with you.

Now you see yourself with new eyes; suddenly you're sexier, more interesting, more exciting. You notice things about your admirer. If you like what you see, you begin to imagine things about the future—how you'll break the ice, how you'll make out, maybe even how this might be the person you've been waiting for. You become the romantic star of an old Hollywood script, written as you imagine you and your lover might co-author it. The future has changed; it holds new possibilities, new challenges. So, too, you have in your present experience changed, as you see yourself anew, in the ways you imagine another sees you.

If you don't like the looks of your admirer, the change is

less dramatic. But still your future changes, and so does your image of yourself. It would be embarrassing to be asked out; maybe if you're not careful the kid will really go off the deep end; you've got to cool it. You know, you're really a heartless, lovable thing.

Not only the future and present change. The past also takes on new meanings in the present moment. Now you know why you've been running into one another so often lately; it's been arranged. Could this explain those phone calls that end as soon as you say hello? No wonder the kid is always so tongue-tied when you ask a question or make a casual comment.

Seeing the unguarded glance, the world you knew has altered. The glance surprised you; looking more closely you find something new in the attitude of the other person. That new thing means that your knowledge of the world—of the other person, of yourself, of the future, of the past, and, all in all, of the present moment—has been inadequate. Seeing things through the other person's eyes puts your experience in a new context. As you take the role of the other, your self-awareness changes.

This homely illustration barely hints at the complexity of this part of Mead's image of the individual and society. Yet it offers a starting point, for it suggests, contrary to common sense, that even our own pasts are not what we might think they are. It is not simply that we forget. Our memories of the past do grow dim and patchy, but something else is going on. Somehow, even the most vivid memories change their meaning. "When one recalls his boyhood days he cannot get into them as he then was, without the relationship to what he has become," Mead told his students.[3]

Thus, Mead anticipated the autobiographical message of Thomas Wolfe: You can't go home again. But he also told us why: In our memories we can return to the past, but we always return as a new self, a self quite different from the self we were then.

---

[3] George Herbert Mead, *Philosophy of the Present* (Chicago: Open Court, 1932), p. 30.

STILL, IN ANY SPECIFIC MOMENT OF LIVING, we are influenced by what has happened. The past is, in a crucial sense, unchangeable. "The world that comes to us from the past possesses and controls us," Mead cautioned.[4] There is a certain "causalness" to the past; that which has happened limits the possibilities of the present. There is a continuity to human experience; if there were not, we would never know what to expect, we would have no feeling of coherence, and social order would be impossible.

The "givenness" of history helps us make sense of our situation. Within the narrow confines of our present situation, "our history gives us the elbow room to cope with the ever-changing stream of reality."[5] So, too, we are influenced by our ecology and biology. But this is the critical point: Searching for coherence in our present moment, we give our own meaning to the world about us.

If a minute ago you were slapped in the face by a "spiteful enemy," the pain will still remain. There is a givenness to what has happened. But if you now see through the spite and discover, or think you discover, that love lies behind it, the meaning of the attack alters. You rearrange it and other memories and anticipations to help you make sense of the present situation. As you can define that situation, so you act: Rather than hitting back, you seduce, manipulate, or mock your frustrated lover.

We are influenced by what has been; yet as we think, choose, and act, we are constantly giving new meaning to what has been. Living in our present moment, we rewrite the past, again and again. And it is the new, rewritten past that is real.

To say we "rewrite" the past does not mean simply that the past changes because we look at it differently. Mead's argument

[4] George Herbert Mead, "Scientific Method and the Moral Sciences," *International Journal of Ethics* (1923), p. 247. Reprinted in John W. Petras, ed., *George Herbert Mead: Essays on His Social Philosophy* (New York: Teachers College Press, 1968), p. 96; also reprinted in Andrew Reck, ed., *Mead: Selected Writings* (Indianapolis: Bobbs-Merrill, 1964), p. 266.

[5] George Herbert Mead, "The Nature of the Past," in John Coss, *Essays in Honor of John Dewey* (New York: Holt, Rinehart and Winston, 1929), p. 241. Reprinted in Reck, ed., *Mead: Selected Writings*, p. 353.

was more profound: The past, as well as the future, is relative to the present. We organize memories of the past and anticipations of the future in ways that will fill in the missing elements that we need to make sense of our present situations.

As long as the "past" and "future" make sense, we cling to them. The "history" that we organized and rewrote yesterday is all we need to make sense of today's familiar situations. We meet minor problems or possibilities with about the same images of past and future that have worked before. They made sense yesterday, and probably will tomorrow. But greater challenges force us to rewrite those histories, as well as our anticipated futures. Confronted with a demanding problem or potential, we rework both history and future in a way that makes sense in the present moment. This new reorganization, involving a new past and future, "serves us until the rising novelty of tomorrow necessitates a new history which interprets the new future."[6] Thus, the continuity and novelty, the stability and change, of our private lives means that we are controlled by the society that has preceded us, and yet we change it.

This view then frees us from bondage either to past or future. We are neither creatures of necessity or of an irrevocable past, nor of any visions given on the mount. . . . Our values lie in the present, and past and future give us only a schedule of the means, and the plans of campaign, for their realization.

George Herbert Mead, *Philosophy of the Present*

This, then, is the key to Mead's answers to the confusions of relativity. In the interplay of emerging self-and-other awareness, we create coherence and order, both in our own lives and in our society. This means we are not simply captives of our own bodies, or products of our environment, or the deluded tools of social order and social institutions. Human beings, as no other things, can to some degree move beyond the demanding influences of biology, ecology, and social institutions. We

[6] *Ibid.*

are capable of being in some ways creators of both ourselves and our society. We cannot create our history and essential being singlehandedly, as many existentialists such as Camus seem to suggest; but we can consciously influence our own lives and even our society.

THIS QUESTION IS basic to Mead's image of the individual and society: How do we come to think of ourselves as objects? Before all else, Mead tells us, it is by recognizing the ways others see us as their objects.[7] For this process, language is invaluable.

The chair is an object in our life, and, if the chair had a consciousness of its own, we would be objects to it. But if a chair is conscious, it does little to tell us so; it just sits there. An animal—a dog or a horse, even a cat—is another thing. If we attempt to treat it simply as our own object, ignoring its subjective life, it might find a way to tell us. The dog whimpers, the cat whines, the horse bucks, and we know that they are unhappy. Still, to some of us the messages are little different from the creak of a chair when we sit in it. Here we must tighten a screw; there we must dish out more food or open the door to let the animal out. We may tell our troubles to the family dog, but the conversation is decidedly one-way.

We get far more feedback from people. They do not simply creak or whimper. Even without words they tell us more: that we are unfair to them, that we are wonderful, that we are showing how weak or strong we are, how considerate or selfish, how nasty or foolish. They tell us about themselves, what they intend to do, what they think we will do, and what we should do. The more they tell us, the harder it is to treat them simply as objects. We begin to see how they see us, and how they see us seeing them.

They tell us these things in many ways, through a variety of languages. Their language may be verbal—a word or sen-

---

[7] George Herbert Mead, "The Genesis of the Self and Social Control," *International Journal of Ethics* (1924–25). Reprinted in Reck, ed., *Mead: Selected Writings*, pp. 283–284.

tence—but it may be simply a gesture, a glance of the eye, or a special kind of grunt or movement of the body. The important thing is that we know what their noise or movement means. Their message is clear: They are about to do something that the rest of us will have to adjust to.

Animals, of course, use such language, but in the human another dimension is added. In our gesture we affect not only others but ourselves as well. We are capable of symbolic interaction—the communication of ideas, meanings, and attitudes that are addressed both to ourselves and to the receiver.

To communicate this way, we must take the role of the other. We speak one way to a salesperson and another to a child; one way to our friend when he is happy, another when he is depressed. We put ourselves in their places, see ourselves through their eyes, and adjust our communication. We speak to ourselves as well as to them. Our speech is their speech; we use the symbols we know are meaningful to them and to ourselves.

Language, then, helps us "see ourselves as others see us," and it enables us to speak to ourselves in the ways others might speak to us. We take the conversations of individuals and groups and use them in our "inner sessions and debate with ourselves." The language we use is ours only because it is the language of others, of the organized human world to which we belong.[8] In the give-and-take of living, communication develops and we learn to take the role of the other—and as we do, we discover not only the other person, we also discover ourselves as we learn to see ourselves through the other's eyes.

Self and Social Control: The Generalized Other

In the child, this self-and-other awareness emerges gradually. At first it is seen in a simple "conversation of gestures." The

---

[8] George Herbert Mead, "National-Mindedness and International-Mindedness," *International Journal of Ethics* (1929), p. 396. Reprinted in Reck, ed., *Mead: Selected Writings*, p. 358.

baby learns to clap her hands when her mother does. Soon she learns that she can start the conversation: when she claps, so will mother. She may laugh and run away when her father growls like a big bear and chases her. This kind of play is also familiar in the mock battles of dogs or in the play of a mother cat with her kittens.

The child soon learns more complex "imitation." Now, when the dog makes a move for the cookies, she yells "No, no" in just the way she herself has been warned off by her mother. She learns to play with a doll, talking to it in the tones her parents use in talking to her. She "plays at" the roles of others: she pretends to be her mother, a teacher, a preacher, a doctor, a pirate, a cowboy. In this play, she is learning the roles of others in her society.

She has not yet learned how those roles relate to one another, however. Now she can play simple games like hide-and-seek that require taking the role of only one other person: She is the hunter or the hunted, even if six others are also being hunted. Such play is only a set of responses to individuals. "The child responds in fairly intelligent fashion to the immediate stimuli that come to him, but they are not organized,"[9] Mead argued. Still, in learning to "take the role of the other," the child has taken an essential step toward self-and-other awareness. In a few years, she takes another.

That step is seen when she learns to play a game involving a number of interlinked roles. Baseball, for example, makes demands far beyond those of hide-and-seek: "The child must not only take the role of the other, as he does in the play," Mead wrote, "but he must assume the various roles of all the participants in the game, and govern his actions accordingly. If he plays first base, it is as the one to whom the ball will be thrown from the field or from the catcher. Their organized reactions to him he has embedded in his own playing of the different positions. . . ."[10]

[9] George Herbert Mead, *Mind, Self and Society* (Chicago: University of Chicago Press, 1934), p. 152.
[10] Mead, "Genesis of the Self," in Reck, ed., p. 285.

This "organized reaction" of others becomes for the child a "generalized other." She still thinks of each player individually, but now she also thinks of all of them together in an abstract way. Somehow, "the team" becomes more than the sum of its parts. In the child's mind, the attitudes she sees in the individual players melt into one another, becoming a "generalized attitude" of the group. "They" want her to come to practice; "they" are upset when she throws the ball to the wrong baseman.

No single player may have exactly the attitudes of this "generalized other"; possibly no one will have some of the generalized attitudes the child imagines. Each teammate may have a different idea of "the group's" attitudes. Yet, if they are to be a team, they must at least roughly agree in their images of the "generalized other." If they do not, they won't be able to act as a team.

Every player has to know that "the team" expects the baseman to stay near his base; that when the bases are loaded "they" expect the guy who catches an infield fly to throw to the catcher at home plate. Each player knows that "the team" expects him or her to take a certain role; each knows that every other player knows what every other player "is supposed" to do. Who says they are supposed to? "They" do. "Everybody" knows that.

IN BASEBALL, rules help the child develop the sense of the team as a "generalized other." With the rules of the game, she is able to see how each player is supposed to act and the ways all of the various roles interlink with one another. As she does, she is learning how to fit into an ordered society. The game introduces her to the ways of the world. Unknowingly, she becomes an accomplice in the effort to make her a conforming, cooperative adult.[11]

This is only the beginning. In the same way that she learns to think of the team as a "generalized other," so she will eventually discover generalized attitudes in more widespread, diffuse

---

[11] Maurice Natanson, *The Social Dynamics of George Herbert Mead* (Washington, D.C.: Public Affairs Press, 1956), p. 13.

groups. She may become "aware" of many other generalized others; even her entire community may become a generalized other. For each, she is able to say that "they" like this or that, expect this thing or that thing, are prone to act in this way or that.

Likely, this "generalized other" is a complicated mixture of attitudes. The child agrees with some and disagrees with others. Whatever the mix, as long as she lives in the community she will act in ways that take that generalized other into account. Even when she does the exact opposite of what she thinks "they" want, she imagines their disapproval. If she thinks that "they" see her as a "troublemaker" or a "tomboy" or a "good girl," eventually she may come to think of herself in the same way.

Most of us, most of the time, act in the ways we think "they" expect us to. In some cases, we conform only because we fear punishment. But usually we conform because we agree with generalized attitudes or because it never occurs to us to act otherwise. For generalized others become powerful actors in the creation of our own self-awareness.

Our thinking is an inner conversation in which we may be taking the roles of specific acquaintances over against ourselves, but usually it is with what I have termed the "generalized other" that we converse, and so attain to the levels of abstract thinking, and that impersonality, that so-called objectivity that we cherish. In this fashion, I conceive, have selves arisen in human behavior and with the selves their minds.

George Herbert Mead, "The Genesis of Self and
Social Control"

When we were toddlers, most of us took our first step toward other-awareness when we learned to take the role of our mothers; then, in seeing ourselves through our mothers' eyes, we took a step toward self-awareness. From that time, social awareness and self-awareness developed together, the one stimulating the other.

With a sense of a generalized other, the tempo quickens and

takes on new qualities. New possibilities of thought arise. Even as toddlers we were able to imagine conversations with our mothers or other specific individuals; now, through a sense of a generalized other, we are virtually able to carry on conversations with our community. We talk to ourselves as we imagine "the community" would—and we respond to what "they" say. Our thinking becomes more general, more abstract; our imagination, too, assumes new qualities; we see ourselves in roles never before imagined, related to others before unknown.

As our thinking and imagination take on these new qualities they also take on new limits. What once seemed possible now seems romantic. Now the child knows she could never be a pirate. "They" would never let it happen. The generalized other becomes a "censor," a gatekeeper, who stands at "the door of our imagery and inner conversations."[12] It tells us what is true and false and what is approved and condemned, not only for us but for all others in our community.

As the "censor" helps hold us in line, it also helps us mature. No matter how inaccurate is our sense of "generalized" attitudes, no matter how they may anger and frustrate us, they help us recognize and criticize ourselves and thus develop an awareness of self. Seeing oneself through the "eyes" of generalized others, we are able to evaluate ourself, to approve and condemn ourself, to pat ourself on the back and attack ourself in anger. In the process, we become aware of who we are, what qualities we have, how we fit into and differ from the rest of society. Our sense of self grows, as we see ourself through the eyes of others, and especially through the eyes of generalized others.

This interdependence of self and others, Mead argued, means that rational men and women can live in harmony and order, without the need for an all-powerful, constraining ruler. "It is only so far as the individual acts not only in his own perspective but also in the perspective of others . . . that a society arises," Mead argued.[13] Only in a coherent society can the self appear.

---

[12] Mead, "Genesis of the Self," in Reck, ed., p. 288.
[13] Mead, *Philosophy of the Present*, p. 165.

This perspective on social order is basically similar, as we shall see, to those of Marx and Weber. It looks to individual action as the basic element of order and change. "That is the reality of the world," Mead insisted. "It is an organization of the perspectives of all the individuals in it. And every individual has something that is peculiar to himself."[14]

In this remarkable vision, then, we see the possibility of a society of organized individuality.

MEAD HAD SET himself a difficult task: to develop an image of the individual and society that allows true individuality, as well as social coherence and change. But what about individuality? To this point, we have seen how traditions and conventions weigh down on us and become part of our very sense of self. We can be "self-conscious," but that might mean only that we will see ourselves as others see us. If that is all there is to "self-consciousness," there may be little possibility of individuality after all: If our self-awareness depends so completely on others, we will simply conform.

Our bondage to society is not so much established by conquest as by collusion. Sometimes, indeed, we are crushed into submission. Much more frequently we are entrapped by our own social nature. The walls of our imprisonment were there before we appeared on the scene, but they are ever rebuilt by ourselves. We are betrayed into captivity with our own cooperation.

Peter Berger, *Invitation to Sociology*

But this sketch of Mead's image of the individual and society is not yet complete, as we shall see in Chapter Four.

Summary and Direction

The influence of some men and women on their societies is enormous. This is most clear in the great religious figures of history, such as Jesus and Mohammed, who bring to life new

---

[14] Mead, *Movements of Thought*, p. 413.

images of man and society.[15] Had Mead known of Weber's writing, he might have called such men "charismatic": they lead others to view themselves and their societies in new, compelling ways (see pp. 208–209).

In these leaders, Mead saw how each individual has the possibility of creating a unique self, even within the constraints of the given society. For the innovative leader is not fundamentally different from other persons: "We call them leaders as such, but they are simply carrying to the Nth power this change in the community by the individual who makes himself a part of it, and belongs to it."[16]

What sets creative individuals off from more conventional persons is a greater tendency to introduce novelty into their own lives and into the lives of others. Creative persons rewrite the past and future in novel ways, giving unexpected meaning to the world about them. They are able to do this to the degree that they have moved beyond the narrow perspectives of their own community. Somehow they are able to take in more of what's happening; they are able to see problems and the sources of frustrations more clearly than others; they are able to consider wider ranges of possible ways to cope with the problems and frustrations.

In large part, innovative leaders are able to do this because they are able to take the roles not only of individuals and generalized others in their own community; they are also able to take the roles of those in other communities. Thus creative leaders are set apart by their abilities to introduce new attitudes, new images, into the lives of their fellow men.[17] They are set apart in this way because they are involved in a self-and-other awareness that goes beyond the involvement of most other men and women.

Facing new problems, they are more likely to break from traditions. Rather than simply following the expectations they have learned—the laws, the meanings, the values of generalized

[15] Mead, *Mind, Self and Society,* p. 217.
[16] *Ibid.,* p. 216.
[17] *Ibid.,* p. 256.

others—they reorganize their experience in unexpected ways. The greater parts of their lives are still conventional, habitual; but in some important ways they make novel replies to their social situations.

To simplify this complicated idea, which carries with it all of the arguments so far seen in this chapter and more, Mead used a simple distinction between the "I" and the "me." The "I" is the individual's response to the attitudes of others; the "me" is the organized set of attitudes of others the person assumes as his or her own. The "me" is the conventional, habitual individual. It involves those responses shared with others; without the "me," the individual could not be a member of the community. But as individuals express themselves, they are reacting to the organized community of the "me"; their novel replies evidence the "I." The attitudes involved are those of the group, but the individual in whom they are organized has the opportunity of giving them an expression perhaps never seen before.

Both the "I" and the "me" are essential to the full expression of the self. A person must take the attitudes of others in order to belong to a community and even to carry on thought. On the other hand, the individual is constantly reacting to the social attitudes, and in this cooperative process the very community to which he or she belongs is changed.

The changes may be humble and trivial ones, Mead admitted. "And yet a certain amount of adjustment and readjustment takes place. We speak of a person as a conventional individual; his ideas are exactly the same as those of his neighbors; he is hardly more than a 'me' under the circumstances; his adjustments are only the slight adjustments that take place, as we say, unconsciously. Over against [the conventional person] there is the person who has a definite personality, who replies to the organized attitude in a way which makes a significant difference. With such a person it is the 'I' that is the more important."[18]

---

[18] *Ibid.*, pp. 199–200.

Both the "me" and the "I" are necessary to the development of "individuality." For individuality cannot develop in isolation; unless we are deeply enmeshed in our society, our individuality withers away. The developing self requires both involvement in the social conventions and a capacity to challenge those conventions.

. . . the "I" is that part of the self, rooted in the biological equipment of the organism, which we identify with impulse, freedom, creativity, subjectivity. . . . The "me" is all of the attitudes, roles, meanings, pressures and values of others organized and taken over into one's self through the agency of role-taking. . . . One without the other would give an extreme and one-sided self. If the self were only a "me," the self would be nothing but a reflection of the social other. . . .

In terms of these two aspects of the self, Mead explains social control (the "me" limits and checks the "I") and social change (the "I" asserts itself within the limits of his society).

Paul E. Pfuetz, *The Social Self*

This is the irony and difficulty of self-awareness: It is only in joining with others that we recognize our individual selves; yet as we express our individuality, we separate ourselves from the group. Individuality requires order and destroys it.

Once again, we face the problem of self and society: Can we find a coherent and workable image of order, change, and individuality? For centuries, men and women have searched for powers in themselves and their social groups that might weld them together in harmony and individuality. Idealists looked to human goodness: to impulses toward brotherhood, toward neighboring, toward some sort of religious communion. But with dispiriting regularity, even the most well-planned and selfless attempts to set up small communal groups have failed. People have been held together by force and fraud, but they have not learned to create an order of free men and women, united by compassion and love.

As we shall see in Chapter Four, Mead asked, Why? The

question—the starting point of social criticism and exploration —grew from his own intense self-and-other involvement. Mead's explorations continually focused on the questions of the creative self, but those questions led him to critically question the ways society was organized and to search for possibilities unrecognized.

In Mead, then, we see the critical sociologist at work. Through the creations of his critical sociology we gain insight into the problems and possibilities of the basic processes of critical sociology—the processes involved in the interplay of emerging self-and-other awareness and involvement.

Chapter Three

The Beats:
Images of Community and Change

"MARK TWAIN ONCE WROTE that the only people that should use the word 'we' are editors, kings, and persons with tapeworms. Yet there is a way of integrating your own ego trip with a sense of community, with a concept of the 'we.' I feel a sense of this most strongly in these massive events. . . . I felt it in Woodstock. . . ."[1]

Abbie Hoffman wrote these words in the hopeful aura of what had been a high point of the youthful search for a new form of community, based on the brotherhood of man. That search had been growing through the fifties and on into the sixties, in the lives of the Beats, then the Hippies and the Street People. And now in Woodstock, as the decade and the movement neared an end, it had reached new depths of satisfaction and excitement in a massive outpouring of fellowship and joy.

To Hoffman and thousands of others, Woodstock was not just a music festival but a way of living, even a way to the rebirth of society. It was a celebration of brotherhood, of a communal bond that would bring new enlightenment, new humanity to America. Yet, only a few months later the myth

---

[1] Abbie Hoffman, *Woodstock Nation* (New York: Vintage, 1969), p. 132.

of Woodstock was sullied in what was to have been a West Coast repeat of the intense experience.

In California, Altamount was planned as the last of the great rock festivals of the decade, a Woodstock West, the last chance for a mass gathering of youth culture to bathe in their own fellowship. Among the happiest of happenings, it was to be the happiest of all, a day of joy and love. But for many it turned out to be a day of terror. By nightfall most who had come with excitement had left with distaste, disillusion, even shock. Four people had died, one stabbed to death in view of thousands, his death recorded on film; others were maimed and beaten.

None expressed the disillusion more sharply and bitterly than the underground papers of nearby Berkeley. "Altamount was a lesson in micro-society with no holds barred," wrote the *Berkeley Tribe*. "Bringing a lot of people together used to be cool. Human Be-ins, Woodstock, even a Hells Angel funeral were creative communal events because their center was everywhere. People would play together, performing, participating, sharing and going home with a feeling that somehow the communal idea would replace the grim isolation wrought on us by a jealous competitive mother culture.

"But at Altamount we were the mother culture. The locust generation came to consume crumbs from the hands of an entertainment industry we helped to create."[2]

In the sixties such self-criticism and self-analyses were rare. But in the seventies they grew common. It was as if the new decade signaled a new face of discontent, less hopeful, less rebellious, more cynical and resigned. In a few long years, the "love generation" had spent its energies and seemed to have grown prematurely old.

There were those who still spoke in easy optimism about a "greening" of America through a new consciousness, of recreating society by creating a new self-and-social awareness, a new

[2] *Berkeley Tribe*, Dec. 12–19, 1969, p. 1.

sense of brotherhood and communal individuality. But with each new year of the seventies, words of communal hope grew ever more rare. Even if a new consciousness were forming in the new generations, it did not seem to have the power to create a new and more humane society.

Now the future seemed less hopeful, the path to human fulfillment not so easy to find. The centuries-old ideals—of brotherhood, equality, and freedom—remained, but they had grown more vague than ever, and it was difficult to tell what they meant in real, human life. Somehow, something seemed to be missing in the communal ideal. It offered a utopian image of life much to be desired, but it seemed unable to suggest a way to get to it. The aged question nagged: Is there no way to create a social order of individual freedom and brotherhood?

THIS CHAPTER CONSIDERS one of the many contemporary searches for an answer to that question, the hopeful, bittersweet search of the Beats for communal brotherhood. Adequate histories of the Beats, and of others who have searched in recent times for communal life, remain to be written; in this chapter, they remain unwritten. My purpose is more limited: to search for possibilities that might further themes introduced by Mead. Not the Beats, then, but critical sociology is the central concern of this sketch. For my experiences in the fifties with some who were called "Beat" and my readings in more recent years suggest that there is much to learn from the lives of those who search as they did for communal fellowship—lessons about the insights and errors of the searchers themselves and about the obstacles and challenges that are faced in our society by those whose lives question its traditions and accepted ways.

In these lessons, we find a variation on the theme of self-and-other involvement that Mead has invited us to consider. Through the example of the Beats, we see that to creatively understand our own private worlds and problems, we must look and live beyond ourselves. To be sure, the problems of our day-to-day lives are problems of our own individual consciousnesses—our own private troubles, anxieties, and indifferences. But our individual problems are not ours alone: If we are to understand them, we must recognize the relationship of our own unique consciousness to the social worlds that surround us. Our private problems—and our possibilities—involve the relation of our inner world of consciousness to the world "outside."

> The inner does not become outer, and the outer inner, just by the discovery of the "inner" world. That is only the beginning. As a whole generation of men, we are so estranged from the inner world that there are many arguing that it does not exist; and that even if it does exist, it does not matter. . . . But without the inner the outer loses its meaning, and without the outer the inner loses its substance.
>
> R. D. Laing, *The Politics of Experience*

In stable times, when the forms of human relationships change slowly, questions about the relation of "inner" to "outer" do not arise. Debate ends before it begins; questions are not asked, for the answers have been given and accepted. Men and women live and die with mute faith in the existing beliefs, and even in suicide accept their truth.

One of the first evidences that a society is transforming, that old ways of thought and belief are eroding, is seen when creative individuals on the peripheries of their societies again ask such questions. They ask them, indirectly and subtly, in the forms of their art, literature, and music, seeking new visions that make better sense of an abrasive and meaningless world. In their search can be seen the basic question of the critically involved life: How can I live with others in this world?

Consciousness, Rejection, and Community

"Human life," Herman Hesse wrote in *Steppenwolf*, "is reduced to real suffering, to hell, only when two ages, two cultures and religions overlap. A man of the Classical Age who had to live in medieval times would suffocate miserably just as a savage does in the midst of our civilization. Now there are times when a whole generation is caught in this way between two ages, two modes of life, with the consequence that it loses all power to understand itself and has no standard, no security, no simple acquiescence."[3] Hesse was writing of another troubled time for Western societies, but his words cut into the confusion of life in our own transforming society.

Even in simple economic terms we can see how unsettling the fifties must have been, especially for those who were young. In the twenty or thirty years since their birth, their society had gone through fundamental economic changes, and they were caught midway between. They had lived their early years in the wake of the Great Depression of the thirties, but they grew to adolescence in a fermenting abundance, in which the threat of scarcity and hunger was hardly visible. For many, their parents' and grandparents' ethic of frugality was shattered by the affluence of postwar prosperity.

Most of their generation who went through that experience saw only hope and high promise: The threats of scarcity and the insecurities of the working life were ending, and signs of new leisure and comfort were everywhere. Prosperity posed no problem: the lure of material well-being made the exchange of their labor seem reasonable. They did not need to be coerced by fear of hunger as many of their fathers and grandfathers had been; they were lured by the certainty of abundance. Jobs were plentiful, and from all sides they were urged to prepare to join in the great drama of building a better world.

In the late sixties and early seventies, as the economy floundered, that sense of mission would grow ever less compelling, and John F. Kennedy's ringing challenge, "Ask not what your country can do for you; ask what you can do for your country," would grow hollow. It was a challenge of life for earlier

[3] Herman Hesse, *Steppenwolf*, Basil Creighton, trans. (New York: Bantam, 1969 [1929]), pp. 24–25.

generations, voicing hopes that most youth in the fifties could recognize: By doing well, productive men would help their country do good.

But, even in the fifties, a few, including those who were to be labeled by the rest of society as "Beatniks," saw the demands of industry and of commerce, government, and other modern organizations as debasing and demeaning. No new values could be seen to take the place of those destroyed by affluence. Society seemed to offer only restraint; escape from poverty did not end the vulnerability of the individual to the society that surrounded him.

For these few, the illusions of old beliefs were shattered, revealing society's other face, the face of exploitation. They had discovered a new, more complete tragedy of uncertain freedom.

When a person moves out of a given social role into another, and the society fails to provide as full and clear-cut a set of meanings and values for the guidance of behavior in the second role as in the first, the person will experience a relative loss of contact with meanings and values (. . . which is experienced subjectively as a sense of "meaninglessness of life").

Arnold Rose, *Theory and Method in the Social Sciences*

The Beats sent up a howl that seemed to voice frustration with the moral poverty of their parents' communities, anger at the human disgrace of their society, contempt of the blindness of their fellow men. A few poets and writers heard in the howl something akin to the infant's inarticulate cry. Some glanced at Marx and saw the roots of the discontent in inequality; others read more closely and saw the roots spreading down into the ways industrial society is organized, into the roles men and women are forced to accept. And a few looked even deeper, following Camus, Sartre, and other existentialists to discover a poverty of culture, an emptiness of beliefs and values, a societal confusion about the very meaning of human life.

All were right, each in his own way. Yet in this spectrum of discontent there was little hope, little vision. It was the discontent of an anti-culture, negative and profound. "What sphinx of cement and aluminum bashed open their skulls and ate up their brains and imagination?" demanded Alan Ginsberg, "Ashcans and unobtainable dollars! Children screaming under stairways! Boys sobbing in armies. Old men weeping in parks!"[4]

As had the labor unions in earlier decades, the Beats saw problems in the ways our society was organized. Why do some people live in luxury, while others starve? Why do some work hard for nothing, while others reap the rewards while doing nothing? They focused on organizational problems: Who does what; who gets what?

But their howl spoke of things far beyond problems of organization. It asked why the military and industry have taken such power in our society, why we follow the dictates of technology, and the demands to produce and consume ever more. The howl spoke of problems in the ways the entire society was functioning, of problems in the future it seemed to be moving toward. It spoke of institutional problems: What is done? With what effects?

Like the labor unions in the thirties, the Beats saw a need for institutional change. The problems of American society could not be solved simply by rearranging the positions of people in the existing organizations. To be sure, rearrangement was necessary, and organizational problems were involved. But those problems demanded institutional solutions. The entire system must be changed, for it was mutilating modern man. They picked up the rebellious sociology of C. Wright Mills, condemning the self-serving purposes of the "power elite," the blindness of bureaucracy, the power of the military, of industry, of the government, the inhumanness of technology. They were anti-war, anti-organization, anti-consumption, and anti-business.

Nor did the rejection stop there. In their more profound depths, the Beats saw that the problems of American society

[4] Alan Ginsberg, *Howl and Other Poems* (San Francisco: City Lights, 1956), p. 164.

were also cultural: We were enslaved to this wayward system by false religions and political ideologies, and by even more fundamental values. Why was society organized the way it was; why did it function in the ways that it did? The Beats were energetically anti-"work," anti-"propriety," and anti-"property."

The Beats' condemnation of the dominant American society was sweeping, and in condemning their society, they condemned themselves. Their rejection was generalized and total; in their eyes, the society they had grown within was worthless, without human meaning. But this meant that the attitudes they had learned through childhood and adolescence—the "generalized others" they had identified in their society—were also worthless and meaningless. And some of these attitudes, no matter how much they are scorned, no matter how inhuman and irrational we know them to be, are not shed easily. Consciously, they can be rejected; but the price may be a nagging guilt, and perhaps even anger at oneself for feeling guilty. To use Mead's terms, the "I" may reject, but the loyalty of the "me" dies slowly, and the self is locked in civil warfare.

THE EFFORT TO REMOLD, in one's own life, the culture one has grown into is heavy with danger. The searcher is likely to be treated as a criminal or madman, condemned and criticized by his own society, ridiculed, even persecuted. Even if he is more fortunate—even if he is simply ignored by others—he must begin his struggle as a cripple. For to consciously reject the "generalized attitudes" of the parent society is to reject positive reference points that have helped him evaluate his actions and accomplishments.

This is the price of freedom on the peripheries. We are able to free ourselves from our parent culture only by destroying parts of ourselves, much as an animal might escape the hunter's trap by gnawing off its own leg. But unlike the wounded animal, the detached person is doubly crippled; however he mutilates himself, he will never quite be free of the trap but will carry it with him in his new freedom. Even if he escapes guilt, the culture he has rejected remains with him; now it no longer reassures him, yet it continues to limit the possibilities he sees in himself and his life.

The burden of his detachment is profound. Cutting himself off from those he has known, he not only loses his old certainties, he loses the familiar means of discovering new things about himself. For, as Mead tells us, "One has to find oneself in his own individual creation as [it is] appreciated by others."[5] We realize our own self by distinguishing ourselves from others— by seeing ourselves as "objects"—human, living objects different from other objects and persons. But the more distant we are from others, the more gross those distinctions, and the less they help us see ourselves.

In our detachment, even when we do discover something about our selves, we feel unsure of it, and unless we can find others to acknowledge the discovery, it withers. For our sense of our unique differences grows and endures only when we see it shared by others who are important to us.

> . . . we are all mysteriously related, because others see us and so become an inalienable dimension of our lives—become, in fact, ourselves . . . our freedom waits for the recognition of other people and needs them to become what it is.
>
> Maurice Merleau-Ponty, *Sense and Nonsense*

But what others? If the society we live in is unsatisfying, perhaps we can find, even create, our own community. Perhaps in the fellowship and inspiration of others who also choose to withdraw, we can find a new sense of self, a way of life more meaningful, more satisfying, more humanly creative.

Once again, in seeking an alternative to the given society, the men and women who would be called "Beats," and later the "Hippies," discovered one another's isolation and drew together. In part they united in defense, to protect themselves against

[5] Mead, *Mind, Self and Society*, p. 324.

the hostility of their society. But they came together also to enjoy the coherence—the self-awareness through social awareness—that individuals can find only as they see themselves in others, and see others seeing them.

Consciousness, Vision, and Community

In many ways the efforts of the early Beats—those who were beat before the Beats were named—were similar to those of a small group of New York artists whose discontent twenty years earlier gave rise to modern abstract art.[6] Sensitive to their own discontent and to others in their detached peripheries, their art announced the early whispers of cultural change that would begin to blow strongly only twenty years later, when its effects would be seen in the struggle of the Beats and the confused musing of students in the fifties.

Each of these New York artists had already gained success and some fame in the conventional art of their times, the troubled thirties; those conventions emphasized paintings with a political and economic message. But the abstractionists chose to start off on new paths and found themselves attacked by critics, cartoonists, newspapers, even those whose favor they once enjoyed.

The rebel artists had an immense advantage over the Beats, one that has eluded most persons in the modern world: they found a reference point from which they could judge their actions, themselves, and their society. They defined themselves in their work. A sense of community grew from the coherence of their individual efforts and their mutual interest in creating new forms in art. Their community and their individual lives were oriented to the struggle for a new awareness of their experience and to ways of expressing it. In their small community, they created visions that foretold the coming discon-

[6] In this discussion of the New York artists, I am especially indebted to Rosenberg and Fliegel, *The Vanguard Artist.*

tent of new generations. Once again, as John Dewey had noted years earlier, "the first stirrings of dissatisfaction and the first intimations of a better future are always found in works of art."[7]

The visionary sensitivity of the creative artist is often noted, but the importance of the community, even to the creative artist, is as often missed. We like to believe that true creation is a solitary thing. But, again, this is only a partial truth. Solitude during the creative act seems to be essential, but creation is also, deeply, a social thing, an achievement of individual-in-society. "It was our community that helped us break through to a world of marvelous possibilities," one of the original group recalled.[8] Even in art the community generates, as well as suppresses, individuality.

Detached from the dominant society, each artist alone was sensitive not only to his own life, but also to the society he had left yet in some ways carried with him. Alone, he was vulnerable to that society; in his community of fellow artists he found not only stimulating ideas and criticism but also the confirmation of his own emerging visions. And he found the security of a small brotherhood of searchers, supporting one another against the rejection of a world they could not forget.

When we began to do non-representational art, we were really undertaking a tremendous adventure. There were some advantages that the feeling of adventure gives you. We also had the advantage of a kind of [spirit] and comradeship that came from talking with other artists who were interested in the same thing. But we were all completely excluded from our society, the society around us. . . . Can you imagine what psychological hazards there were in this kind of thinking?

> A New York abstractionist, quoted in Bernard Rosenberg and Norris Fliegel, *The Vanguard Artist*

The message of the abstractionists was essentially that repre-

[7] John Dewey, *Art as Experience* (New York: Minton, Bilch & Co., 1934).
[8] Rosenberg and Fliegel, *The Vanguard Artist*.

sentational art was inadequate to human experience in a rapidly changing society. Coherence, if it is to be found, must be found in relativity rather than in the emergent modes of organization that had been passed to us by our culture. This profound message ultimately would call into question the institutions of contemporary society. But the focus of the artists' message was on the artistic expression of the experience.

The Beats never achieved such a unifying vision. Perhaps it is not surprising, for the Beats were among the first to express in their daily lives the general cultural discontent that had been growing through the twentieth century. Whereas the New York artists could be creatively troubled by early whispers of the coming change, the Beats felt the full force of its brutal gusts. Whereas the New York artists expressed their discontent in art and only somewhat unconventional ways of life, the Beats lived their discontent in vibrant confusion. As such, the Beats enjoyed less coherence, less security and protection in their communities, and they suffered reactions far more severe.

As a discernible movement, their defeat was announced almost in the moment that the rest of society noticed their existence. For until journalists and officials began to speak of "Beatniks," coffee houses in North Beach in San Francisco, in Greenwich Village in New York, and in other corners of large cities, generated communities of discontents that gave at least a vague focus and support to individual unrests, and provided human contact and communal warmth. They thought of themselves as somehow different, somehow superior to the rest of society, and in this self-identification of brotherhood they found comfort and stimulation.

The public label, the publicity, and the attention probably were in themselves enough to destroy the effort. Lacking a coherent image of themselves, of their own community, even of the society they were trying to reject, the Beats found it difficult to resist the temptation to accept the label, to revel in the attention, to live up to and exceed the expectations for eccentricity and deviance. Other young people swarmed to

Telegraph Hill and the Village, often simply aping the public image, no more than mouthing the negative condemnations that for others had taken form in the bitterness of their lives.

The Beat communities, joined by little internal coherence, could offer scant resistance to the attention and harassment of their society. Communal feelings paled as the numbers of would-be Beats increased; a sense of meaninglessness and impotence became more complete, internal strife escalated along with theft, assault and drug dealing, bringing increased publicity, police control, and unofficial harassment. The vague images of the alternatives they searched for were sullied, and age took its toll.

The Beat communities faded. Individuals stopped thinking of themselves as "Beatniks," and then they stopped thinking of one another as Beat, or even as an "us." Losing their sense of being different, they lost their vague sense of community.

Summary and Direction

In the lives of the Beats, the aged dreams of brotherhood once again had taken living form, and once again those dreams had failed. But the howl of the Beats seemed to echo in the discontent and energies of new generations of youth. Through the sixties, strains of indifference and retreat played through new experiments in brotherhood, strikingly in the "drug cultures" and "hippie communes." But these, too, were short-lived. For most, the time of hope could be counted in months. As with the Beats, the promise of the experiments fashioned with their lives quickly gave way to frustration, disillusionment, and, for some, despair.

Now the critics, many of whom who had shared in the failure of the vision, roared their bitter condemnations. "What he could not give voice to," wrote Norman Mailer, again of himself, "was a voice large and endless in its condemnations of himself and the friends of his generation and the generations which had followed, an indictment of the ways they had used their years, drinking, deep into grass and all the mind illuminants beyond the grass, princelings on the trail of the hip . . ." What was the product of this history? Mailer's answer was unforgiving: ". . . an unholy stew of fanatics, far-outs, and fucked-outs where even the few one loved were intolerable at their worst, an army of outrageously spoiled children who cooked with piss and vomit while the Wasps were quietly moving from command of the world to command of the moon."[9]

Just as men and women are stripped out of the context of past and future, leaving only a raw present, so too their art and their religion and their lives disintegrate into kicks. After the kick subsides, the person is left precisely where he was before—in the bored morass of self. . . . The beat and the square, more than either realizes or admits, are cut from the same cloth. The dilemma is that of [the] character who has "nowhere to go but everywhere." Since there is no basis for choosing one direction over another, the final alternative is to lapse into that dark inertia which is just beneath the neon surface of American life.

Elwin H. Powell, "Beyond Utopia"

Still, communal hopes lingered on. In the early seventies small bands of individuals continued to turn to more coherent communes, limited in membership and economically self-supporting through collective farming or craftsmanship, even through permanent jobs in the "outside" world. Occasionally even middle-aged and older persons joined together in communal households, while continuing to work in established ways. And as the seventies progressed, religious converts downplayed the old moralities, emphasizing the communal inspirations of Jesus, Buddha, Hare Khrisna, Aurobindo, and Mahara Ji. The age-old dream endured of saving men and women, even society, through brotherhood.

But a half-century earlier, George Herbert Mead had rec-

---

[9] Norman Mailer, *Of a Fire on the Moon* (New York: Little-Brown, 1970), pp. 389–390.

ognized a problem in that dream. Communal involvement not only unites men and women to one another, it also divides and alienates.

THE BEAT COMMUNITIES NEVER FOUND the kind of coherence the early abstractionists had discovered in their lives together. Many of the Beats, especially in the early days, were struggling poets, writers, and artists, yet they lacked the unifying vision that had united the New York artists and gave focus to their work and meaning to their community.

Yet among at least some of the Beats an awareness of profound importance seemed to be emerging, as they struggled to make sense of their mutating worlds. That awareness told them to look for the sources of their personal troubles and to seek the possibilities of their lives not only in their own inner worlds nor only in the world outside, but in both.

In the Beats, we have seen how dangerous this search can be. For to critically look for sources of personal troubles and individual possibilities often leads a person to challenge and reject the "generalized attitudes" of the parent society. To do this is to reject the positive reference points that have given coherence and meaning to one's life. Critical involvement, then, lures the individual into the confusions of relativity. But critical involvement also offers hopes of an answer to that confusion. For in moving together with others who are also critically involved, searching for answers to the questions of how to live creatively with one another, individuals may create new order and meaning and find new coherence in their lives.

Still, that coherence may be short-lived, no matter how sincere and open we may be in our mutual search. In the example of the Beats we recognize one reason why: If an alternative community is to endure within a larger society, it is not enough to howl. The defects and limitations of the larger society must be seen clearly. So too must its strengths and possibilities. That means it is not enough to be involved in one's self and the immediate community. Such involvement may give

us a way of looking at ourselves, but if we are critically involved we will soon find the limitations of that view as well
and move on to search for a fuller vision.

This, too, is a lesson of critical sociology we find in the Beats:
the ways we see and think about ourselves and about our society
sensitize us to some possibilities, but at the same time they blind
us to others. A way of looking is also a way of not looking.

Contrary to popular images, Beat communities were not lifeless and devoid of energy and effort. They were vital and exciting; there was an air of electric expectation, an energetic, ner-
vous searching. There was also subdued violence, a roiling anger
and suspicion, a merciless rejection of others that told of their
own insecurity. For—as in most desperate subcultures—with
each new year, they were held together not so much by a
common allegience or by shared values but ever more by the
feeling that it is "them" against "us"—a cohesion through
shared hostility that George Herbert Mead traced to the very
roots of individual and social order.

Chapter Four

The Invitation in Mead: II

"WHAT WAS MOST EUPHORIC, however, was us and what we were to each other." That's a battle veteran writing—a veteran of the student takeover of Harvard's University Hall, one of the final scrimmages between students and administrators in the sixties. In the camaraderie of battle, she had discovered some important things about herself and about others: "For those few hours we were brothers and sisters. . . . You had to realize, whatever your politics, and whatever your tactics, that we were very beautiful in University Hall, we were very human, and we were very together."[1]

She was not alone: a similar excitement runs through the "I was there" reports of campus rebellions of the sixties and early seventies, emphasizing something that is often overlooked in "explanations" of youthful dissent: Whatever its issues, whatever its costs, whatever its successes and failures, a shared struggle offers its own rewards—a sense of togetherness which brings a heightened sense of self. Mead would have recognized these rewards as the spoils of virtually every war, every community battle, every communal struggle to recover from the ravishings of floods, tornadoes, and other disasters. We search

[1] Cited by Fred M. Heckinger (New York Times Service), *San Francisco Chronicle*, June 2, 1969.

for meaning, awareness and self-respect, and often we find them most easily in our shared struggles.

All too often, Mead saw, men and women draw together not in brotherly love, but in a shared hostility to others. In the midst of "The War to End All Wars"—today known as "The First World War"—William James had recognized the powerful bond that unites men and women when they join against a common enemy. War touches something deep in us, making us forget our differences, drawing us together as does nothing else. But can we find such bonds only in organized murder? Is there no moral equivalent of war?[2]

That question bothered Mead deeply, adding to the difficulties of his quest for an image of the creative individual in an ordered society. For he saw that the response to battle is only one expression of human appetite for hostility, an appetite that interlinks with the desire to feel superior. We draw together in resentment and hatred of "outsiders"; we unite in our feelings that it is "them" against "us," that "we" are better than "they." It is not only the victims of our hostility who suffer. For to the degree that we unite in hostility, our own individuality is suppressed.[3]

Mead's hard-headed awareness and realistic insights mixed with complacency about the present condition and optimism about the future of man and society. He was both "tough-minded" and "tender-minded," and it is the tension and interplay of the tough and tender that makes his work potentially so valuable to critical sociology. What has survived in American sociology, however, is mostly the tender Mead; this is the part most compatible with the hopefulness of his day and with the complacency of modern social inquiry.

---

[2] William James, *The Moral Equivalent of War*, in Henry James, Jr., ed., *William James, Memories and Studies* (New York: Longmans, Green, 1911), pp. 265–296.

[3] George Herbert Mead, "The Psychology of Punitive Justice," *The American Journal of Sociology* (1918–1919), pp. 577–602. Reprinted in John W. Petras, *George Herbert Mead,* pp. 130–150; also reprinted in Reck, ed., *Mead: Selected Writings,* pp. 212–239.

It is time, then, to revive the tough Mead that has for half a century remained hidden beneath his kindly optimism.

MEAD LIVED in one of the most dramatic periods in the development of the Western industrial society. In those years, capitalism turned monopolistic, even while businessmen continued to boast of "free enterprise"; organized labor movements emerged with volatile energy, the First World War introduced the twentieth century to unimagined death and destruction; the Bolshevik revolution in Russia ignited new hopes and fears throughout the world; the postwar depression in the twenties and the Great Depression that followed again reduced the world to bitterness.

He lived to see fascist governments rise in Europe and the hopes for a League of Nations die. He saw the ideals of classic democracy in America grow vague and archaic, in the dawning of new ways of industrial competition and negotiation, new tensions in international relations, and new methods of propaganda, manipulation, and governmental control. He was profoundly concerned about war and about man's apparent appetite for stupidity and legal injustice.

He saw these tragic facts of human life, but even they failed to depress him. He reflected the enthusiasm of a generation dazzled by newly discovered possibilities. It was a time of unequalled optimism among American intellectuals. At the turn of the century, as the world moved toward its first great war of modern technology, they had discovered that knowledge can bring power. The knowledge need only be properly used, and the intellectuals could show how. They would bring new enlightenment to society. They would stimulate and help direct social change. They would create a new reasonableness in the management of society.

Though there was no great need to worry about man's future, there was an urgent need to work. The vision of utopia was only a hope, and Mead knew it; his own theories insisted that tomorrow's society might be far from utopian. Evolution leaves the future ever open to question: "We are on the way, but we do not know where," he confessed.[4] But men and women, aware and active, can take part in their own evolution, charting their progress, even influencing their own development and the thrust of their society.

In his gentle and unassuming way, Mead had no desire to shine in the limelight. He saw himself as an ordinary soldier in the battle for social and intellectual reform and did not aspire to lead the troops. His profound devotion to scientific inquiry was always controlled by his desire to contribute his share to the betterment of mankind. "We determine what the world has been," he wrote just before his death, "by the anxious search for the means of making it better."

Lewis A. Coser, *Masters of Sociological Thought*

There is some justice to the charge that "Mead's assumption that an increase of knowledge would bring an increase of virtue does credit to his heart if not to his head."[5] In Mead's view, thus far, the individual seems simply too good to be true. Yet if we look further, we see that, despite his optimism about the future, Mead recognized that conflict and hostility were deeply embedded in humans and had helped shape and misshape individual and social history through the ages.

This part of Mead's thought has been given little attention, perhaps because he only occasionally discussed the problem of conflict and its relation to social change and order. But when he did, his terms were unmistakable: Conflict is not only a fact of life; it is a necessary part of an organized world of self-creative persons. The flaw in modern men and women was not in their willingness to struggle with others; it was in their failure to struggle in ways that create rather than destroy.

---

[4] Mead, *Movements of Thought*.

[5] Hugh Dalziel Duncan, *Communication and Social Order* (New York: Bedminster, 1962), p. 102.

Conflict, Self, and Society

To Mead, even conflict is an expression of the self. The members of a highly organized society share many interests, but at the same time they are in conflict over numerous others. Clearly, this conflict can destroy an organization. The baseball player who is hungry for success can get into the limelight only by playing the game. But there are various ways to play baseball, and a few jealously competing individuals may wreck the team. So, too, blind egoism can destroy an organization, even a society.

But it is also possible that conflict will increase social integration. Indeed, conflict can be creative, for both society and human individuality develop as oppositions between individuals and groups are worked out. Even in a pack of wolves, more than fear keeps one from another's throat. Hostile impulses are held in check and modified as each animal learns to adjust to others in somewhat complex relationships. In this controlled conflict, they "negotiate" an ordered relationship in which hostility rarely gives way to serious attack.

In humans, able to use more powerful languages, adjustment is far more complex. Yet the process is similar. The attack on other individuals of one's own group "is modified and softened so that the individual asserts himself as over against the others in play, in courting, in care of the young, in certain common attitudes of attack and defense, without the attempted destruction of the individuals attacked."[6]

Consider the familiar human impulses toward self-protection and self-preservation. These impulses are usually expressed in rivalry and competition, and especially in economic competition. But these same impulses also lead us to protect one another in our social groups. This protection intensifies our sense of union and interdependence. Thus, rather than destroying

[6] Mead, "Psychology of Punitive Justice," in Reck, ed., p. 214.

the group or the nation, the conflict of self-and-other involved men and women becomes, indirectly, the way to increased social unity, coherence, and coordination.

As individuals in groups and societies attempt to resolve the conflicts that trouble them, they reconstruct their community; that reconstruction may result in a wider social organization. Conflict within a clan, for instance, may lead its members to join with a larger tribe, in which old hostilities are harmonized or stifled by the newly formed power. Thus, even the leaders of nations, fearful of the results of hostility, attempt to develop some sort of international community, such as the United Nations. In such ways, the conflict and discontent within the society, rather than destroying, may bring recreation.

Social conflicts, that is, demand the reconstruction of a group or society. The vehicle of reconstruction, as we have seen, is always individual consciousness: "For it is their possession of minds or powers of thinking which enable human individuals to turn back critically, as it were, upon the organized social structure of the society to which they belong . . . and to reorganize or reconstruct or modify that social structure."[7]

In this way, men and women discover unity in their diversity, creating consensus out of conflict. And in the process they create and maintain their sense of self. Individuality and order, then, emerge from creative conflict. But, as we shall see, it doesn't happen quite this easily.

THERE IS SOMETHING enjoyable about other people's troubles. Even in our sorrow for a close friend, we may feel quiet pleasure at his bad luck. Our sympathy may be real enough, yet there is a certain satisfaction that misfortune struck him, and not us. To Mead, this "primitive enjoyment" about the misfortunes of others was one of the hardest things to explain about human experience.[8] But his image of self and society led him to a telling insight: We are most pleased by those misfortunes of others that tell us we are better than they are.

[7] *Ibid.,* p. 308.
[8] Mead, *Mind, Self and Society,* p. 206.

This is why we laugh when someone else falls down. "If a person does actually break a leg we can sympathize with him, but it was funny, after all, to see him sprawling out." What makes it so funny? The fact that we put ourselves in his place and then realize we are safe: "We do, so to speak, start to fall with him, and . . . our laughter is . . . a release from that immediate tendency to catch ourselves."[9] It was, after all, not we who fell; it was that poor clod over there. Even as we help him up, excitement lingers beneath our polite response. Our sympathy may be real, yet we feel amused and superior.

We get those same feelings from the social blunders of another, even from his failure and defeat. We may be very careful in what we say to him, but still we feel superior: He, not we, has done this unfortunate thing. Even if we remember a similar blunder or defeat in our own lives, his troubles tell us that he is no better, and perhaps far worse, than we.

When we discover that others share our feelings of pleasure, we draw closer together, united by an agreement that we are all superior to such an unfortunate person. The unity we find in comparing ourselves to others is all the more powerful when we also share a dislike for the others. Our shared hostility— kept in check, but very much part of our individual pleasure at the misfortune of our friends—now becomes an underlying bond of our group.[10]

It is easy to study this in everyday situations. Gather ten or fifteen of your acquaintances and make the subject of your conversation the admirable qualities and services of someone known to all. Then change the subject . . . to someone for whom all have a common dislike, and note how much warmer is the sense of at-oneness of those who are engaged in common disparagement. . . . The hostile attitude is particularly favorable to social cohesion.

George Herbert Mead, "National Mindedness and International Mindedness"

---

[9] *Ibid.*
[10] *Ibid.*

In our gossip, each of us makes the claim that he is in some ways superior to those flawed characters of our excited stories; and when others support the claim, we draw closer to them. We discover that we share certain values and encourage one another to believe that those values are better than others. We may all be deluded in our agreement, but it is an agreement we encourage, for it helps each of us enjoy a sense of superiority and self-respect. There is no easier way to express and renew that agreement than in hostility to those who are "different."

When we identify with a group, that sense of superiority is magnified. Our team is better than theirs; our club, our political party, our race, our religion are the best, no matter what others may say. "We all believe that the group we are in is superior to other groups," Mead noted. "We can get together with the members in a bit of gossip that with anyone else or any other group would be impossible." This shared hostility unites men and women as nothing else can. Leadership may be important in pulling us together and exciting our loyalties, "but on the whole we depend upon recognition that other people are not quite as good as we are."[11]

This is most blatant in nationalism. To the patriot, it seems perfectly legitimate to proclaim the superiority of one's own nation over all others. In his own country, in most times, the patriot meets little opposition, for others share his basic biases. As we brand other peoples with ugly colors, we enhance our own ways of life and assure ourselves of our own dignity and self-respect. We pull closer together, in our shared hostility.

Whatever its costs, at times this shared hostility can be useful in the struggle for selfhood. If it is only through hostility and conflict that self and society can be maintained, Mead concluded, then that's the way it must be. "To realize the self is essential, and if that has to be done by fighting, it may be better to keep at least the threat of a fight."[12] For human conflict may arise from real and individually important differences

[11] *Ibid.,* pp. 207–208.
[12] *Ibid.,* p. 317.

in interests and purposes—as in the antagonism between capitalists and workers, between producers and consumers, buyers and sellers, subjects and rulers.

When antagonism arises from the frustration of human efforts to maintain a sense of self, aggressive conflict may offer the only hope. Indeed, when faced with authority that is arbitrary, even revolution is "almost necessary."[13] For under even the most benevolent dictator, men and women cannot express their own purposes. Constrained and directed, allowed only to respond and obey, they are denied a sense of self.

The Destructive Bonds of Hostility

The more our hostility to others is backed up by the group, the closer we draw to one another; the closer we draw, the more fully are we socialized into the common hostility. Thus we are cut off from our enemies, our opponents, our competitors, from all who are in any way "outsiders."

This means, for one thing, that society is splintered, divided within itself. We have just seen that this may be necessary, at least at times, to some degree. Indeed, when men and women differ in their meanings, attitudes, and values they must somehow hold themselves apart from one another while they work out new ways to live together without destroying their individuality. Only in this way can they create "unity in diversity."

But to the degree that we are united by shared hostility, we are blinded to the lives of our enemies: we treat outsiders as typifications—as "hippies" and "Establishment Pigs" and "Up-Tight Mothers" and "Young Creeps," as "Niggers" and "Honkies." Unaware, uninterested in the individuality of "them," we miss the possibilities of discovering unity with them; we fail to consider accommodations and adjustments that might help us live together in harmonious individuality. What

[13] Mead, *Movements of Thought,* p. 12.

might have been creative conflict turns into hostile rejection, repression, and brutality, even into violent destruction.

In this blind conflict, Mead saw, we lose new possibilities of self-awareness. For we discover ourselves through the eyes of others, which means our sense of self is limited to the groups we belong to. So long as we are cut off from the lives of "outsiders" by our shared hostility, we are denied that enlarged self-awareness they might make possible.

But just as hostility divides a society into antagonistic groups, it can also break down those divisions. This happens when men and women set aside their differences to join in warfare, not only against the enemies in other lands, but also against the criminals and deviants in their midst. And, Mead saw, when an entire society unites in battle, self-and-other awareness suffers even more.

USUALLY WE ARE CAREFUL not to let our hostilities to outsiders show too clearly; they are subtly expressed in tendencies to treat "them" differently from the ways we treat "us." Indeed, often our hostilities and prejudices are hidden by masks of morality. These masks may be so familiar that they hide our aggression even from ourselves. When we "respect the law," we feel our own goodness and sensibility. After all, without such respect, what would happen to society? Clearly, those who break the law must be taught a lesson: those who go outside legal channels to challenge it must be controlled.

But, Mead saw, even respect for the law could become a cover for hostility. Rather than an instrument of justice, the law could turn into a "ponderous weapon of defense and attack."[14] As it does, hopes of helping the lawbreaker or of creating more humane institutions of justice are lost.

This shared hostility has an important payoff. Whatever other differences may separate us and our groups, in the cry of "murderer" we join together against a common enemy. "Seem-

[14] Mead, "Psychology of Punitive Justice," p. 586, in Petras, *George Herbert Mead*, p. 137; in Reck, ed., p. 221.

ingly, without the criminal the cohesiveness of society would disappear," Mead argued. "The criminal does not seriously endanger the structure of society by his destructive activities and on the other hand he is responsible for a sense of solidarity, aroused among those whose attention would be otherwise centered upon interests quite divergent from those of each other."[15]

The law has become the weapon for overwhelming the thief of our purses, our good names, or even of our lives. We feel toward it as we feel toward the police officer who rescues us from a murderous assault. The respect for the law is the obverse side of our hatred for the criminal aggressor. . . . Thus we see society almost helpless in the grip of the hostile attitude it has taken toward those who break its laws and contravene its institutions. Hostility toward the lawbreaker inevitably brings with it attitudes of retribution, repression, and exclusion.

George Herbert Mead, "The
Psychology of Punitive Justice"

In the same way, we unite against external enemies. Especially in a popular war—that is, in most wars—the sense of solidarity breaks down the customary barriers that separate us from one another. In the fighting mood we identify with our movement or our nation and discover a bond with those who are fighting alongside us. United by a common cause, our own rivalries and differences of opinion tend to disappear. In times of war, resistance to the national effort vanishes, friction gives way to eager cooperation, and we thrill in marching with those who in daily life are competitors, rivals and opponents.[16] Through these experiences powerful emotions arise, emphasizing for the time being what the whole community stands for and condemning the individual who is opposed or indifferent.

But the price paid for such solidarity is great and at times disastrous. For to the degree that we organize by hostility, we suppress individuality. Even in a political campaign, members may so fully surrender themselves to the party that in the

[15] *Ibid.,* in Petras, p. 141; in Reck, ed., p. 227.
[16] *Ibid.,* in Petras, p. 147; in Reck, ed., pp. 234–235.

battle they become nothing more than "Republicans," "Democrats," "Socialists," or cogs of some other party. The party symbol expresses everything; the individual's own goals are unexpressed. However controlled and subdued, the heated campaign battle is much like the battle of nations; it is a battle for the survival of the right party and the death of the wrong.

At most extreme, we even lose sight of our own purposes, deceiving ourselves that we are struggling for certain goals— perhaps to save the free world, to end the threat of communism, to combat crime and evil, to help wipe out injustice, racial discrimination, and poverty. But, whatever our initial purposes in joining the battle, we turn our energies from those goals to the struggle itself.

Now the struggle is valued in itself, for in it we renew the unity of our group and thereby renew our own sense of self and self-respect. United against the enemy we reach the ultimate form of self-assertion—but the self that is being asserted is a self whose existence calls for the destruction or defeat or subjection of the enemy.

THIS IS THE CRITICAL POINT: No matter how necessary or just the struggle, as we join in hostile battle we lose the ability to think of ourselves and our society in terms of our own individual lives. What is "good" and "valuable?" What does it mean to be a "responsible" member of society? We face the enemy, and through him we find our answers: To be good is to not break the law or the rules, to not oppose our group or our society; to be responsible we need only obey the rules and help punish those who don't.

Thus, in defining "the criminal" and "the enemy" we define ourselves and our society—but it is a negative definition. We have seen this in the "counterculture" of the Beats; but now we can also see it in the stance of "respectable" society toward its enemies and those labeled as "deviants."

Property, for instance, can be defined in terms of its positive social uses for human life. But in our agreement that we must stand together in the struggle to protect property those positive uses are forgotten. "Property" becomes sacred not because of what it does for us but because in its name we are united. Armed with the law, we punish those who threaten it and are blinded to the meaning of what we are protecting.

In the same way, as we unite in hostility against the lawbreaker, we come to think of "personal rights," "family rights," and the "rights of government" as something abstract, beyond our individual lives, sacred in themselves. Anyone who falls outside the rigid terms of these "rights" is condemned. He is persecuted not because he destroys or threatens the society but because he has not honored the "rights" we agree on.

Thus, Mead has taken us to the roots of the conserving bias of human societies. We struggle to retain the social order, for in that order we recognize ourselves; as we unite to protect it against dangers, real and imagined, we discover a new solidarity in our shared aggression. But now we see how much such conservatism can cost; for as we unite in hostility to conserve the social order, we lose our potentials of individuality.

Thus, as nations battle, self-awareness withers away. And thus the "deviant" unknowingly has revenge on the society that crushes him: Concentrating our energies on his punishment, we are paralyzed in our efforts to examine the human meanings of our institutions, our actions, our lives.[17]

In defending our institutions against real or imagined enemies, we accept those institutions as "good" in themselves. As we must defend society against its enemies, society must be "good" in its present form. With our backs to what we protect, we forget or never discover what is inherently valuable about the law, the church, the family, the government we protect. We neglect to ask how those institutions, as they exist, serve and suppress the men and women who support them. United in hostility, we do not seek to discover how to creatively reform our society; we seek to destroy those who differ from us. As we

[17] *Ibid.,* in Petras, pp. 140–141; in Reck, ed., p. 226.

do, we blind ourselves to the lives of others, and we lose sight of the critical questions of our own needs and lives.

HISTORY OFFERS ONLY a negative answer to William James's question: There is no moral equivalent to war and punitive justice. People can be held together by force and fraud. They can come together in their shared hostility to outsiders and to deviants within their own groups. But when they attempt to join in brotherhood and love, they fail. To Mead, that is the deepest tragedy of human society.

"We come back to our original questions," he wrote near the end of his life. "How shall we get and maintain that unity of society in which alone we can exist?"[18] Is there no productive way to create a bond of brotherhood among individuals and groups in a large social order; must we always be united and divided by hostility and aggression?

> There is something profoundly pathetic in the situation of great peoples, that have been struggling up through long centuries of fighting and its attendant miseries, coming closer and closer to each other in their daily life . . . and realizing only intermittently the spiritual life which this larger community confers upon them, and realizing it only when they could fight for it. . . .
>
> George Herbert Mead, "National Mindedness and International Mindedness"

Mead thought he saw a way out of this historical fate. His solution is unworkable, yet it rests on a profound insight that takes us an important step closer to a useful image of the individual and society. Again his insight springs from the ability of the individual to take the role of the other.

Summary and Direction

Mead, remember, started with the existential human, what he called the "biologic individual." The existentialist, as we have seen in the brief portrayal of Camus' thought in Chapter

[18] Mead, "National-Mindedness," in Reck, ed., p. 359.

One (pp. 9–11), tells us that the individual constructs himself, his essential being, through his actions and, at the same time, he constructs his world. Thus, in the existential image, human individuality is assured. But the cost is high: The existentialist's image ignores the power of economics, politics, and organizations on our inner lives, and it ignores the profound influences of socialization.

Mead's image is somewhat more complete than the traditional existential view. Both begin with individual minds and work out through society; but Mead begins at the same time with society, which works into the individual mind, through the processes of communication. This is the genius of Mead's image: He begins with both parts of the interplaying processes of individual and society and shows how the two processes—individual and social—are one, yet at the same time distinct.

The individual takes society into himself, and as he does he influences the processes of his society; society responds to the innovative individual, yet the social processes go on integrating. Through role-taking, the individual becomes aware of others and his relationship to them, and as he does he also grows aware of himself. To be individual the person must be social; even his thought is social, for it goes on only as he assumes the roles of others.

Yet, clearly, the ability to take the role of the other is alone no guarantee that humans will live in creative harmony. Many who are gifted at "taking the role of the other" use the ability to exploit others. Mead did not couch the problem in these terms, yet he was aware of it. It demanded, he saw, that each individual recognize how his own actions and attitudes interlink and depend on others. To act effectively—whether in cooperation or rebellion—each must be able to recognize how his or her life and individuality relate to others'. With the recognition goes the doing.

Here Mead found the key to hope in a tragic world. In the ideal society, individuals would act in their individuality, yet—self-and-other aware, recognizing how their individuality interlinks with that of others in mutual interest—they would act in creative unity with others. Their societal awareness would be part of their self-awareness; their self-involvement would include a societal involvement. Even conflict would be creative, leading not to destruction but to negotiation and reform that increase the human satisfactions and coherence of both individual and society.

But how is this possible in the giant and complex societies of modern times; how can we even hope to take the attitudes of the numberless others who in one way or another are involved in our actions? Relationships are so complicated they seem to overwhelm the capacity of any individual to take the roles of all those whose lives interlink with his.

"And yet," Mead argued, "though modern life has become infinitely more complex than it was in earlier periods of human history, it is far easier for the modern man than for his predecessors to put himself in the place of those who contribute to his necessities, who share with him the functions of government, or join with him in determining prices."[19] It is not the number of participants, or even the number of different roles in a society, that is of primary importance. The important question is whether the others' roles are recognized as important to and interlinked with one's own life.

If that question is to be answered positively, somehow the social and psychological barriers that separate individuals and groups from one another must be broken down.

MEAD, AS WE HAVE SEEN, FOCUSED his critical sociology on questions of self-awareness and involvement. Doing so, he gave only passing attention to the nagging questions of racial inequality and economic exploitation that today plague us so insistently.

In this light, Mead's hopes for man seem blindly optimistic. If society is so organized that some persons live in wretchedness while others enjoy unearned luxury, then what is needed is not to break down the barriers that separate them, but to

19 Mead, *Mind, Self and Society*, p. 291.

break down the inequality. Indeed, at times the barriers may even be useful, for behind them the exploited can gather together, marshaling their forces to compel the privileged and powerful to change.

In an important way, however, such criticism is unfair. Mead, remember, was aware that conditions in modern society could demand aggressive conflict, perhaps even revolution. At times, such conflict could even help reform society, to allow more creative individuality to more men and women. If he gave the abrasive conditions of modern society only passing attention, it was at least in part because his vision was fixed on even more fundamental questions of human consciousness and social order.

For Mead saw that even when individuals are not separated by undeniable barriers of inequality, still they remain estranged from one another. Loyal to their special groups, they miss the enlarged self-awareness they might find in others. Separated and insensitive to the lives of others, their conflict is not creative but destructive. Not only do they fail to find the possibilities the others might offer; within their own groups they continue to organize around their shared hostility to those others.

We must overcome distances of space and time and the barriers of language, convention, and status so that we can take the roles of those who are involved with us in the common undertakings of life. Our only hope is our curiosity, which may be called "the passion of self-consciousness." This teaches us that "we must be others if we are to be ourselves."

Hugh Dalziel Duncan, *Communication and Social Order*

Some of the barriers that separate individuals and groups from one another are obvious; language differences, geographic distance, age differences, differences in tastes, values, and beliefs. Yet even if these can be surmounted, other, more fundamental, barriers remain: the barriers erected, as we have seen, to protect the individual's sense of self. For self-awareness is rooted in the groups whose roles the individual is able to take;

to give up those distinct groups is to give up the inner coherence and feelings of well-being they make possible. To lower
the barriers that separate our special groups from the rest of
society, to step beyond our groups into other relationships is
threatening. To do so, we risk the security of the known for the
possibilities of the unknown.

Now Mead's question—how can we create social unity without destroying the individual—can be stated more fully: How
can people be encouraged to venture from the confining security of their present groups, to interact with "outsiders" in
ways that allow and encourage them to enter into one another's
lives—to take one another's roles, discovering themselves in one
another's eyes, and creating new unity in their discovery? To
answer that question we must find out what it is that divides
and unites individuals, what encourages and suppresses their
individuality.

Here Mead's vision failed. He had posed the critical question
of consciousness in our times, the basic concern of a critical
sociology. Yet, with a persistent focus on self-and-other involvement, he failed to look fully in the directions his question
must take us. Those directions lead to a critical view of the
existing society and to an exploration of the possibilities that
are emerging and that might be created within that society. In
Marx and Weber we find invitations to take these directions.

EVER OPTIMISTIC, Mead believed that the ideal society was
within our grasp if we would only reach for it. Like Marx, he
looked forward to a utopian tomorrow. But unlike Marx, he
thought that the present thrusts of organized society could take
us there. A new society was evolving, and though conflict and
struggle were still necessary, there was little need for any sort
of violence or abrupt "revolution." For the contradictions of
capitalism were not increasing; rather they were lessening, as
men and women learned to "take the roles" of ever more others,
linking together in ever larger social and geographic areas, moving toward a humanistic, "functional" society.

In this ideal "functional" society, men and women would be

truly intentional; all individuals would possess a "perfected social intelligence"; each would be able to take the attitudes of every other individual. Thus conflict would be creative, not destructive, as the opposition of individuals quickly brought changes, leading to ever more coherence and harmony in both self and society. In their diversity, individuals would discover their unity; through enlightened conflict—the conflict of men and women self-aware and socially aware—they would continually recreate a society that serves all individuals.

But Mead's hopeful vision of the coming society was a philosopher's dream, his image of a functional society one more example of the misworkings of liberal humanism in American thought. Like other well-meaning men and women of his time, such as John Dewey and Jane Adams, he taught of a new society of harmony and creative brotherhood. But in his radical visions he failed to see that he was asking individuals to adjust to a political-economic society that was cynically indifferent to their lives.

The new radicals assumed that it was possible, as William James had said, to find a "moral equivalent of war"—a moral equivalent of evil of all kinds. . . . The new radicalism nevertheless led to an attack on social problems which in some of its implications was the reverse of radical . . . the manipulative note was rarely absent from their writings: the insistence that men could best be controlled and directed not by the old, crude methods of force but by "education" in its broadest sense.

Christopher Lasch, *The New Radicalism in America: 1889–1963*

Mead—who had so incisively penetrated the processes of social psychology—had given little attention to the political and economic nature of his society. To be sure, with each new decade, it seemed that society was growing ever more "functional"; but as it did, the humanistic ideals that had inspired Mead seemed ever less realistic. In the brute facts of organizational life, Mead's dream, like those of other liberal humanists, seemed to be turning into a nightmare.

Part Two

CRITICISM
The Invitation in Marx

Heavy physical work, the care of home and children, petty quarrels with neighbors, films, football, beer, and, above all, gambling filled up the horizon of their minds. . . . To keep them in control was not difficult. . . . And even when they became discontented, as they sometimes did, their discontent led nowhere, because, being without general ideas, they could only focus it on petty specific grievances.

GEORGE ORWELL, 1984

Chapter Five

The Invitation in Marx: I

In the mid-seventies bare buttocks livened the pages of our daily newspapers as students turned to a new fad, "streaking": men and women running naked through a crowded street, onto an opera stage, even across the Golden Gate Bridge. A few officials growled, but to most people it was a welcome sight: Students were finally turning their backs on major issues, exposing things that some observers considered rather trivial. It seemed a return to the serenity of the fifties, when college presidents had little to worry about beyond springtime panty raids and autumnal excesses of excited football fans.

In the years between panty raids and streaking, however, television and newspapers had been filled with stories of campus anger, demands, and violence; the emotions and energies of students were charged by issues that led many of them to a growing involvement in questions about their lives and the lives of distant others.

It was difficult for many of their elders to understand the activism of these years; it seemed only destructive, self-centered, and irrational. Yet, ironically, many of the youthful activists seemed to rebel in the name of the ideals of their elders.

Karl Marx had recognized the revolutionary potentials

of "rising expectations."[1] As long as men and women are blinded by poverty, able to see little hope of improving their lot, they remain resigned to their fate. But when things begin to improve, hopes soar. The situation is volatile, for however fast their lives improve, expectations rise faster, and opportunities never seem to keep pace.

A similar thing may happen as other social conditions improve. As the nation finally turns attention to social injustice, as the constraints of rigid discipline and regimented schooling loosen, as emerging nations are freed from outright colonial exploitation, as the energies of world leaders turn to discussions on avoiding war and establishing international justice, as Presidents begin to speak not of simply ending poverty and abject misery but of establishing a "great society" and a nation of justice—as such things happen, men and women begin to dream of new utopias around the corner.

But realities are not so responsive to human hopes. Dreams give way to frustrations that, just as the frustrated hope of the economically underprivileged, are politically explosive.

The college students among whom the youth culture and campus unrest emerged . . . were part of the first generation of middle-class Americans to grow up in the post-Depression American welfare state under the tutelage of a parental generation that embodied the distinctive moral vision of modern liberalism. . . .

And as they brought their parents' high-minded ideals to bear on American society in a thoroughgoing way, their vision of that society changed radically. . . .

William Scranton *et al.*, *The Report of the President's Commission on Campus Unrest*

Like those who placed their hopes in brotherhood and communal living, many of the young activists were deeply involved in a critical search for ways to live with others in our times. But unlike their "communal" counterparts, they turned to po-

[1] Karl Marx, *Wage-Labour and Capital* (New York: International, 1933), p. 33.

litical dissent as the way to pursue their search and to struggle for their ideals of a better society.

In effect, they interpreted the howl of the Beats, bringing to political debate the qualities of American culture. In the Beat's inarticulate questioning, linking private problems to public issues, we have seen three levels of critical involvement (see pp. 42–44):

1. An indignation focused in the question: "Who does what?" This is an organizational criticism, a questioning of the structures of society and the roles that are allocated in society. Why do some people live well, others in poverty; why do some work hard for nothing, while others reap the rewards?

2. A rejection focused in the question, "What is done?" This is an institutional criticism, a questioning of the ways functions in society are allocated. Why have government, military, and industry taken such overwhelming power in contemporary society? Why do we follow the dictates of technology, ever expanding our production and consumption, making human lives secondary to economic growth?

3. A frustrating anxiety, focused in the question, "Why is all this done?" This is a cultural criticism, a questioning of the meanings, values, and goals of society, a rejection not only of the institutional structures and organizational relationships but of the entire social bond. Even the most basic and honored values and beliefs are questioned and found wanting.

In this spectrum of critical questioning, radicals have raised questions that formerly were beyond politics, that in American traditions had been reserved to the arts and letters.[2] To the radicals of twentieth-century America, every aspect of human existence is ultimately a question for political decision. Politics is useless unless it improves the quality of individual human life. That is a message we also find in Marx.

---

[2] Christopher Lasch, *The New Radicalism in America (1889–1963): The Intellectual as a Social Type* (New York: Knopf, 1965), p. 90.

IN THE SIXTIES a new wave of interest in the political Marx surged through American campuses and into Third World movements. Once again, radicals saw in his theories a formula for revolution and a way to end inequality and alienation. But in practice the formula proved difficult, and soon it was again being said that for American radicalism "Marx is dead." It was not the first time he had been laid to rest, nor was it likely the last. For our Western traditions of thought offer few other images of the individual and social change that can give such hope to the powerless and impoverished. When discontent men and women seek an image that will help them make sense of their world, they have few places to turn. Again they conjure up spectors of Marx to inspire their labors of change. But time and again the image fails them, for they expect too much of Marx and understand him too little. So too do those who fear his name.

To many Americans, the one key to Marx's thought is revolution—abrupt, violent, and destructive revolution. This is unfortunate for, as we shall see, Marx meant something quite different by "revolution," something that could be helpful in understanding contemporary change. It is also an error, for there is no single key to his complex thought. To understand Marx a large set of keys is needed.

In this chapter and Chapter Seven a few of those keys are briefly displayed: his ideas on consciousness and praxis, his ideas on ideology and social class, his ideas on social conflict and social change. Others could be added, and must be added by those who would truly understand Marx. But these will do for now; in them we can see the outlines of his image of consciousness, conflict, and social change.

Alienation and Consciousness

"The most important concept for understanding the student movement is Marx's notion of alienation." It was 1964 in

Berkeley. The speaker was Mario Savio, a figurehead of the Free Speech Movement, which marked the beginning of a wave of activism on American campuses. Recent months had been hectic, and it was difficult to think clearly. Mostly, people felt things: the daring, the excitement of their demands, the inspiration of their leaders, the justice of their cause. Given the situation, Savio's lecture on alienation was impressive.

"Its basic meaning," he explained, "is that the worker is alienated from his product. But the concept is applicable to students, too, many of whom don't come from the working class. Somehow people are being separated off from something. The students are frustrated; they can find no place in society where alienation doesn't exist, where they can do meaningful work. Despair sets in; a volatile political agent. The students revolt against the apparatus of the university. This is the mode of power of the movement."[3]

Savio had caught a critical point, not only about the student movement but about Marx's most basic beliefs. For Karl Marx was not simply against poverty, as is so often thought. His dream was not only to more equally distribute the wealth of a productive society and to end economic injustice and exploitation. True, he sought these things, but only as a part of more profound human goals. For he recognized that economic abundance for all might bring only a more comfortable slavery, what C. Wright Mills would later describe as a society of "Cheerful Robots."[4]

This is the reason Marx sought an end to the inequality of capitalism: a capitalistic society alienates man not only from others, but also from himself.

"ALIENATION" is a vague, ill-defined term. Perhaps due partly to its vagueness, the word seems to carry a poetic curse to the twentieth century. These days it cavorts through casual

[3] Mario Savio, "The Future of the Student Movement," speech at a symposium of Young Socialist Alliance, Westminster Hotel, Berkeley, November 20, 1964.
[4] C. Wright Mills, *The Sociological Imagination* (New York: Oxford, 1959).

conversations and political rallies and weaves into the fabrics of popular film, fiction, and drama. In an age of intellectual fads, the idea shows surprising endurance.

The persistence may be due, in part, to the personal satisfactions offered by the idea of alienation. It helps describe our feelings of aloneness, justifying our most bitter complaints about society without demanding that we actually withdraw from it. It allows us to live with our discontent and to locate its sources outside of ourselves. It appeals to those who would separate their lives from certain others in order to gain the advantages of being part of a brotherhood, of an "us," who find the warm. pleasure of being different from "them."

Thus, "alienation" is also a natural vehicle for messages of generational discontent. It is no accident that discussions of alienation continue to be most popular among the young, for the young are more likely than their elders to be psychologically on the periphery of society; they are the ones most anxious to know life's meaning and least satisfied by the answers of their parental culture.

The questions posed by the ambiguous idea of alienation are basically those that Mead had raised: questions of the relationship of our being to our consciousness, of existence to essence, of subject to object, of the "inner world" to the "outer world." These questions have plagued men and women through our century with a persistence that goes beyond the fact that we like to play guessing games and to compete with one another's brilliance. For the relationship of being and consciousness is one of the most fundamental problems of contemporary awareness.

Marx's ideas on alienation and the qualities of human life are developed most fully in his youthful writings.[5] For years after his death, those writings were unknown to Marxist and anti-Marxist theorists. Only in the 1930's did they appear in English, and even today many scholars—mostly those of the older generations reared on the "mature" Marx—refuse to accept them

---

[5] Principally *Economic and Philosophical Manuscripts of 1844,* in Karl Marx, *Early Writings,* T. B. Bottomore, ed. (New York: McGraw-Hill, 1964).

as the "real" Marx. They were written, they claim, before Marx became a Marxist.[6]

It is true that as Marx aged, his concerns for the quality of individual human lives seemed to fade into the background of his image of the individual and society. Yet Marx had not rejected those concerns. Even in his most mature works with Frederick Engels they flow like insistent currents beneath the surfaces of his words and now and then boil turbulently to the surface.[7]

Within the capitalist system all methods for raising the social productiveness of labor are brought about at the cost of the individual laborer; all means for the development of production transform themselves into means of domination over, and exploitation of, the producers; they mutilate the laborer into a fragment of a man, degrade him to the level of an appendage of a machine, destroy every remnant of charm in his work and turn it into hated toil; they estrange from him the intellectual potentialities of the labor process. . . .

Karl Marx, *Capital*

As he matured, Marx concluded that the only way to realize his youthful visions of humanity was to change society; that the individual alone can do little even to change himself, much less the lives of other persons. In all but the rarest moments of inspiration, most persons are imprisoned in their social situations, blinded to the sources of their misery, betrayed by their own minds.

[6] See, for a good example, Sidney Hook, *From Hegel to Marx: Studies in the Intellectual Development of Karl Marx* (Ann Arbor: University of Michigan Press, 1962). See also Lewis S. Feuer, *Marx and the Intellectuals* (New York: Anchor, 1969).

[7] For discussions of the position that there is no fundamental rift between the works of the younger and the older Marx, see Robert Tucker, *The Marxian Revolutionary Idea* (New York: Norton, 1970); Istvan Meszaros, *Marx's Theory of Alienation* (New York: Harper, 1972); Erich Fromm, ed., *Marx's Concept of Man* (New York: Ungar, 1961); and S. Avineri, *The Social and Political Thought of Karl Marx* (Cambridge: Cambridge University Press, 1968).

We would err to ignore the young Marx, then, for his writings reveal the heart of the older Marx, whose worries about capitalism and revolution shook the world. And they reveal a depth in Marx's thought that might be missed by those who read only the works of his mature age. For even before he passed the age of thirty, Marx had presented a striking development in the history of man's efforts to understand himself.

LIKE MEAD, the young Marx saw that our senses can be formed only in their interaction with objects outside them. In that interaction even the "so-called spiritual senses, the practical senses (desiring, loving, etc.), in brief, human sensibility and the human character" can come into being. "It is therefore not only in thought, but in *all* the senses that man is affirmed in the objective world."[8]

It is only in relating ourselves to the objective world that the world becomes real to us and we become real to our selves. Thus through our actions—through "praxis," or "practice"—life creates life; our being and our consciousness, our existence and essence, emerge together. Praxis, then, is a creative interplay between our needs and the conditions, the material and human relations around us. In the actively productive life, we relate to the objective conditions, including other persons, not just with our consciousness but with all of our senses, each of which has its own needs.

Thus the young Marx departed radically from the German traditions in which he had matured. Emphasizing the individual's actions, he took Emanuel Kant's question, "How can we know?" from center focus and replaced it with the existential question, "How can we live?" Yet Kant's question is never far from Marx's theories, for implicit in them is the idea that somehow we can influence our history—that under certain conditions we can know, can see our self and our world; that our

---

[8] Karl Marx and Frederick Engels, *Marx/Engels Gesamtausgabe* (Frankfurt: Marx-Engels-Archiv, 1927), Vol. III, p. 191.

mind is not simply a response to the demands of our body and surrounds.

But if we are to act, we must also be able to choose, and if we are to choose, we must be able to think at least somewhat independently of our surrounds. Thus Marx reverses Kant's priorities: We do not live in order to deal in knowledge and rationality; we gain knowledge in order to live, and in true living comes awareness and rationality.

In his youth Marx asked the question so common in our times: Why is modern man unable to feel himself to be a whole person? He agreed with Hegel that society, especially industrial society, is at fault. But there Marx and Hegel parted company. For Hegel, the answer was that society alienates man from the essential Truth. To become whole, one must seek to perfect his Ideas; we realize ourselves in our intellectual and spiritual striving.

To Marx, we realize ourselves in our everyday actions; but most persons, in most times, are unable to freely choose their actions, for they fail to see their needs clearly. To Hegel, ideas are the route to salvation; to Marx, they are usually the stumbling blocks to progress, masks that hide our brutality to others and to ourselves.

With his usual amount of modesty, Marx proclaimed that his perspective resolved what others had seen to be the "conflict between existence and essence, between freedom and necessity, between individual and species. It is the solution of the riddle of history and it recognizes itself to be the solution."[9] If consciousness is part of our being, then actions are the fundamental concern; it is what we do that influences our development. Actions are the stuff of history and of human life.

THERE IS A SUBTLETY to this argument that is missed by those who simply repeat Marx's phrase out of context, that "it

[9] Marx, *Economic and Philosophic Manuscripts of 1844* (Moscow: Foreign Languages Publishing House, 1961), p. 127.

is not the consciousness of men that determines their being, but, on the contrary, their social being that determines their consciousness."[10] Through omission, a complex argument is reduced to a straw man that can be accepted or rejected as a matter of taste.

Marx held that the language of real life is the individual acting in response to his body and his surrounds; but he also recognized that from this action emerged ideas and that ideas in turn influenced future action and perceptions. The individual consciously interacts with his environment, perceiving his world in terms of his present intentions, knowledge, basic needs, and level of technological development.

It is often thought that Marx believed that only economic and productive roles determine the person's being. True, Marx saw these as the most fundamental influences on human history. But he also recognized the part played by ideas and ideals. These do affect both behavior and being. In fact, the very heat of his arguments against Hegel and other idealists rises from his respect for the power of ideas and ideals.[11]

What effects social change is the reaction of human consciousness to ripening conditions—the understanding, the decision, and the resulting action. The movement of history is not due to the creative activity of Absolute Mind, nor to the result of a dynamic urge within life and matter; neither is it imposed from without by the irresistible force of economic pressure. It develops out of the *redirective activity of human beings*, trying to meet their natural and social needs by . . . economic and social changes.

John Lewis, *The Life and Teaching of Karl Marx*

There is an interplay of ideas and activity; in our actions, we are influenced not simply by material or physical conditions, but

[10] Karl Marx, "Preface" to *A Contribution to the Critique of Political Economy* (Chicago: Kerr, 1904), p. 12; for a fuller statement, see Karl Marx and Frederick Engels, *The German Ideology* (New York: International, 1960), pp. 1 ff.

[11] George Lichtheim, *The Concept of Ideology and Other Essays* (New York: Vintage, 1967), pp. 20–22.

also by our ideas of those conditions and our relations to them. In the interplay of ideas and our surrounds, we can act consciously, thereby not only altering our own consciousness but also changing our world so that it is more appropriate to our needs. But only if we act with what Sartre later called "good faith"—only if as we act we subjectively relate to the objects of the world—will the world become real to us and will we become real to ourselves. Thus life creates life: from the creative interplay—the "dialectics"—of subjective man and objective world emerges true consciousness, true awareness of oneself.

Marx, then, did not say that human consciousness is simply determined by the body and its environment, as many of his interpreters and critics have claimed. Rather, the young Marx argued what George Herbert Mead and Max Weber half a century later would turn into a basic proposition in their images of man: that true consciousness arises as we meet and solve our problems and that in this interplay arise social relations, organizations and institutions.

Mead, as we have seen, elaborated this basic proposition in subtle and exciting ways. But the young Marx had other things to do. He developed his informing perspective—a sociological image of the critically involved individual—and then, with Engels, moved to concerns more politically demanding and volatile.

Ideology and Exploitation

We have the potential of creative involvement. Still, usually that potential is unfulfilled. Looking about him at industrializing Europe, Marx saw that somehow—even from the actions of individuals who seemed to be pursuing their own ends—a social order emerges that is so overpowering it effectively determines goals, actions, and even thoughts. Why this overwhelming influence of the social surrounds?

Marx saw two fundamental reasons. First, each of us, even

when pursuing our own goals, is limited by the activity of other persons around us, especially those within our day-to-day groups. They coerce and constrain us and limit our actual choices; they also interact in such ways that our actions have virtually no influence in creating new social orders.

But most of the time we do not even attempt to act in ways different from our fellow men, even when it would be possible, even when it would be creative or enjoyable. For we are held captive by our own ideas. History repeats this irony of human life: usually our ideas and ideals do not enlighten us and free us to act in our own best interests; rather, they blind us to our selves and our world and blind us to the processes and injustices of our society.

Through history, Marx argued, most persons have been the slaves of their own beliefs and habits of thought. Despite our capabilities, we are then the dupes rather than the creators; we are used, and don't know it. Indeed, we cling to our ignorance, willingly participating in our blindness, for our ideas and ideals help us make sense of lives that are otherwise unbearable. This blindness prevents us from recognizing our true human needs.

If there is tension between our needs and what is offered us, we believe that it is we who are at fault, we who must adjust to the demands of the world. Where there might be meaningful action—a productive interplay between our subjectivity and our objective conditions—there is simply responsive behavior.

More than anything else, we are blinded by the view we have of ourselves and our world. We accept political beliefs that, in fact, are masks that hide the truth of our own lives and hide the truth of our social world. "Among the many forms of alienation," writes Erich Fromm, "the most frequent one is alienation in language. . . . The *word* 'love' is meant to be a symbol of the *fact* love, but as soon as it is spoken it tends to assume a life of its own . . . and soon I say the word and feel nothing, except the *thought* of love which the word expresses. . . .

The same holds true for all other achievements of man; ideas, art, any kind of man-made objects. They are man's creations;

they are valuable aids for life, and each one of them is also a trap; a temptation to confuse life with things, experience with artifacts, feeling with surrender and submission."[12] These masks are not the creation of the individual alone; they are largely determined by the social conditions. Socially imposed rules separate individuals from themselves, from others, from their world.

This is especially true in industrial society, where productive energies are diverted into the meaningless labor demanded by industry, which twists a human into a "crippled monstrosity." Labor that is forced, that the individual does not freely choose, with all of his being, "alienates man from his own body, external nature, his mental life and his human life."[13] In capitalist society especially, human labor becomes a commodity, something to be bought and sold rather than freely chosen. Thus, the labor is alienating; through it, individuals become things, not only to their bosses, but also to themselves.

The fundamental terms of reference in Marx's theory of alienation are "man" (M), "nature" (N), and "industry" or "productive activity" (I). . . . Marx pictures the relationship . . . in the form of a *threefold interaction* between its constituent parts. This can be illustrated as follows:

As we can see, [this] means that "man" is not only the *creator* of industry but also its *product*.

Istvan Meszaros, *Marx's Theory of Alienation*

In one of his early manuscripts Marx identified four kinds of alienation individuals suffer in industrial labor. First, they are alienated from the objects they produce with their labor. Even though they make the products, they lose control of them, and the products come to enslave the people. Second, they are alien-

[12] Fromm, ed., *Marx's Concept of Man,* pp. 45–46.
[13] Marx, *Economic and Philosophic Manuscripts of 1844,* p. 103.

ated from their labors, because those labors are not related to their innermost creative needs. Third, because their activities are unrelated to their needs, their lives are alienated from their own essence. Finally, alienated labor alienates them from other people.[14]

In these youthful ideas on alienation and in his later works, Marx saw that the root problem of men and women living under capitalistic systems of production was that they cannot recognize themselves as active agents in their social world. Rather, the world seems to be beyond or above them; it is an object to be experienced passively and receptively. And if individuals are also parts of that world they see "outside" themselves, they come to see themselves as objects, divorced from their own feelings; they become "things" even to themselves. They, too, are only objects to be passively experienced.

But it doesn't have to be this way, Marx believed. He had a dream of a glorious, utopian future. When alienating labor has ended, individuals will be able to live truly, in Sartre's "good faith." This was true praxis: "Every one of your relations to man and to nature must be a specific expression, corresponding to the object of your will, of your real individual life. If you live without evoking love in return, if you are not able, by the manifestations of yourself as a loving person, to make yourself a loving person, then your life is impotent and a misfortune."[15] In the perfect society, self-and-other involvement would flourish.

History shows the individual forced and lured into acting in "bad faith." Still, it is possible for some men and women, some of the time, to engage in "true" activities. But when they do, they are necessarily critical of their alienated activity, which leads them to be critical of the society that has placed them in their alienated roles. They become "radical," for "to be radical is to grasp things by the root." For man the root is man himself.[16]

[14] Marx, *Early Writings,* pp. 124–125, 138.
[15] *Ibid.,* pp. 193–194.
[16] *Ibid.,* p. 52.

Thus, the critical involvement we have seen in Mead leads to social criticism, to an effort in Marx to penetrate the illusions that separate us from others and from our selfs, to tear off the masks that hide the injustices and brutalizations of our society.

MARX'S IDEA OF REVOLUTION is not what most Americans think it is. We know, from years of being told, that America was born of "revolution." But there is something quite different between that revolution and the kind that Marx anticipated. What we think of as our Revolution—the Revolution of 1776 —left the basic structures of American society virtually unchanged. There were exceptions, but in the largest part, those who had been powerful and wealthy remained so; those who had been underprivileged remained underprivileged.

By contrast, Marx dreamed of a revolution in which an established society is changed from within to form a new society. In the Marxian vision, in response to internal pressures, the very centers of society change. Thus Marx was little interested in the American revolt of 1776; rather he found a model in the French Revolution that erupted only thirteen years later.

That revolution was the first in which revolt was seen not just as a way to correct things which are felt to be wrong; it was seen as a means to the rebirth of a society. In the French Revolution of 1789 the very centers of society were changed, though not in the way its leading spokesmen hoped. That pervasive central change—not the violence and bloodshed that helped bring it—is what Marx saw as a true revolution.

The revolution had been long in developing and marked the death throes of a society based on feudalism. For as new systems of trade and economy developed, and as new methods of production and industrialization spread, the old agricultural systems no longer worked.

The French Revolution was encouraged by the demands of peasants for more land, by Parisians sick of hunger and poverty and bureaucratic repression. But the most important revolutionaries were the new middle classes. They had come to new wealth and now grew frustrated at being denied the right to vote and other means of political power that might match their economic power. Years of conflict followed the revolutionary violence, but it hurried the transformation of France from feudalism to capitalism.[17]

By the mid-nineteenth century, it appeared to Marx that other countries in Europe were on the verge of the same kind of transformation. But this time it would not be the aristocracy, but the middle class who would be overthrown.

Marx . . . was the first thinker who saw that the realization of the universal and fully awakened man can occur only together with social changes which lead to a new and truly human economic and social organization of mankind.

Erich Fromm, *Beyond the Chains of Illusion*

No one was more sensitive to the signs of discontent than Marx. He was fascinated by the French Revolution, for in it he saw that middle-class businessmen, growing strong and restless in a feudal economy, had risen to overthrow the very system that created it. But this was to be just one step, a necessary preliminary, to the great revolution. The next step would come, he believed, from the discontent of the workers. Just as the middle class had been most deprived by feudalism, so the workers were the most exploited under capitalism. For capitalism forced them from lives of security in feudalism and gave them little in exchange.[18]

The roots of insecurity among the poor and powerless twist deeply into the groundworks of Western civilization. Those roots sprouted as industry and technology made their impact on the culture of Western Europe. Marx saw clearly that the industrial revolution had a catastrophic dislocation on the lives of the common people. Prior to industrialism, most common

---

[17] For a succinct discussion of the effects of the French Revolution on Marx and on Western images of man, see E. H. Carr, *The October Revolution: Before and After* (New York: Knopf, 1969), pp. 2–7.

[18] The following paragraphs draw on Karl Polanyi, *The Great Transformation* (New York: Farrar & Reinhart, 1944; Beacon, 1957).

people enjoyed a basic economic security. Even the peasant, little more than a slave with a few political and legal rights, "belonged" to a plot of land. No matter whether the land was that of a master or was a "common land," on which the peasant worked with others of his village to earn a bare living by raising sheep: The land provided a certainty to his life.

The commercial and industrial revolutions uprooted these farmers from their land, to turn them into commercial and industrial workers. They were freed from their slavery to the land and master. But the freedom they gained was troublesome. Under feudalism they had little choice but to struggle with their land for subsistence, yet they were secure in their right to struggle. Under early capitalism, they could choose to starve without work or to work for an uncertain life.

Nor was it only the worker who was thrust into insecurity by the industrial and commercial revolutions. Throughout capitalistic Europe, owners often treated the workers in ways arbitrary and unfair; but often they were virtually forced into injustice. For they, too, were captives of their industry's insecurity, as they struggled for survival in an impersonal market. Medieval "businessmen" had been protected by an image of a "just price" and by the professional sanctions of guilds. Financial returns were low, but they were secure. In free enterprise systems, by contrast, the businessman had a chance to grow very wealthy, but he also ran greater risks of failure. He was more vulnerable now to the problems of open competition, less protected from economic depressions, fearful of inventions that would make his own product obsolete, subject to the fads and fashions of consumers. His insecurity, as much as his hope, was reflected in monopolies, combines, "fair trade laws," procedures to protect his inventions, to gain control over and even suppress new inventions. But, somehow, the system seemed to work in fits and starts, generating a relentless tide of economic ups and downs.

Discontent mounted rapidly. The average income per worker rose markedly but so did feelings of insecurity. Every day men went to work in fear that tomorrow they would be dropped from the payroll. England was the first to respond to the new problems: Early in the nineteenth century, Parliament passed a sort of guaranteed-wage law, whereby the government supplemented the wages of workers who did not earn a set minimum amount—a sort of "guaranteed wage" plan rather like those again being debated today in various governments. But the act failed to establish a feeling of security within the capitalistic economy. Lacking a personal commitment, a social bond, to one another, both the employer and worker took advantage of the government's protection. Employers depressed wages below the minimum, allowing the government to subsidize their industry. Workers loafed on the job with little fear of losing their incomes.

Often an ill-conceived plan not only fails to bring reform, it destroys chances for future reform. The failure of the guaranteed-wage programs undermined the influence of those who were concerned with the welfare of the workers. When the ineffectual law was repealed in 1834, labor was left more than ever at the mercy of the employers, and the workers' temporary sense of security plummeted. Economic depressions, each seemingly bringing more unemployment, brought ever greater despair.[19]

This was the misery of the worker that Marx saw around him. As debates undulated over the virtues and vices of guaranteed annual wages, demoralization and demands escalated. Pressures increased for laws to provide social security, minimum wages, relief, and welfare. All the while, men and women grew more desperate, at times to the point of courage. And from desperate courage, rebellion grows.

Summary and Direction

In the discontent of the workers Marx saw the end of capitalism. But Marx was not simply against capitalism. Rather, he

[19] *Ibid.*, pp. 77–102.

recognized in it a power never before seen in history, and a necessary stage in man's journey to a utopian future. "The bourgeoisie," he wrote with Engels in *The Communist Manifesto,* "during its rule of scarce one hundred years, has created more massive and more colossal productive forces than have all preceding generations together. Subjection of nature's forces to man, machinery, application of chemistry to industry and agriculture, steam-navigation, railways, electric telegraphs, clearing of whole continents for cultivation, canalization of rivers, whole populations conjured out of the ground—what earlier century had even a presentiment that such productive forces slumbered in the lap of social labor?"[20]

Capitalism had emerged in the revolution from a feudal society, and it in turn would give way to socialism and the beginning of man's true history. Just as feudalism finally created a new middle class, so capitalism created a new class: the workers, whose lives were made monstrous by their labors in suppressive factories. This working class needed only to recognize that its unhappiness was caused by capitalism. Then it would rise with explosive energies to bring an end to the power of capitalists and create once again a new society. But this time, it would be a society in which the true potentials of man might be realized.

The superstition that used to ascribe revolutions to the ugly intentions of agitators is a thing of the past. Today everyone knows that whenever a revolutionary upheaval takes place, its source lies in some social need that outdated institutions are not meeting. The need may not be felt strongly enough or widely enough to obtain immediate success, but any attempt at brutal repression will only make it more powerful.

Karl Marx, *Enthullungen uber den
Kommunistenporzess zu Koln*

The industrialized, free-enterprise economies of Europe, Marx saw, generated forces unparalleled in history. Capitalism was

[20] Karl Marx and Frederick Engels, *The Communist Manifesto,* in *Selected Works,* Vol. I (Moscow: Foreign Languages Publishing House, 1951 [1848]), pp. 38–39.

not only unique in its enormous productivity, it brought new forms of society—of family relations, political authority, music, art, and values and beliefs. These new forms both excited and angered him, for with new possibilities, they brought new miseries and new myths to delude those who suffered.

To Marx, capitalism was an unavoidable stage in the history of man, but he was impatient for its decline and fall. He heaped scorn on all who seemed a part of the inhuman system. Not one man, nor any groups of men were to blame; it was everyone: industrialists, merchants and rulers who exploit others for their own gain or pleasure, intellectuals who excuse the exploitation, even the workers, as long as they remained unaware of their slavery. His condemnation was complete; all involved in the brutalizing society were the targets of his anger.

IN BACK OF THE HOSTILITY of workers and their unions, George Herbert Mead believed, lay the struggle of workers to gain a sense of who they are. For even in the early decades of the twentieth century, Mead saw, it was impossible for many workers to gain a sense of "selfhood" in their work or in the lives that their work allowed them to live. In such conditions, it was impossible to become involved in the critical concerns of self-and-others; it was impossible to move beyond the narrow perspectives of one's immediate groups, to take the roles of distant others and thereby gain a deeper awareness of one's self.

And, Mead saw, the individual who is unable to gain a sense of who he is may rise to challenge the order of his society. When situations grow extreme, when men and women are allowed only to respond and obey, when they feel only constrained and directed, they take whatever chances they get to "bind themselves together by hostile organizations to realize their common purposes and ends and thus assume the selfhood which society denies them."[21]

Marx shared this commitment to self-awareness for all persons and like Mead recognized that individuals who are united

[21] Mead, "National-Mindedness," p. 396. Reprinted in Reck, ed., *Mead: Selected Writings,* pp. 369–370.

in struggle can bring creative change to their society. Both recognized how brutally destructive unenlightened conflict and violence can be. But where Mead pursued the meanings of this insight for individual growth and change, Marx pursued the possibilities of large-scale, continuing conflict as a means of bringing not only change but rebirth to a society.

Marx saw more clearly than Mead that the struggle against economic injustice was not only a struggle for a sense of self but also a struggle for physical satisfaction. To be sure, the questions of human freedom and responsibility were the critical questions of human life for Marx; but as long as there was scarcity and inequality in the world, he saw, those questions held little intrigue for most persons. For the energies of hungry men and women are directed toward more fundamental questions: questions of necessity.

Mead had criticized and explored possibilities of his society, but always as contexts for the critical questions about self-and-others. In Marx, we see much the same range of concerns, but they are emphasized in ways that virtually reverse Mead's priorities. For Marx recognized how difficult it is for most individuals, in most societies and most times, to escape the constraints and limitations imposed on them.

It is not so much human nature or human capacities that are at fault in the modern world, Marx tells us; it is economic and political systems. Capitalism has created a new breed of men and women, humans who have been brutalized by the new processes of technology and economics. To be sure, capitalism has created possibilities never known to earlier men and women. But it also calls out the worst in us, dividing us from one another, blinding us to our own lives.

Whatever the problems in this argument, they should not obscure the critical lesson it offers: to understand ourselves and our society, we must become social critics, struggling to expose the errors and deficiencies of our society, persistently asking the kind of questions we have seen in the spectrum of radical discontent—critical, irreverent questions about the organizations of our society, about its institutions, about its culture.

Chapter Six

The Unions: Images of Conflict and Change

VIOLENCE PLAYED an important part in the emergence of recent activism—and in its failure. The process generally ran something like this: As demands and counter-demands escalated, the dissenters' threats turned to destruction. Windows were smashed, street lights broken, police cars overturned and even burned. This touched off an "overkill" response, in which police, governors, and other authorities moved to the offensive. Tear gas and arrests became familiar on campuses, then scatter-guns, bayonets, and rifles, and new arsenals of "crowd control" weapons. Just as in the union movement of earlier decades, given anger, fear, and weapons, it was only a matter of time until death became part of the scene. As it had earlier been the workers, now it was mostly the young who suffered.

The violence and counter-violence brought new life and new supporters to the ranks of both the forces of "law and order" and the dissidents. This, too, seemed to parallel the experience of the unions in the thirties, when violence attracted new support for both the "oppressed workers" and the "beleaguered management." The open struggle demanded attention, luring and forcing men and women to take sides, polarizing communities.

Thus, the violence and deaths helped the cause of the dissident unions, winning the active support of middle-class men and women who had until then been passive or indifferent. In this way, union history shows, minority dissidence may grow into major social conflict of such thrust that some change, in one direction or another, is inevitable. But the parallel was faulty.

In this chapter, then, we will look more closely at the history of conflict and violence in the rise and success of the labor unions in America. In that history, we shall see that the relationship of violence and conflict to change is not so simple as the young activists seemed to think.

UNLIKE THE RECENT RADICALS, most Americans think of violence as irrational, even as "un-American." They are shocked at the waves of rioting that sweep through the urban ghettos, at the brash speeches of black activists and young white "revolutionaries," at the "takeovers," "trashings," and battles between police and students on our campuses.

Underlying this shock, as Michael Wallace points out, is an "historical amnesia."[1] We have believed for so long in the Horatio Alger myth—that anyone can rise from rags to riches—that only the most controlled and "tasteful" conflict seems justified. If some people can't succeed through legal channels and peaceful competition, it is because they are not really worthy; only gangsters and others who are selfish and lazy resort to violence to gain their ends the "easy" way. There is no need for collective violence; hard work, patience and restraint will bring all people, regardless of birth, to the comforts of a middle-class life. Thus in this restricted view violence is an aberration, a mistake, a sickness.

It is true that much collective conflict is ill-conceived, offering its authors little chance of success. Some, certainly, is little more than a howl, a violent exasperation, an "acting out" of deep despair. But even this violence may not be so irrational as

---

[1] Michael Wallace, "The Uses of Violence in American History," *The American Scholar* (Winter, 1970), pp. 81–102.

it seems. It may spring from a desperate discontent that can find no effective voice in the established and changing society.

The great visionary poet William Blake wrote half a century before Freud that "Unacted desire breeds pestilence." Enacted desire, on the other hand, even if, in the absence of alternative channels, it be expressed through social violence, may help clear the air.

> Lewis A. Coser, *Continuities in*
> *the Study of Social Conflict*

Collective violence is usually a response to the demands and deprivations that develop as new forms of society replace older ones. The history of Western society shows undulating fevers of collective violence at those times when political and economic structures are in flux, when old forms of organization show signs of weakness or inadequacy, when new kinds of men and women gain influence and wealth but are denied power, when others are displaced or held in a disadvantage grown obvious.

Collective violence, then, can be seen as an expression of discontent: the discontent of those who feel they have lost something valuable, and seek to regain it (reactionary discontent); the discontent of those who feel deprived of rights or things they think they deserve (reforming and revolutionary discontent); the discontent of those satisfied with the direction things are taking, but disturbed by the demands of others (conserving discontent).[2]

Reactionary Discontent

The early impact of industry gave rise in European societies to a rash of "reactionary" violence from workers bent on destroying the machines they thought would take their jobs. It is

---

[2] This differentiation of types of discontent was stimulated by Charles Tilly's essay, "Collective Violence in European Perspective," in *Violence in America: Historical and Comparative Perspectives,* Hugh Davis Graham and Robert Gurr, eds. (Washington, D.C.: Government Printing Office, 1969), pp. 5–34.

tempting today to see their rebellions as irrational. But it is probably more accurate to see them as reasonable efforts to defend traditional ways of life against the urbanization and centralization that came with industry.

In the early nineteenth century, for example, the "Luddites," calling themselves an "army of re-dressers," took up battle against the power looms and shearing frames. It was not simply that they as craftsmen of the handloom detested the new weaving machinery. Something more far-reaching was at stake: in the new political economy of industry, the Luddites saw themselves as being cast aside by industry and authorities alike. It wasn't simply their economic well-being that was threatened; with their jobs would be lost a whole way of living. They were fighting for their lives or, more accurately, for deeply valued ways of life.

The Luddites' rebellion was not a lone reaction to isolated and momentary misery. Their fears were but one crest of the waves of discontent that swept through European societies as they industrialized and centralized. So, too, other peoples in other places and times of the early nineteenth century revolted against tax collectors, against military conscription, against policies on the ownership of land.

They even rebelled against the selling of food, which to us today seems to be simply normal business practice. But to those who had grown within feudal ways of life, only a mercenary would sell food, especially to people who had no real chance to earn enough to buy their way from hunger. They fought to save the traditional guarantees of a feudal society—the right to earn life's necessities by working at one's craft or by farming land even if they themselves did not own it. The rebels knew that justice was on their side.

Persistently those who seek popular revolution see themselves as the enemies of despotism; they struggle for democracy, equality, and enlightenment. But, clearly, the rebels' views and values are not shared by men of power. On the surface, and probably to themselves, the demands of nineteenth-century dissidents appeared practical and down-to-earth: give us land, food, jobs, and security. In fact, they demanded things far more profound. For to meet such demands required a change in economic distribution—not simply a change in who was getting the land, food, and jobs but in the forms of distribution. They required a change in the character of jobs, in the systems of ownership, in the structures of power.

The rioters were asking not simply for changes in business and political organizations; they were asking for changes in the institutions of economics and government—for changes in "blueprints" of how the economy and polity should run. Those institutions and the ideologies that supported them had dramatically transformed as capitalism and industry replaced feudalism.

The rebels called for a return to the old institutions, and in their call they challenged the legitimacy—the very right to exist—of the new systems of government, commerce, and production. Though they appeared to hope for simple reform—that is, a slight reorganization of business and government to give them an improved position—their demands required something more like a revolution. For to meet their demands would require changes in the very centers of society—in the institutions of industry, commerce, and government. Such changes require in turn changes throughout the other institutions of society. For, as Karl Marx saw, social change is "systemic"—changes in one part of society call out changes in other parts. When the systemic changes fundamentally alter the central institutions, a society has been truly revolutionized.

It is accurate, then, to call the reactionary violence of the Luddites and similar rebellions against the effects of industry and urbanism "counter-revolutionary." For, in fact, the Luddites were living in the midst of a revolution—of systemic change that swept through the institutional and organizational structures of society. In their demands and violence, they sought to reverse the industrial revolution. But as we recognize today, revolutions and counter-revolutions are not so easily mounted.

THE REACTIONARY MOVEMENTS of nineteenth-century Europe differ strikingly from the early American labor movement. The dissent of the reactionary is justified by an ideology of earlier times: The reactionary has not accepted the changed views of human justice that emerge to support the new institutions, much less the utopian ideals of those who dream of even further changes from what has been. Rather, the reactionary continues to hold old ideologies and is disturbed, even incensed, to see them violated.

As the labor movement took form in America, the ideologies of European feudalism were all but forgotten. In nineteenth-century America, a union movement was able to advance on one front alone, the demand for improved material conditions. In the face of economic depression, this single demand—based on the individual aspirations of the workers rather than on the sense of a shared fate, or a "class consciousness"—proved inadequate. When jobs were secure, the workers would join the unions, making their demands for higher wages and better working conditions, but when depression hit and unemployment soared, the members left the union rather than face the danger of being fired for their membership.[3]

America did not feel the full impact of the industrial revolution until around the time of the Civil War. Even then the workers were hesitant in their demands; and for two decades after the war, unionism remained tame, even fearful. Most attempts to win better conditions ended quickly, often disastrously for the workers. Faced with a demanding and insensitive industry, American workers yearned for an end to misery, for better wages, easier work, and shorter hours. And as conditions slowly improved, they began to envision a better world.

[3] See J. David Greenstone, *Labor in American Politics* (New York: Vintage, 1969), pp. 18–21; and Patrick Renshaw, *The Wobblies: The Story of Syndicalism in the United States* (New York: Anchor, 1967), pp. 1–11. For a brief history of the American labor movement, see Henry Pelling, *American Labor* (Chicago: University of Chicago Press, 1960); for a more readable account, highly sympathetic to labor, see Louis M. Adamic, *Dynamite: The Story of Class Violence in America* (New York: Chelsea House, 1931).

Revolutionary Discontent: The Wobblies

In the early years of the twentieth century, new images—visions of a glorious future—danced in the minds of union leaders and members. Even the most pragmatic union men could hope that material betterment would bring not just an end to hunger and fear but other social and human rewards. They dreamed of a comfort and fulfillment thus far enjoyed only by the middle class. That meant, at the least, basic changes in the social, economic, and political life of America. For the radical few, the vision went far beyond these pragmatic changes. Their vision was truly utopian, and thus truly revolutionary.

Every period in history has contained ideas transcending the existing order, but these did not function as utopias; they were rather the appropriate ideologies of this stage of existence as long as they were "organically" and harmoniously integrated into the world-view characteristic of the period (i.e., did not offer revolutionary possibilities). . . . Not until certain social groups embodied these wish-images into their actual conduct and tried to realize them, did these ideologies become utopian.

Karl Mannheim, *Ideology and Utopia*

What was required was a pervasive institutional change—not just a reorganization, but a change in the system, in the forms of organization. The utopian unionists recognized that their vision was revolutionary; rather than seeking justice in yesterday's ideologies, as had the Luddites, they found it in a utopian tomorrow.

Most striking of these idealists were the "Wobblies," the Industrial Workers of the World.[4] As had the Knights of Labor before them, the Wobblies sought to build a union so big that, through massive support, it would be able to capture control of all industry and thus destroy capitalism. Their inspiration was Marxian, and, somehow, their programs failed them.

---

[4] See Renshaw, *The Wobblies* (New York: Anchor, 1967); Aleine Austin, *The Labor Story* (New York: Coward-McCann, 1947).

The Wobblies represent a profound yet neglected lesson of human history: Radical goals require images and ideas that are socially aware—images that will help an inspired leadership develop a kind of organization that is able to wage its battles in a hostile world. The more radical the goal, the more fundamental the change required in society; and the more fundamental the change, the more it will be resisted, not only by those whose power, prestige, and wealth are threatened, but even by others who, though less well placed, have come to value the established ways of life.

The Knights of Labor and the Wobblies did not even begin to succeed. Whatever else they lacked in their idealism, they were unable to find an image of the individual and society that would help them develop an organization that could not only express their inspired hopes but help them cope with the world they faced.

The IWW, formed in 1905, was known to millions of workers and was dedicated to organizing not just a select few, but the mass of workers.[5] Yet its membership never reached more than 120,000. Neither it nor other radical union movements commanded the loyalties of massive memberships or enjoyed the success of the more pragmatic unions. For their ideals seemed as strange and distasteful to most workers as they did to the more privileged.

It is not surprising that the Wobblies inspired fear. They generated a free speech movement and mounted soapboxes to advocate violence, direct action, and "sabotage." For all their words, they conducted few strikes, and in their activity there were but few instances of planned violence; most often they sought to discourage all but the most ordered confrontation. Yet violence plagued them. The Wobblies' reputation made them an easy target for repressive action by owners, authorities, and vigilante groups of aroused citizens. Their members were beaten and harassed, their offices and halls destroyed.

[5] Philip Taft and Philip Ross, "American Labor Violence: Its Causes, Character and Outcome," in Graham and Gurr, *op. cit.*

When they attempted to organize lumber workers in Centralia, Washington, for example, their union hall was wrecked, during a Red Cross parade. The IWW tried again, but as soon as they opened a new hall threats began, and fears mounted. During an Armistice Day parade in 1919, members of the IWW were barricaded in their hall, determined to protect it. When the hall was attacked, they opened fire. Four members of the American Legion were killed, one apparently from gunshot wounds inflicted by a Wobblie named Wesley Everest, who was also, ironically, a war veteran.

Vengeance was quick; that night Everest was lynched by a citizen mob. More legal methods were used against the others. Eleven members of the IWW were tried for murder. One was released, two were acquitted, and seven were convicted of second-degree murder. Justice was served—or was it? Whoever was guilty in the shoot-out, it is clear that in Centralia the Wobblies were victims: Their violence was a response to attacks made upon their members for exercising their constitutional rights. Yet only they were convicted by the supposedly impartial law.

Nor was it only in Washington that radical ideas struck fear and brought violence down on the Wobblies. In 1917, the state of Minnesota passed a criminal syndicalist law forbidding the advocacy of force and violence as a means of social change. A number of other states followed suit. In quick order, several hundred members of the IWW were tried; thirty-one were sent to the penitentiary in Idaho, fifty-two in Washington, and one hundred thirty-three in California.[6]

The experience echoes through the decades: Men were convicted for their ideas, not for acts of violence. The case of the Wobblies, then, presents what many see as but part of a continuing practice of legal vigilantism, a tendency of the powerful and secure to turn their idealistic challengers into political prisoners, in direct contradiction to the First Amendment.

[6] *Ibid.*

Reforming Discontent: The AFL-CIO

The violence suffered by the Wobblies was only a more extreme case of what happened to unions in general in the late nineteenth and early twentieth centuries. Most unions in America were far more pragmatic than the IWW. From the beginning, most unions demanded only higher wages, retirement funds and other fringe benefits, safety and improved working conditions, and—what often generated the most violence—the right to organize.

Still, even the most pragmatic movements were, in an important sense, utopian. In another important sense, their utopian images differed from the more radical idealism of the Wobblies. Unlike the "reactionary" movements of the earlier industrialism, both pragmatic and idealistic unions were "forward-looking" and envisioned an improved society, not just for themselves but for the entire society. But where radicals demanded change of revolutionary scope—that is, change in the institutional forms of society—the pragmatists' dreams were less grand. They sought only organizational changes: improved wages, hours, and working conditions. In final analysis, they wanted no fundamental changes in the way society was going, they simply wanted a better deal for themselves.

Still, at least until the time of the Second World War, even that practical demand was utopian, for it seemed to be a struggle against great odds and for something never known to Western man: the end of poverty and economic injustice. Through his union, the worker could feel himself part of a modern drama, a battle to win a more just society.

The practical and limited demands of the American Federation of Labor (AFL) gave it an advantage over more idealistic unions such as the Wobblies and the Knights of Labor. For AFL members could see progress in minor organizational reforms that benefited only certain groups of workers. Whereas the Wobblies had hoped to change things for everyone, in one massive movement, AFL leaders could believe they were making progress by organizing strong and durable organizations of a few select types of workers. From the beginning, they excluded nonworkers, organizing skilled tradesmen who could easily see that they had a shared interest in reform.[7]

This new type of unionism flourished under the leadership of Samuel Gompers. It rejected the Marxian ideas of class war and even the idea of the Wobblies that workers could progress through "one big union." Reform would come by winning demands for specific locals, but the local union could succeed only by maintaining a strong loyalty to the national organization.

Even the most practical demands of the AFL and smaller "pragmatic" unions were seen as threats by men of power and affluence and others who valued the security of ordered community. Often, striking workers came up against laws of the state and federal governments. For those laws were weighted in favor of business and social stability. Union demands were feared, not only because they threatened the profits of industry but also because they threatened the established order of things.

Most violence in labor disputes erupted over the right to organize, and the odds were heavily in favor of the employer. Not until the mid-thirties did the workers gain a legal guarantee that they could organize. In the absence of legal support many workers were denied the right to union membership on threat of losing their jobs. Efforts of union members and leaders were usually frustrated, and even the intervention of friendly government officials provided little more than morally persuasive power. The laws, assisted with police protection, favored the owner.[8]

---

[7] For discussion, and bibliographic references on the American Federation of Labor and the Congress of Industrial Organizations, see Lewis Lorwin, *The American Federation of Labor* (Washington, D.C.: Brookings Institution, 1933); Pelling, *op. cit.;* Greenstone, *op. cit.;* and Taft and Ross, *op. cit.*

[8] For examples of owner's resistance to union organizations, see the excerpts in Leon Litwack, *The American Labor Movement* (Englewood Cliffs: Prentice-Hall, 1962), pp. 82–112.

Employers in no other country, with the possible exception of those in the metal and machine trades in France, have so persistently, so vigorously, at such costs, opposed and fought trade unions as the American employing class. In no other Western country have employers been so much aided in their opposition to unions by the civil authorities, the armed forces of government and their courts.

Lewis Lorwin, *The American Federation of Labor*

With monotonous regularity, currents of violence in labor disputes served to strengthen the hand of the owner, gaining the union nothing of immediate value. In only a few cases did violence seem to help the unions gain their immediate ends.

To many observers, this is conclusive evidence that the conflict and violence of the union movement was simply wasteful and destructive. But actions do not have only immediate effects. They also have long-run consequences—latent effects that become apparent only after some time, when joined by the effects of countless other actions. If we look only at the immediate payoff, it seems that the unions gained little in the first half-century of their efforts. But in longer perspective we see that in the early decades of this century the workers were, unknowingly, gaining by losing. In the thirties, as the nation struggled against the problems of the Great Depression, those gains paid off, in a ground swell of union agitation, government action, and public support.

WE STILL KNOW little about collective dissent. In part, I believe, this is a result of a tendency in our society to embrace images that emphasize the harmony and balance of social life and simply to assume that collective conflict is an evil thing, a sickness or deviance.

Procedures have been established, it is argued, to work out grievances in our system. True, the procedures don't always work, but as long as they are followed, there is a good chance, the best chance we have, that "orderly" conflict will benefit not only the dissenting groups but the entire society. The collective conflict of political parties, for example, may be irritating and inefficient, but in the long run it is constructive, and through it the community escapes the destructive effects of "irrational" conflict.

So, too, the argument continues, the modern conflict of labor and management can be productive, as long as the rules of arbitration, negotiation and demonstration are followed. But if those rules are broken—if management sends goons to break the picket line or if strikers resort to rioting, threats of bodily harm, or illegal acts—the chances of constructive outcome are lessened. Thus, it is argued, until the government stepped in during the Great Depression of the thirties to bring order to the confusion of labor-management battles, little was gained by the labor movement and much was lost to the nation. Every labor demand, every strike, every instance of civil disobedience simply brought further unrest and social destruction.

There is one trouble with this view: It does not recognize the way that decades of growing sentiment can suddenly take focus in times of crisis, providing direction and inspiration not only to common people who are seeking ways to express their discontent but also to government officials who are seeking to return the country to "normalcy."

It is true that labor and the unions enjoyed few clear victories before the National Industrial Recovery Act of 1933 announced their right to organize and the Wagner Act, two years later, set the ground rules for collective bargaining. But, I suspect, it is unlikely that the government would have stepped in so decisively if there had not been the decades of agitation, disturbance, and illegal strikes that brought into clear focus the nature of the problem.

Nor is it likely that the workers would have responded so eagerly to the legislation. The Great Depression had brought hard times, and the Roosevelt administration had cleared the way for unions to express discontent and to make demands. But it was half a century of union agitation that showed the way, that provided the image that gave focus to the discontent. In the desperation of the thirties, workers flocked to join the AFL and the newly formed Congress of Industrial Organizations (CIO). Union membership shot up from three million members in 1933 to over eight million in 1939. So, too, did union activism. In little more than four years, from 1933 to 1937, some ten thousand strikes drew out five and a half million workers.[9]

As strikes and the repressive violence that so often resulted continued, sympathy spread for the unions and for the right to organize. The seeds of this growing sentiment had also been planted by the earlier union activities. For as the coercive repressions of the unionists and strikers persisted through the early decades of the twentieth century a sense of moral outrage grew in the land, and with every broken strike and bloodied head it grew stronger. At times even violence precipitated by the workers brought new waves of public outrage against the owners, for worker violence was invariably met by even more violent repression.

This warfare of the worker with industry continued through the thirties, but even before the outbreak of the Second World War, it was clear that the unions were winning their battle to be recognized and to engage in collective bargaining. The unions seemed to be gaining other goals as well, as they turned their weight behind the national Democratic party and the policies of Franklin Delano Roosevelt, helping stimulate a growth of welfare programs unparalleled in history in this country.

Many, including recent activists who embraced violence as a means of change, have seen the unions' success as a confirmation of Marxist theories of class warfare. But there is another side to this union "success." Certainly the strikes and the organizing efforts of the unions themselves played a part in the concessions finally made by management; certainly, too, the government under Roosevelt contributed; certainly, too, gen-

[9] "The Industrial War," *Fortune* (November, 1937), p. 140. Reprinted in Litwack, *op. cit.,* p. 119.

eral public sympathies were involved. But victory depends not only on one's own fervor, luck, and wisdom. It also depends on the condition of one's opponent and on the general resources available to the contestants. And from the late thirties on, both economics and changes in ways of business organization have been kind to the worker's dreams.

EVEN SO FAR AS the union's ideals of the thirties have become reality, then, it is not clear that the success could be repeated or that similar programs of involved conflict today can hope for the same degree of success. For between the Great Depression and the aftermath of World War II, an economic miracle had occurred. The workers, as most others in our society, enjoyed its payoffs.

Still emerging from the hardships of depression in 1939, when Germany attacked Poland, the U.S. economy felt the narcotic kick of a war industry. When Japan attacked Pearl Harbor on December 7, 1941, the economy leaped to a new high of mobilization, production, and employment. Hundreds of thousands of able-bodied men left their jobs for combat or the battles behind desks. For the majority of the workers who stayed behind, wages skyrocketed, and unemployment all but vanished. Morale mounted with patriotism and payrolls, and the workers' desperate hopes of the thirties turned to complacent expectation.

Still, the experts were worried. The economy had been given a temporary reprieve, but what would follow? Through its history in the United States and western Europe, capitalism had suffered periodic deflations, and another was certain to follow when the war machine closed down. Then, zealous radicals anticipated, the labor movement would regain its direction and spirit.

But the economy fooled them. Rather than sharply contracting, it continued to expand, with every year bringing new increases in the gross national product, in the cost of living, in production. Wages went up, houses sprouted like mushrooms, and new highways interlaced across the country. Again stimulated by the Korean War in the early fifties and by the ever growing "World War III industry," the economy boomed, and hard times faded from the memories of those who had known them. Pay envelopes grew fatter; cars poured from the factories and into the garages of workers and the "middle-class" alike. Good times had come, and better ones were on the way. The workers had gained their desperate goals, many of them, but they had been helped by economic conditions that even today appear amazing.

At the same time, business organizations were transforming in ways that would aid the unions. As we shall see more fully in Chapter Nine, corporations were developing new capacities, new resiliencies, new flexibilities. Most important of all, owners were giving up the reins of management to professionals. The new men of management were less ego-involved, less rigid in their attitudes about private property and the rights of dissent, more open to the persuasive arguments of profit and loss.

Yet here, again, the decades of union agitation before the thirties may have played a part, preparing at least the more flexible and the more heavily pressed owners and managers to recognize the necessity of giving in to union demands. For only the most selfless of men will respond willingly to human suffering and social injustice, especially when it is something they only read about in the papers or see on the screen. Besides, few industrial or political leaders easily agree on what is just and unjust, nor do they readily consider the social roots of human misery.

But industrial leaders do tend to be practical men. Labor's battles forced them to consider not only the human suffering involved in the worker's condition, but also the practical consequences of worker discontent. For the cost of labor's efforts went beyond the deaths and personal unhappiness brought by wage strikes and efforts to organize: they could also be calculated in dollars, in factory damage and interrupted production —costs that finally made arbitration and concession appear economically profitable and even necessary.

Conserving Discontent

In the turbulent forties, the American labor movement lost momentum, as it gained in organizational strength. By 1950, the idealism that had reappeared in the thirties had again vanished, and the unions settled to a more or less routine chanting of a simple cry for "more." In this change, they became increasingly tied to the government and industry. Since the Second World War erupted, strikes have continued, but according to a formula.

The issues of strikes—almost always over pocketbook issues involving union members' well-being—are so clearly defined by laws and arbitration procedures that unrest can hardly spill over to other sectors of society. There is conflict, but it is controlled and focused, allowing the larger society to go on with minimal disturbance while the strike issues are being settled.[10]

This system of controlled conflict benefits industry and government, and it benefits the unions as well, making it easier for them to gain at least limited goals for their members. But not all workers belong to unions, and not all those who want to work can find jobs.

Once in the hard times of the late nineteenth century and again in the thirties, union leaders spoke of bringing all workers under their wing and of winning employment for all who sought it. But today union goals are more limited. Within the unions there is little remaining of the sense that they are creating a new society, and it seems that their mission has been redefined. The AFL ideology has prevailed over the utopian visions of the Wobblies and the early CIO; the goal of today's union is not to reach out to all workers, but to protect their own, and those they cannot protect are regretfully forgotten.

Excepting for their collaboration with a few recently aroused groups such as seasonal farm workers, public employees and university professors, the unions seem to have closed their ranks

[10] Litwack, *op. cit.,* pp. 153–176.

against outsiders, helping preserve the status quo against those who are still deprived of income and political influence. Nor is it only the organizational leaders who seem to apply different formulas of "justice" than their fathers did when it was the workers who fought for reform. Indeed, the leaders often seem more open to change than the general membership: the energies of rank-and-file members, so hopeful in the thirties and forties, have given way to cynicism and complacency. The dreams that inspired the movement to press for change have turned into myths that justify the way things are and resist new efforts to bring fundamental reform. Far from the revolutionary force of Marx's vision, today's unions have joined the struggle to maintain the status quo against the discontent of those left behind in poverty.

Now when three million workers have been organized—a greater number than was supposed necessary to secure complete victory over the enemy—the party is endowed with a bureaucracy which, in respect of its consciousness of its duties, its zeal, and its submission to the hierarchy, rivals that of the state itself; the treasuries are full; a complex ramification of financial and moral interests extends all over the country. . . . Thus from a means, organization becomes an end.

Robert Michels, *Political Parties:
A Sociological Study of Oligarchial
Tendencies of Modern Democracy*

Believing that they and their fathers have "pulled themselves up" by their bootstraps, many workers see little reason that others can't do so. But in this bitter advice, they fail to see fundamental differences between the poverty of today and the poverty of the working classes of fifty or a hundred years ago.

It is true that the demands of the young Third World Americans or the more mild requests of the older minority communities are similar to the expressions of the discontent that charged the labor movement in earlier decades of this century. It seems, as well, that the ghetto riots are kin to the spontaneous outbursts of workers in the nineteenth century, before the rise of unions. But similarities should not blind us to differences. For the fields on which today's poor must mount their battles are vastly different from those on which the workers took their stand. The struggle of the racial minorities is something new in American history.

Today's movements differ from the union movement on many counts. For now, it is enough to mention two of them, for these two alone show the blind inadequacy of challenging the minority poor to "pull themselves up" the way the workers have in the past century.

RACE IS THE MOST OBVIOUS of the differences. Today there is a racial quality to militant poverty that the labor movement never knew, a virtual "caste" struggle of minority groups against the oppressive social and economic system of a white majority.

As the decades of the twentieth century passed, "lower class" and "non-white" became more and more intertwined, especially in our urban areas. Today there are still many whites who are deprived, but with each passing year it has become increasingly difficult to identify any ethnic, religious, or national groups among them. In earlier decades, the racial minorities shared their poverty with white ethnics—Scandinavians, Irish, Italians, and Poles and other East European ethnic groups.

It was hard enough then to endure the poverty of ghetto life, when other groups could also be seen as discriminated against because of their cultural backgrounds or the way they looked. But today, the white ethnics, aided by their unions, have moved from the ghettos to working class communities, leaving behind the blacks, Puerto Ricans, Mexicans, American Indians and, though not so clearly, the Orientals.

Still it can be objected that even today poverty isn't really racial. In fact, in 1972, the U.S. Bureau of Census classified over 16 million whites and only 8.3 million "Negro and Other Races" as "below low income level." But look a bit closer: in 1972 the census showed approximately 182 million whites and

26 million "Negro and Other" in America. That meant that 32 percent (8.3 million out of 26.3 million) of the total black population lived in poverty, compared to only nine percent (16.2 million out of 182 million) of all whites. Put another way, since racial minorities comprise between 12 and 13 percent of the population, if race weren't involved we would expect between 12 and 13 percent of all "Negro and Others" to fall below "poverty level." But according to the census, over two-and-a-half times as many do.[11]

The racial quality of the current dissent from poverty is further increased by the fact that many of the whites who are poverty-stricken live in small towns and in the countryside, removed from the urban unrest. The racial minorities, by contrast, have moved in large numbers into the hearts of the largest cities. There, in the concentration of human energies, the impetus for change and the threat of violence link all the more closely.

THE OTHER DIFFERENCE APPLIES to the poverty-stricken regardless of race, but again its effects are magnified in the minority ghettos of our large cities. Unlike the unionizing workers, the poor today have been excluded not only from the profits of an expanding economy; they have also been denied participation in the industry. Increasingly, machinery, automation, and cybernation are taking over not only the jobs that once required brute energy but also those demanding only routine operations. But these are the jobs that unskilled groups once used as stepping stones, to move from disadvantage to comparative security. Today these means of survival and mobility are rapidly disappearing. Even those remaining jobs that do require little preparation are being filled by others who have enjoyed better training than is available to those who grow in poverty.

---

[11] *Statistical Abstracts of the United States, 1975* (Washington, D.C.: Government Printing Office, 1975), pp. 26, 389. Also published as *The U.S. Factbook* (N.Y.: Grosset & Dunlap, 1975), pp. 26, 389.

This means not only that jobs and a satisfying income are beyond the grasp of the poverty-stricken. It also means that in their dissent, activists lack the weapon that proved to be the key to union demands: They cannot seriously hurt the economy by withholding their participation. For the unions, violence was almost always only a secondary tactic, and usually to be avoided. The strike was the thing: Through the strike management and government learned that it is more profitable to make concessions to workers' demands than to resist.

But it is difficult to make such a point if your services are not needed. For some who dissent, the violence itself takes on the meaning that the strike once had: it is the means by which the powerful are convinced that it is less costly to meet the dissenters' demands. In this light, even what has been denounced as a "rage of destruction" can be seen as a desperate demand for improvement. Frustrated in other efforts to gain attention, the discontented take to the streets, just as workers had turned to violence when other forms of collective bargaining were denied. However ill-conceived, however unplanned and uncontrolled, the black riots of recent years can be recognized as modern efforts at "collective bargaining by riot."[12]

At a street-corner meeting in Watts when the riots were over, an unemployed youth of about twenty said to me: "We won." I asked him: "How have you won? Homes have been destroyed, Negroes are lying dead in the streets, the stores from which you buy food and clothes are destroyed, and the people are bringing you relief." His reply was significant: "We won because we made the whole world pay attention to us. The police chief never came here before; the mayor always stayed uptown. We made them come." Clearly it was no accident that the riot proceeded along an almost direct path to City Hall.

Bayard Rustin, "The Watts 'Manifesto' and the McCone Report"

---

[12] E. J. Hobsbawn, "The Machine Breakers," *Past and Present* (1952), pp. 57–67.

According to this formula, the greater the destruction and suffering, the higher the cost, and the more likely the powerful will give in, making concessions to these demands. But the powerful have other options, above all the option to suppress the dissident minorities by force. The powerful are often fearful, confused and angered by dissent, especially when it smacks of disobedience or violence. Repeatedly in America and elsewhere, disobedience and violence—and even dissent that is clearly legal—has been met with escalating force, and mounting public disfavor.

Summary and Direction

In the union story, we have seen collective violence as a response to the demands and deprivations that develop as new forms of society replace older ones. Today, that lesson grows compelling. For many of the personal troubles and public issues of our times can be understood, in part, as another in the history of reactions to the breakdown of old forms of power, economics, and social status.

Today, just as in Marx's Europe, as outdated economic and productive relations crumble, the social order is in turmoil. Established ways of doing things no longer work; authority is questioned, and discontent grows on all sides. As we have seen, such discontent may arise among those who have been underprivileged (reforming and revolutionary discontent); it may also come from those who have been, and continue to be, privileged (conserving discontent); it may also come from those who yearn for a return to valued ways of life they have lost (reactionary discontent).

Thus, the working poor mobilized into unions to win greater privileges and pay; the owners, the wealthy, and the powerful, struggled against both. Today, as the jobless poor struggle for survival and a sense of dignity, the historical situation has changed, but the basic pattern seems to hold: When men and women seek to share more equally in wealth, privilege, or power, violence is the likely result. And, more often than not, that violence is authored by the privileged and powerful.

. . . well-intentioned liberals point out that our social and technical system is a delicate Swiss watch that can be fatally deranged if due process is not observed. It is a complicated machine, but it is not so delicate as all that. . . .

I myself am a pacifist, but I think that our system can bear, and ought to get, a good deal more roughing up than it has. And I do not much distrust that the young, white and black, know where to draw the line. The most brutal and destructive acts will continue to come from those in power.

Paul Goodman, *New Reformation:*
Notes of a Neolithic Conservative

In this perspective, the history of the union movement again demonstrates that our society—as almost all societies, at almost all times—is deeply conservative. In its early phase, a new collective movement is usually viewed as "deviant," not only by those in privileged and powerful positions but by most others who value the conditions the activists oppose. Earlier in its history, it was the union movement that was considered illegal by the larger society. But this lesson is ignored: In recent decades, the majority of union members have joined in condemning new movements.

This conserving response seems to be more intense when more sweeping changes are demanded by the new movement. The AFL demands for higher wages—which required only minor organizational reform (that is, a slight change in the practices of management)—were resisted; but the CIO's demands for the right to organize brought on far more violence and bloodshed. For the CIO sought a minor institutional change —that is, a slight change in the "blueprints" of management, which would bring some rather major changes in organizational practices. Yet even this response was less extreme than the violence that met the demands of the Wobblies and the Knights of Labor, for their demands would have required sweeping institutional and organizational change.

Our history offers ample illustration of this conservatism, for much of the collective violence in America has been repressive: owners have repressed the workers, strikes have been crushed, slave revolts have been put down, radical organizations destroyed, newly arrived ethnic groups exploited and constrained. There is good reason, as Wallace suggests, that such phrases as "labor violence" are gross distortions. A more accurate label might be "industrial violence" or, more generally, the repressive violence of those in privileged positions against those who are seen as threats.[13]

Here we find a base irony in the union story, an irony not simply of union history but of human society. For the conflict and violence of the workers was often, and most harshly, directed not at the owners and factories. It was directed at other workers who were less privileged, less able to protect themselves. As workers climbed a rung up the ladder of income and security, they reacted bitterly against all who seemed to be threats to their jobs and their ways of life. Scabs—men who crossed their picket lines to keep the factories running—were harassed, brutally beaten, and killed.

The repressive violence was all the more harsh when race was involved. The bloodiest cases were seen in the late decades of the nineteenth century, when Chinese laborers were victimized by owners and persecuted by white workers who detested these immigrants who willingly sold themselves into virtual slavery. The riots, raids, hangings, and mass murders of Chinese families, as well as the legal harassment and exclusion, are not simply an example of the evils of the industrial system. They are a fundamental part of the history of worker insecurity and discontent in America.[14]

That part should not be forgotten, even by those who find inspiration in the success of the union movement, for it suggests

---

[13] Wallace, "Uses of Violence in American History," pp. 81–102.
[14] *Ibid.*

that working-class conservatism stems in large part from the fear and resentment that arises when men and women feel threatened and see valued ways of life challenged. This conservatism, then, is not simply bigoted and blind; it is both, to some degree, but it is as truly the resistance of people who have reason to feel deeply threatened by disorder and change.

The enemies, real and imagined, are those the workers think are threatening their ways of life, their economic well-being, their values. For they are on the edge of the privileged centers of American society; and in times of riot, high unemployment and other social stress, they are vulnerable, and they know it.

Thus, the resistance of working men and women to demands of the minorities is not simply "racist." Racism is clearly involved, but so too are fear and frustration. The workers see hard-won privileges, perhaps even their jobs, families, and homes, threatened by the rise of the poor. The feeling that jobs are becoming more scarce, that money is tight, that the national economic pie is shriveling, increases their insecurity and their resentment of ethnic demands. For if deprived minorities are to gain economically and politically, it seems that others must lose. The workers, including successful black workers, see themselves—often rightly—as the likely candidates.

THE PARALLEL of recent activists with early union organizers, then, is both suggestive and faulty. For the unions of the thirties were made up of men and women whose labors were needed by the corporations they struck against. But the young radicals, like the impoverished blacks of the sixties and seventies, had no clear way to economically cripple the "Establishment" they opposed, short of outright destruction.

A few among the activists took this possibility seriously, planning explosive attacks on banks, public offices, and utilities—attacks that could seriously interfere with "business as usual." Through a continuing plague of such attacks, they argued, a small minority of dedicated revolutionaries could bring the "paper tiger" to its knees.

Though their radical violence was futile in itself, it was linked to the elaborate rationalization that violence and destruction would dramatize the radical cause; right-wing forces would try to repress the radicals and that would bring liberals to their support. This would radicalize the liberals. Eventually, the country would be "polarized."

Besides, the rationalization continued, violence generates a "consciousness" in the minds of people otherwise numbed to the realities of corporate thinking and military imperialism. Even kids from the slums and working classes could identify with street violence and looting. Thus there could be created a solidarity of youth united by a struggle for survival and of older liberals who had been radicalized by the "fascist reaction" of the establishment.

But the formula didn't seem to work. Few Americans shared the radicals' deep discontent with their society, and many who did, could not believe in the activists' "solution" through violence. But even if the violence had been able to generate more support, the youthful activists had little chance of repeating the success of the union movement.

For the unions enjoyed another fundamental advantage: Their demands involved at heart pragmatic, "bread-and-butter" issues that could be met by specific concessions from management. But the idealistic demands of the young radicals were often sweeping, impractical, and unclear, demands that even the most benevolent and responsive government would have been unable to meet.

They were, roughly, demands of the heart: They demonstrated a search for self, even a critical involvement in the lives of others. But, like Mead, most of the young activists—despite their radicalism and political fervor—had given too little attention to the political and social nature of the world they lived in. To be sure, some of them looked to Marx for their inspiration, but few seemed to recognize the profound lessons that lay beneath the surfaces of his critical rhetoric.

Chapter Seven

The Invitation in Marx: II

EARLY ONE SPRING, the first spring of the seventies, young activists attacked the Bank of America building that nestled in the student community near the University of California at Santa Barbara. The bank was set ablaze; so too was an idea. Protest by fire soon visited the nearby Irvine campus, and within a year Bank of America branches in California were hit by more than twenty arson attacks and bombings, while other activists went to work on other targets around the country. Within another year, the wave of violence had all but spent itself. With it the rebellious spirit that had grown through the past decade seemed to grow tired, and radical challenges became more studied and responsible. Still, memories lingered into the seventies, and occasional bombings and other outbursts brought new fears and new hopes of militant radicalism in modern America.

The attacks on the Bank of America, the largest banking corporation in the country, were hailed by radicals and near-radicals who saw in them a double imagery: a dramatic objection to their country's involvement in war and exploitation and a rejection of the "Establishment's" most cherished "myth" —the value of private property.

"Anything that contributes to the end of war is an act of

love—not an act of violence," Robert Scheer, Peace and Freedom candidate for U.S. Senator from California, declared only a few days before voters were to go to the polls. "Burning the bank calls attention to the fact that it is a major prop of U.S. imperialism. If you don't want to see the Bank of America burned down, get the Bank of America out of the war. I don't see the burning of buildings as an act of violence. I don't have any respect for private property."[1]

If Scheer—once a political science professor at Michigan State University—meant to shock his public into thought he may have succeeded, although the thoughts of most were not the kind that would take him to the Senate. For an attack on the "right of private property" strikes at the heart of our most cherished beliefs. Isn't the right to private property the mark of freedom, the foundation of our democracy, the fundamental law of economic success? The question seems to be rhetorical, offering its own obvious answers. The achievements of our society lend ample proof of the fundamental value of private property—not only economic achievements but political and social advances toward true democracy, equality, and brotherhood.

But to those who view these concepts with an eye to the excesses and injustices of our society, it seems that something is wrong. Our images of democracy, equality, and brotherhood do not fit reality; our institutions contradict our ideals; the ideologies that justify and hide the contradictions are myths. As long as men and women uncritically accept the ideologies, the radical insists, they will fail to see the contradictions of their institutions and their ideals, and they will fail to recognize their own roles in a society that is unjust and destructive of human consciousness.

In these radical charges we can hear Marx's voice telling us that we are blinded to our lives by ideologies that serve the rich and powerful, that in the service of money and property we destroy our own consciousness.

[1] Quoted in the *San Francisco Chronicle*, Oct. 28, 1970.

WHERE OTHERS SAW the confusion, vibrant expansions, and simple inequalities of an industrializing Europe, Marx saw the transformation of an entire social system as it adjusted to the demands of a new technology. The means of production were owned by a small segment of the population, smaller than ever before in man's history. These owners appeared to buy the labor from the masses of non-owners. But the appearance was deceptive. The workers seemed to be free, selling their services in an open market. But Marx saw through those appearances and discovered a new form of slavery.

Marx did not say that everyone's belief and attitudes flow from his class position. Marx said that the ruling ideas of an epoch are the ideas of the ruling class. . . . To put it bluntly: if society is ruled by a minority with special privileges, the ideas that the majority have about the social order must be distorted or biased towards the perspective of the ruling minority, or else the social order would be unstable.

David Horowitz, *Radical Sociology*

From one perspective, in societies such as Marx's and such as ours, individuals lose touch with the economic processes which, at base, are their own creations. We accept a mystical idea that there are economic "laws" magically beyond human life, and self-sufficient. Believing this, we accept the idea that we are ruled by these laws. We fail to recognize that economic laws are fictions of our own making, created in our own inability to comprehend our own actions.

So long as we fail to recognize the reality of economics and the way economics and other social relations emerge out of our actions, Marx insisted, we are blind to our own lives.[2] That blindness cannot be cured by individual efforts of psychological or spiritual purging. For the blindness is imposed by the existing society; that society not only coerces and seduces us to con-

---

[2] For a lucid and critical look at Marx, see Raymond Aaron, *Main Currents in Sociological Thought,* Vol. I: *The Sociologists and the Revolution of 1848* (New York: Anchor, 1968), pp. 145-236.

formity, but offers ready-made arrays of ideas—ideologies—that make the conformity seem sensible. This allows those in power to regard the actions and words of reformers as treasonous, as challenges not simply to the social order but to human survival. The threat of competing political and economic and social systems comes to be seen as the threat of social chaos.

Thus, exploitation is part of society itself. Responsibility for what capitalism does cannot be laid to any single industrialist or group of capitalists. They, too, are blind to themselves and their world. Those in the privileged positions of an organized society can be persuaded to correct some incidental defects, but their human psychology keeps them from recognizing the need for fundamental social reform. Thus, Marx believed, they participate in their own overthrow. They will fail to recognize when the time has come for change, when the beliefs and values that support their social organizations have had their day.

This main line of Marx's mature thought pivots on the ideas of social class and conflict. Here is the link between his image of society and his image of social change; here, too, is the point on which his criticism of capitalist society turns.

Social Class, Conflict, and Change

In every society, Marx argued, we can see the basic importance of economic relationships. But Marx was not basically concerned with production, distribution, and consumption of things. These are important, but they are not the real problem. What is crucial are the social relations and social organizations that develop in the production of things.

In the economic organizations, individuals are given roles in the production, distribution, and use of goods. These economic roles are based on divisions of labor: Some persons control and manage, others labor, others trade, others persuade, and some simply consume and enjoy. These divisions give rise to "class" differences: broad strata of people who share similar economic roles also come to share common interests, values, styles of life, and access to political power. All other institutions are fundamentally based on the economic. Even differing ways of family life, bringing up children, courtship and love, emerge from differing economic conditions and relationships.[3]

But class differences are important to social change only if individuals are conscious of them; only when they recognize their shared differences from others can they be considered a class. "Insofar as millions of families live under economic conditions of existence that divide their mode of life, their interests, and their culture from those of other classes, and put them in hostile contrast to the latter," wrote Marx, "do they form a class."[4] However many differing groups and ways of life an observer might discover in history, each technological era of the Western world seems to have generated only two self-conscious classes, locked in opposition to one another: the owners versus the nonowners.

Looking back over history, Marx saw that people organized themselves around available technology in four different ways. In one mode—seen in ancient China—all persons are virtually slaves of the state. The other three are seen in Western history. The ancient mode of production is seen in the relation of slave to master; the feudal mode of production in the relation of peasant to lord; the bourgeois mode in the relation of wage earner to owner. Each represents a stage in man's exploitation of man; together they reveal the progress of Western society toward a utopian future. That utopia will emerge, Marx believed, only when men and women have created a socialist economy, in which the means of production and political power are in the hands of those who do the actual productive work.[5]

Economic institutions reflect changes in technology. Indeed, revolution and progress result from technological change, for

[3] Karl Marx and Frederick Engels, *The German Ideology* (New York: International, 1947).
[4] *Ibid.*, p. 109.
[5] Marx, "Preface" to *A Contribution to the Critique of Political Economy,* pp. 11–13.

new technologies release new capabilities and potentials, upsetting the system of relationships that had developed around the older technologies. Then those in exploited or underprivileged classes begin to question the roles that have been allotted them by the old system; then they begin to search for new roles more adequate to the new technologies of production. They recognize the conflict of interests that was basic to the social class differences all along. Unless those in positions of power and privilege creatively respond to the new technologies and the discontent of the lower classes, rebellion is inevitable.

But the privileged and powerful cannot change, for what they must do is give up much, even most, of their privilege and power. Rather, they seek to reestablish the old order. When others will not freely cooperate—when the ideologies that support arrangements are no longer accepted—the powerful must ever more resort to coercion. They must, that is, reveal the true face of violence and exploitation that had been hidden behind the masks of ideologies. Then, when exploited men and women are suppressed by force, their discontent grows all the greater and more sharply focused. They see through their false beliefs, and seek new visions and beliefs that will direct their energies of discontent.

This, in gross form, is the heart of the sociological model that can be seen in Marx's stinging criticism of bourgeois capitalism. Basic to that model is the idea of social conflict, and class conflict in particular, as the major vehicle of change, the fundamental reality of human history.

Others of Marx's century argued that the problems of industrial society were due to "cultural lag"—to the contradictions between the new ways of life generated by the industrial revolution and the old ways appropriate to the feudal society of before. Marx recognized the importance of such conflict, but —building from the work of Hegel—saw what he thought to be a more important insight: that societies in general, and the capitalist societies of his day in particular, generate their own contradictions.

Thus, all societies are unstable, and all carry within them the seeds of their own destruction. In capitalism, Marx saw these seeds in the exploitation of workers for capitalist profits and the inevitable cycles of depression and wild expansion of capitalist markets, both of which increased the proletariat's misery and helped them recognize that their misery was due to capitalist exploitation. For Marx, then, social conflict between classes of men was inevitable. The history of society is a history of class conflict, and conflict is the source of social and historical change.

Comte, Marx, and Spencer . . . despite all differences amongst them . . . agreed that sociology had to lay bare the inner structure of the new industrial society and to consider whether men could live in it without God. . . .

Marx—after a century of refutations—is the one sociologist who cannot be ignored. His notions on class conflict, on the process of change in society, on the conditions for the emergence of ideology and social awareness, his general and ill-specified view of "alienation" as the human condition in capitalist society, have infused all of sociology.

Norman Birnbaum, *Toward a Critical Sociology*

In this remarkable insight that societies generate their own contradictions and in the conflict that results become the authors of their own failure and their own rebirth, Marx struck an image of social change unrecognized in earlier centuries. He looked, as we have seen, to the French Revolution for his inspiration, but he saw something that even the architects of that revolution had missed: that societies change not through violent "revolution" but through evolution. Old institutions cannot simply be overthrown and replaced with new. Rather, within the constraints and forms of the established institutions, new ways of thought and relationship emerge to challenge the old institutions. Feudalism had destroyed itself, but not until it had created its own gravediggers. That, too, would be the fate of capitalism.[6]

---

[6] Karl Marx, *The Grundrisse,* David McLellan, ed. (New York: Harper & Row, 1971).

With the challenge of new ways, old forms give way, but this cannot occur without competition and conflict, perhaps even violence. Although the process of change is evolutionary, at times the evolution can become intense, even violent and destructive in the form of an abrupt overthrow. But unless the violence reflects the basic social contradiction—that is, unless the frustrations with the existing organization are widely and powerfully shared throughout the population and express emerging social possibilities—a violent revolution cannot succeed. Widespread violence, then, must be evolutionary if it is to be anything more than destructive.

It is true, then, that Marx extolled the social potentials of violence. But he did not see it as necessary to all revolution, nor did he see it as desirable in itself. For Marx, as was suggested early in this chapter, the processes of revolution involved pervasive, fundamental changes in the basic relationship of people to one another—what today might be called a "systemic change," involving profound changes even in the centers of society.[7] Under some conditions it was possible that such revolutionary change could take place without violence.

IN HIS WRITINGS about revolution and violence, the social rootedness of Marx's ideas is again seen. For the creative potentials of force have been extolled in middle-class Western societies for the past three hundred years and continue to be worshiped today. The English, French, and American revolutions are idealized. So too are America's "heroic" victories over the Spanish, the Mexicans, and the American Indians. Politically and intellectually influential people, even in America, warmly greeted the Russian Revolution of 1917, the German Revolution of 1918, and Castro's Revolution of 1959—at least at first. Indeed, force, as long as it is exerted by those in favor, is seen in Western society not only as necessary to preserve the status quo but as a creative element in human history.

In this light, Marx's conception of force is less militant than

---

[7] See Tucker, *The Marxian Revolutionary Idea,* pp. 10 ff.

those embodied in some other Western traditions. For Marx saw that violence cannot create; it can only give the final push to political and social developments which have already virtually taken place. It is not the mother of a new social order; rather it is the "mid-wife of every old society pregnant with a new one."[8]

Marx's view suggests another important thing about a violent revolution: The new institutions that emerge from the conflict will be like both the old and the new cultures, yet will be unlike either. Revolutionaries may hope for complete replacement, a complete restructuring of society. But no matter how thoroughly they plan, they fail. Somehow, a revolution escapes the revolutionary. For new forms always use the old, and there is always an unpredictable outcome. The outcome depends, in some undefined ways, on the unique conditions and contradictions of the times but it also depends on the character of both the old forms and their evolving alternatives.

To Marx, this insight meant even more: To be effective agents of change, we cannot sit idly in speculation and theory building. Rather, we must enter the processes of the ongoing movements; discover the gradual forces of developing counter-cultures, identify what the coming changes might possibly be, choose the most desirable, and then work to bring them about.[9] Marx labored to do this. He knew that it was an enormous project and strained to meet its challenge. Yet its demands were far beyond what even he could master.

IT IS EASY to show how wrong Marx could be. In a way, he set himself up for the abuses of both his followers and critics. In many of his works, he avowed an ideal of powerful intellectual analysis and sought to build the foundation for a "scientific" study of society. But he was also a man who fought passionate battles, using his pen as a sword. His frankly political

[8] Karl Marx, *Capital* (New York: International, 1967), p. 837.
[9] For a brief summary of Marx's perspectives for research and action, see Irving M. Zeitlin, *Marxism: A Re-Examination* (Princeton: Van Nostrand, 1967), pp. 152–155.

tracts—the *Communist Manifesto* is but one of many—are pregnant with phrases and simplified arguments chosen to excite imagination and action. As happens with writers of genius and passion, the excesses crept into his other works. There they offer critics easy targets and confuse even the industrious reader.

But these difficulties do not require, or even justify, rejecting the totality of Marx's monumental work. "I believe that Newton's Law of light was unsound," the young George Bernard Shaw wrote of Marx's detractors in 1889. "But I do not therefore affirm that the phenomena which he sought to explain by his theory do not exist, or that all his theories were fallacious and his statements false. For instance, I do not believe that a mixture of blue and yellow paint will be orange, or that if I jump out of a window I shall soar . . . to the skies. In the same inconsistent way, I believe that Marx's theory of value was unsound . . . and yet . . . I'm quite willing to allow, in the handsomest manner, that Marx was the Aristotle of the 19th century."[10]

Shaw, tongue in cheek as usual, must have enjoyed the excesses of Marx's admirers who likened their hero to Aristotle. The title left little room for John Stuart Mill, Herbert Spencer, and other geniuses of his century. However flattering the comparison to Aristotle, it misses Marx's most enduring contribution. For Aristotle, like political and economic writers who followed him through the centuries, had doggedly focused on one specific political or economic subject, with little attention to the ways that subject interlinked with the rest of the social milieu. That is, they focused on a part and neglected the whole. The magnificent scope of Marx's theories contrasts with these classical analyses, for Marx did not narrowly focus on politics or economics as if they existed in some sort of vacuum. For Marx, social organization—society itself—was central.

In Marx is seen a new way of man's reflection on himself and on his history, an effort to grasp the nature of the social. Social

[10] George Bernard Shaw, in R. W. Ellis, ed., *Bernard Shaw and Karl Marx: A Symposium* (New York: Random House, 1930 [1889]), pp. 186–187.

organization and change served earlier writers only as contexts for their specific topics—contexts usually ignored. For Marx they become the focal problem. That focus, however, is fluid and diffuse. In Marx's work, it ranged not only over the breadth of his society, it moved from society to society, and back and forth through history.

Like other men of genius and vision, Marx lived on the periphery of his society. Despite endemic poverty, he enjoyed a psychological freedom in which he could feel the early whispers of change that stirred in the nineteenth century. As a young man he stormed the University of Bonn, but his radical atheism found little favor, and he failed to win a university appointment.[11] That failure allowed his mind to roam, unfettered by academic pressures and conventions, and the boundary lines of academic specialization. Free from the demands and distractions that burden those who enjoy more secure positions in a community, Marx developed an imaginative, intuitive grasp of his world. His view was discerning and complex; his mind restless and always questioning, and his question always, finally, was "Why?"

> Marx is concerned not only with what is or is not going to happen, but with *why*, with the underlying structural mechanisms of events and trends. Accordingly, to confront his theories adequately, we too must go into the "why". . . . Any man can think only *within* his own times; but he can think *about* the past and future, thus attempting to expand "his time," constructing out of its materials the image of an epoch. That—to a brilliant extent—was what Karl Marx did.
>
> C. Wright Mills, *The Marxists*

Whatever his errors, Marx's perceptions of his moment were incisive. In them we see a new awareness emerging of the relation of individual and society, in dynamic conflict and recon-

[11] For a readable biography, see John Lewis, *The Life and Teaching of Marx* (New York: International, 1965); a more extended treatment is offered by Robert Payne, *Marx* (New York: Simon & Schuster, 1968).

struction. His is an image that brings together many of those elements of humanistic imagination that are fundamental to our still-developing social thought: the ways institutions influence our behavior, the ways ideologies can rationalize the interplay of our needs, conditions, and ideas that make up the fabric of society; the ways social conflict and discontent can be productive; and, perhaps most importantly, the ways a society can generate its own self-contradictions.

The difference was not just that Marx was more critical or more angry than others of his time. Nor was the difference one of intellect, imagination, or effort: John Stuart Mill probably would take second place to no one of his century in operating intellect. In large part, the difference was of perspective and thrust of imagination. To Marx, it was not enough to ask what was happening, nor even what was going to happen. He had to ask why—Why this, why not that? Why here, not there? Why now, not then?

He wrote of the nineteenth century as if it were a cloud passing down the wind, changing its shape and fading as it goes . . . [while others] sat comfortably down before it in their offices and study chairs, as if it were the Great Wall of China, safe to the last until the Day of Judgment with an occasional coat of Whitewash.

George Bernard Shaw in R. W. Ellis,
Bernard Shaw and Karl Marx: A Symposium

He was not the only one to ask such questions; nor, in seeking answers, did he alone probe the underlying mechanisms of events in ways unimagined by men in earlier times. Even before Marx, de Tocqueville, Saint-Simon, Proudhon, Comte, and others began to awaken men and women to the society around them and to the interlinkings of individuals and their societal forms. In their works can be seen a society growing aware of itself, and a sociology emergent.

But it is Marx's view that speaks most clearly from the nineteenth century to our contemporary experience and discontent, whose images of the individual and society suggest most fully the roles of living individuals in the structures of social life and the processes of change. His perspective, all but lost in the years of debate over his political ideas and revolutionary visions, is, I believe, Marx's greatest contribution to the twentieth century.

Summary and Direction

There is far more to Marx's theories than is even suggested here. Yet even in this brief sketch, we can see a sociological perspective of unusual depth and scope, an emerging image of the individual in relation to social structure and to social change. At its core is a creative interplay of being and consciousness, expressed in the actions of the conscious, praxic person. But people are not necessarily so aware of themselves and their world. At all levels of society, in all walks of life, men and women are generally the dupes of history, drugged with religion and other false images.

Although Marx did not so laboriously spell it out, a distinct image of the individual and society can be seen through his work—a view similar at base to those more fully developed a half-century later in Germany by Max Weber and in America by George Herbert Mead. In this view, the society that we are born into is seen to present us with sets of roles—more or less coherent arrays of expectations for the ways we should act, and the ways others should act toward us.

These sets of expectations are carried in our minds and emotions. For most of us, they overlap with fair compatibility; they group around various human activities and goals, in such a way that we can talk of another abstraction: social institutions. Institutions are essentially large-sized blueprints for human behavior, agreements on ways to act in diverse roles. Our ability to think of ourselves and others in abstract, interlinked "roles" and "institutions" brings coherence and stability to our relationships.

Ideally, institutions are direct representations of the actions we have rationally and freely chosen, out of our clearly perceived needs. But, too easily, the link between human need and social prescription is lost. Out of hope, fear, and blindness, we simply follow the blueprints, uncritically and uncreatively.

This gives rise to a basic question: Why do we, even when moved by our own needs to do otherwise, so doggedly follow the blueprints? In part, Marx said in essence, because we are coerced, or seduced, by false promises. But more often it is because we are duped by elaborate sets of beliefs that make the conformity seem reasonable, that mask the reality of our situation and the reality of those who profit from our conformity.

These sets of beliefs, shared by men and women throughout society, are called "ideologies." They are, virtually, the "masks" of institutions, leading us to identify incorrectly the sources of our troubles and to fail to see our possibilities. They even mask their own sources, leading us to think they are given by a god or that they have emerged through the working of human rationality over the centuries.

With deadly accuracy, Marx focused on our capacities to hide the realities of our social life from ourselves; to disguise or ignore the pain we inflict on others in gaining our own ends; to accept the masks of those over us as authentic. Whether we are the exploiter or the exploited, Marx tells us, we are alienated from ourselves and from others.

For Marx, the true source of consciousness was in individuals' actions, and hence in their systems of production. Thus, if we are to be free, we must recognize our slavery; we must see that modern capitalism rose out of the same source as other movements of history: changes in technologies, which give rise to intolerable conflicts in social relations, bringing the downfall of old systems and generating new ideas, ideologies, and religious beliefs—all of them, all too often, nothing more than distorted reflections of social relations and veils of fantasy.

It is not enough to understand individual men and women, nor even to understand one's self-and-other involvement. Society itself must be understood as well, if the inequities and alienations of human life are to be combatted. Critical involvement that ignores the invitation to societal criticism risks blindness.

But the reverse also holds risks: Social criticism that is divorced from one's own involvement in self-and-others, from praxis, is also blinding.

MEAD HAD RECOGNIZED the failing of the communal dream: Brotherhood not only unites individuals in small groups, it divides them from others. His insight emerged directly from his basic view of the relationship of individual consciousness to social order. From this view, too, he created a utopian dream of "functional society," a massive, complex arrangement of men and women who live in creative harmony, each playing an important part in his society. In this vision, each person performs a necessary function in the larger organization—and thus, despite the complexity and size of the society, they are creatively united, for each individual is able to "take the 'functional' role" of the rest.

In the light of modern radical discontent, we can see that Mead's utopian dream fails—not so much because his basic perspective on consciousness and society is wrong, but because it is incomplete. Incisive in his social psychology, Mead failed to look critically at the political and institutional levels of social life.

This is what Marx had done, brilliantly, building from much the same basic ideas about the relationship of consciousness to society as had Mead. Where Mead emphasized the emergence of consciousness and order, Marx had turned to questions of conflict and change; where Mead was politically naive, Marx was incisive and informed. In their perspectives on the individual and society, each remains stimulating and valuable. But their limitations must also be recognized.

If Mead's liberal humanism fails in the light of radical criticism, so too does Marx's. Indeed, so does recent radicalism itself. For none alone offers a perspective that encourages a critical awareness of the contradictions, the thrusts, and the possibilities of contemporary society and yet retains at its very center the development and creative expression of individual consciousness.

This, even more than Mead and Marx, is what Weber struggled to gain. In his works we find an invitation not only to involvement and criticism, but also to exploration.

LIKE MARX'S, Weber's life and thought centered on the problems and predicaments of human freedom, creativity, and responsibility. But Weber, even more than Marx, struggled to understand the possibilities of modern society as well as its contradictions and thrusts. Marx's achievement had been monumental; indeed, it was a profound inspiration to Weber, whose relentless explorations found critical points of departure and communality in Marx. The basic difference between the two, I believe, is one not of kind, but of emphasis. Both were masters of exploration and criticism, but before all else Marx was a social critic; Weber a sociological explorer.

Both sought an answer to the existential question we have heard so often in the confusions of our times: How can I live? Both believed that the answer must be found in terms of individual freedom, creativity, and responsibility. Both implicitly recognized what Mead spelled out: The question can be truly answered only in the awareness of self-and-other involvement. Both were excited by the basic questions of sociological exploration: Why here, why not there? Why now, not then? Why to these, not to those? Both asked these questions of the rise of capitalism and of the thrusts of Western societies.

But here they differed. Marx found in his answers a stinging criticism of modern society, and he carried that criticism to political battle. His achievements were enormous; his basic perspectives on the contradictions, frauds, and ways of change were breathtaking. Yet, once satisfied that his answers about alienation, freedom, and responsibility were meaningful for the political battles that he saw must be fought, Marx seemed to grow lax toward them. He continued to refine and modify his theories, but he no longer asked the most basic questions of them. He used them, that is, to uncover the errors in the roots of his society, but in his mature works he seemed to neglect to seek energetically for inadequacies in the roots of his own theories.

To Weber, the passionate end was not criticism, but understanding; not the uncovery of error, but the discovery of possibility. Criticism and debunking, he saw, are an essential part of exploration; the involved explorer cannot avoid struggles with the injustice and ignorance of his social order. But if we are to avoid self-delusion and political blindness, we must continually turn our critical questions on ourselves and our ideas.

We must recognize that we ourselves are part of the problem we are exploring. Recognizing this, we are forced to question our ideas: Why did this occur to me now, why not earlier? Why to me, why not to someone else? Why in this social milieu, in this society, in this historical era; why not in other times and places? How valid, how adequate, how generalizable is what I've said? What have I missed? What have I been blind to, in the limitations of my own special involvement and awareness?

Weber's restless pursuit of such questions, fermenting in his study of the Protestant Ethic, helps us understand the experience and discontent in our own times. For in his studies of ancient religions and the medieval city, we begin to see how societies change and crystallize and the parts that are played in those changes by individual men and women and collective movements.

Part Three

EXPLORATION
The Invitation in Weber

The most important property of man's image, however, is his ability to change it. Without this, we may be trapped in images which are . . . reinforced in defiance of experience. It is the skill of learning which is the greatest hope of the human race. It is the will to learn which is its greatest question mark.

KENNETH E. BOULDING, "The Place of the Image in the Dynamics of Society"

Chapter Eight

The Invitation in Weber: I

BEN FRANKLIN, we all learn in grade school, was very wise. "Remember, that *time* is money," he advised his fellow colonists of New England. "He that can earn ten shillings a day by his labor, and goes abroad, or sits idle one half of that day, though he spends but six pence during his diversion or idleness, ought not to reckon *that* the only extent; he has really spent, or rather thrown away, five shillings beside." But he loses even more than five shillings and six pence: "Money can beget money, and its offspring can beget more, and so on. Five shillings is turned into six . . . and so on, till it becomes a hundred pounds. . . . He that kills a breeding-sow, destroys all her offspring to the thousandth generation. He that murders a crown, destroys all that it might have produced, even scores of pounds."[1]

  Max Weber was fascinated. Franklin's moralisms would have outraged men and women of other times and places. In America today his little sermons sound ludicrous to those who are disenchanted with the business ethic. To many of us, it seems that a penny saved is a penny not enjoyed. Even those who are still compulsive about "doing" things find little wisdom in Frank-

---

[1] Quoted in Max Weber, *The Protestant Ethic and the Spirit of Capitalism*, pp. 48–49 (extracted from Franklin's *Advice to a Young Tradesman*, 1748) (New York: Scribners, 1958).

lin's admonition that "He that idly loses five shillings' worth of time, loses five shillings, and might as prudently throw five shillings into the sea."[2]

What kind of man would write such things, Weber wondered. More important, what community would listen attentively, inspired by the "obvious" truth?

WEBER FACED the same basic question that had driven Marx: How can humanness and freedom survive under the inescapable progress of capitalism? But fifty years separated the two. Capitalism was a half-century more advanced, the complexities of administration more pronounced, the intricacies of its influence on human life more clear.

It is not capitalism itself that people must fear most, Weber argued; it is the organizations that capitalism encourages. Marx had failed to see the "organizational revolution" that had already begun in his time. To Weber, it was clear: the incentives of poverty are gradually replaced by organizational incentives —not ownership, but administrative status is becoming the main focus of the individual's actions. Not property (as in feudal societies) nor even wealth (as in capitalist societies) but status— one's position and prestige in the society—is becoming the most important key to success in a bureaucratic order.

For Weber, Marx's question mutated: How can the individual survive the increasing organizational demands and seductions of his society? How is it possible to save individual freedom of action? How can the power of organizations be controlled?

The Spirit of Capitalism

Taken out of the context of his times, Ben Franklin appears greedy and unscrupulous in his pursuit of wealth. "The sound of your hammer at five in the morning, or eight at night, heard by a creditor," he wrote, "makes him easy six months longer; but if he sees you at a billiard-table, or hears your voice in a

[2] *Ibid.,* p. 50.

tavern, when you should be at work, he sends for his money the next day. . . . It shows, besides, that you are mindful of what you owe; it makes you appear a careful as well as an honest man, and that still increases your credit."[3]

This smacks of crass hypocrisy. It seems to be no more than an early Dale Carnegie sincerity, a lesson in impression management and manipulation. If you are honest only because it assures credit, then all you must do is appear to be honest. In fact, over-honesty would be wasteful. A virtue is a virtue only if it is useful to the individual, and that which is useful is productive. Thus, the good person will earn and produce more and more, using whatever means are necessary. This means that, in private life, the individual must be frugal, punctual, and industrious and avoid all spontaneous enjoyment. It is not only acceptable, but expected, that he or she be demanding, even brutal if need be, in dealings with others.

In his times, however, Franklin was seen not as a hypocrite, but as a sage, for he voiced the beliefs and ideals that dominated his New England of the eighteenth century. He preached not simply how to succeed, but a peculiar ethic, a philosophy of avarice, a way of thinking in a society where, Weber noted— quoting a satirist who seems to echo Marx—"They make tallow out of cattle and money out of men."[4]

What was new in this capitalistic spirit was not greed, however. That is as old as human life; a lust for money sticks to man throughout his history. "The greed of the Chinese mandarin, the old Roman aristocrat, or the peasant, can stand up to any comparison," Weber noted. Indeed, the most selfish and unscrupulous pursuit of money is not seen in the capitalists of America or Europe. It is seen in countries that are industrially and economically backward, for they tempt the "capitalist adventurer," such as the Dutch sea captain who "would go through hell for gain, even though he scorched his sails."[5]

All over the world and in many historical times, merchants

[3] Weber, *Protestant Ethic,* pp. 49–50.
[4] *Ibid.,* p. 11.
[5] *Ibid.,* pp. 56–57.

have appeared, loans have been made, and even public bodies have been financed by private moneylenders. In Babylon, Hellas, India, China, and Ancient Rome, rich men used their money to finance wars and piracy, contracts and building operations. They have appeared as planters with slaves; colonial entrepreneurs in all sorts of speculative, manipulative, and bloody efforts. The capitalistic adventurer, Weber argued, has existed everywhere, even in modern Western countries and in some parts of large-scale international trade.[6]

But something new has been added in modern times: the organization of "free" labor. The success of Western capitalism rests on other factors as well, especially the separation of business from the household and the development of rational systems of bookkeeping. But the key factor is a rational organization of legally free wage earners who work not because they are coerced by law or the threat of physical punishment, but because they *choose* to.[7]

For centuries it was an article of faith that ordinary people labor only to escape hunger and poverty; their choice to work is not free, but forced. "As a path to happiness," Freud wrote, "work is not highly prized by men. They do not strive after it as they do other possibilities of satisfaction. The great majority of people only work under the stress of necessity, and this natural human aversion to work raises most difficult social problems."[8] The argument is popular even today, in criticism of welfare programs that are said simply to put food in the mouths of the lazy to keep them from trying to lift themselves by their bootstraps.

But to Weber the "human aversion to work" was not simply "natural." The fact that people have traditionally resented their jobs may be due not to their own laziness or other psychological qualities, but to the work they are forced to do. But neither is it unnatural to feel an obligation to one's job.

[6] *Ibid.,* p. 58.

[7] *Ibid.,* p. 22.

[8] Sigmund Freud, *Civilization and Its Discontents* (New York: Norton, 1962), p. 27.

Work may be a mere source of livelihood, or the most significant part of one's inner life; it may be experienced as expiation,
or as exuberant expression of self; as bounden duty or as the development of man's universal nature. Neither love nor hatred of
work is inherent in man, or inherent in any given line of work. . . .

Whatever the effects of his work, known to him or not, they
are the net result of the work as an activity, plus the meanings he
brings to it, plus the views others hold of it.

C. Wright Mills, *White Collar:*
The American Middle Classes

It is not surprising when a man like Ben Franklin learns to
love his work. But it is of some interest when a whole community
begins to agree that the meaning of life is somehow tied to one's
work; that production and economic growth are ends in themselves; that one has a duty to do one's best in business and industry.

As capitalism emerged in Europe and America, more and more
men and women came to accept the idea that they had a "duty"
to their vocations. Resistance to work remained widespread, but
it was being overweighted by a feeling of obligation to one's
job, by the idea that work is an end in itself, a duty. Even the
desire to make money and accumulate possessions became a
duty: The wealth was not to be enjoyed and consumed, but
saved and amassed.

Today such ideas are familiar, even to those who find them
distasteful. But to the pre-capitalist man, Weber noted, they
were grotesques, "so incomprehensible and mysterious, so un-
worthy and contemptible. That anyone should be able to make
it the sole purpose of his life's-work, to sink into the grave
weighted down with a great material load of money and goods,
seems to him explicable only as the product of a perverse in-
stinct. . . ."[9]

It seems even more strange that these ideas would appeal to
the people of Franklin's New England. In industrializing Europe they might make sense, as Marx had seen; but the methods

[9] Weber, *Protestant Ethic*, pp. 71–72.

and riches of the industrial revolution had not yet reached the colonies. Few of the people to whom the ideas seemed so "reasonable" had any chance to get rich quickly or even slowly; and if one did amass any wealth there were few satisfactions to buy with it. For virtually every man and woman hard work could lead only to the irrational sense of having done a job well. Something unusual was going on in colonial New England.

What did people gain from the kind of life Franklin urged? Their penny-pinching, somber efforts yielded few of the satisfactions wealth had brought to people of other places and of other times. What was in it for them? Why were they so different from men and women in other backwoods places in other times?

Such questions—basic to the differences that separate us from one another today—bothered Weber. In his search for answers, he cut to the fovea of the Marxian image of man and society and discovered a blindness there.

THROUGH THE CENTURIES, Weber pointed out, it was traditionally accepted that most men and women did not want to earn more and more, but only enough to live in those ways they were accustomed to accept as comfortable. Some years later, in the early twentieth century, efficiency experts discovered the same thing. Armed with knowledge of how to increase productivity in American factories, they journeyed to eastern Europe, boasting that they would raise not only production, but also the income and standard of living of each individual worker. They failed dismally: when workers found they could earn as much in a few days as they had previously earned in a week, they simply worked for a few days and spent the rest of the week in more pleasant pursuits.

This was no news to those who knew the workers' minds. For centuries before the spread of capitalism, laborers had stubbornly resisted the appeal of the dangling carrot. Most employers knew this. Indeed, among the captains of industry another theory had grown popular: Labor is spurred not by the carrot, but by the stick. The way to increase production is to lower wages, to make people fear starvation and deprivation, for that forces them to work harder to earn the same amount as before. Low wages, thus, lead to high profits. This, it will be remembered—though the capitalistic owners might have been shocked to hear of it—was a Marxian view of the relation of labor to management, of proletariat to bourgeois.

Marx had seen clearly the changes in the mentality of the middle class in the wake of the industrial revolution, and noted that changes were reflected in the mentality of the workers. The workers, he argued, were being duped: the new economic relations would benefit only the middle class, and the new values and ideas simply blinded the workers to the fact. And, Marx argued, capitalism generates a surplus population, enabling it to keep wages at a bare-bones minimum: though industrial capitalism increases production and therefore profits, it must keep wages low, or the workers will slack off and production will fall. Low wages had brought high production for centuries, and in Marx's times it seemed reasonable to assume that relationship would continue.

But Weber saw the limits of that theory. Writing with almost a half-century more experience with the new forms of capitalism, he saw that low wages fail wherever there is need for skilled labor to run expensive machinery that is easily damaged or where sharp attention or initiative is required. "Here low wages do not pay," he wrote, "and their effect is the opposite of what was intended. For not only is a developed sense of responsibility absolutely indispensable, but in general also an attitude which at least during working hours, is freed from continual calculations of how the customary wage may be earned with a maximum of comfort and a minimum of exertion. Labor must, on the contrary, be performed as if it were an absolute end in itself, a calling."[10]

The success of capitalism depended on dedicated labor, and capitalism was indeed succeeding, at least in its own terms.

[10] *Ibid.,* pp. 61–62.

FOR A REVOLUTION HAD OCCURRED. Like all revolutions that have succeeded, the triumph of capitalism in nineteenth-century Europe and America is now seen as inevitable. We learn that it came as a relentless movement, that from its first efforts it was destined to dominate Western systems. But the facts differ: Capitalism was a pretender in its youth, and only after generations of struggle was its title established. For it involved striking changes in human relations and codes of conduct, in social ethics and both churchly and national laws.[11]

So questionable an innovation [as the new spirit of capitalism] demanded of the pioneers who first experimented with it as much originality, self-confidence, and tenacity of purpose as is required today of those who would break from the net that it has woven. What influences moved them to defy tradition?

> R. H. Tawney, Foreword to Max Weber, *The Protestant Ethic and the Spirit of Capitalism*

Those who first experimented with the new ways of doing things, those who demanded change, had to make great efforts and sacrifices to break the web of society that surrounded them. Why did they do it? Where did they find the new principles, the new images of the individual and society that would replace those they rejected?

Marx, as we have seen, had ready answers to such questions. New forms of social life, in the final analysis, are due to changes in the economic environment. Principles are simply rationalizations that distort the inequities in the new social forms and hide their true relationship to the economic environment. To Weber, such an explanation was confused: Marx thought he saw the *cause* of social change when all he actually saw were some of the conditions that permitted it to develop.

Even though the seventeenth and eighteenth centuries were in many ways favorable to the rise of capitalism, they were by no means unique. Other times, other places seemed equally or even more favorable in their economy and commerce. Why

[11] R. H. Tawney, "Foreword" to Weber, *Protestant Ethic,* p. 1 (c).

hadn't capitalism developed in those places? Why was it only in the European societies that a capitalism emerged, based on the free enterprise not only of the privileged, powerful, and monied, but also of the workers, who barter their time and effort for wages?

Once again, Weber turned to Ben Franklin's "state of mind." According to Marx's argument, Franklin's ideals—the kind of ideals that could support capitalism—should not have emerged until after the rise of capitalism. But reality disagreed with Marx's theory: In Franklin's New England, the ideals of capitalism appeared before capitalism itself.

"There were complaints of a peculiarly calculating sort of profit-seeking in New England, as distinguished from other parts of America, as early as 1632," wrote Weber. "It is further undoubted that capitalism remained far less developed in some of the neighboring colonies, the later Southern States of the United States of America, in spite of the fact that these latter were founded by large capitalists for business motives, while the New England colonies were founded by preachers and seminary graduates with the help of small bourgeois, craftsmen and yeomen, for religious reasons. In this case, the causal relations were certainly the reverse of that suggested by the materialistic standpoint."[12]

To Weber, the example was convincing: Marx's model of man and social change was inadequate. "To speak here of the reflection of material conditions in the ideal superstructure," Weber wrote with scorn worthy of Marx, "would be patent nonsense."[13]

But to show that Marx was wrong wasn't Weber's purpose. For the questions remained, and he wanted an answer: Why here, not there? Why now, not then? How could the kind of business activity which was at best only tolerated in far richer and more productive centers—where the economic bases for capitalism seemed so firm—turn into a duty in such an un-

[12] Weber, *Protestant Ethic,* p. 56.
[13] *Ibid.,* p. 75.

likely place as "the back woods small bourgeois circumstances of Pennsylvania in the eighteenth century, where business threatened for simple lack of money to fall back into barter, where there was hardly a sign of large enterprise, where only the earliest beginnings of banking were to be found?"[14]

Weber, just as Marx, saw that a social and cultural revolution had occurred. Marx's description of the change was brilliant, but it was incomplete and thus distorted. The behavior of individuals in their everyday lives, Weber reasoned, had changed because changes had occurred in the ways those persons thought about themselves and about their relations to others and to established routines. Some of these changes in ideas and ideals Weber labeled "the spirit of capitalism."

Marx had argued that such changes in images were nothing more than reflections of changes brought about by technology. But to Weber, this was only part of the story: in the change there seemed to be a peculiar interplay of ideas, ideals, and technologies that Marx had missed.

Clearly, technology played an important role. But, equally important, the culture had been prepared for the rise of capitalism as men and women tried to cope with two profound crises in Western society. Weber traced the roots of those crises to two interrelated themes of Western history: the loss of belief in the mystical and magical and the increasing rationality in the relations of individuals to one another.

WEBER WAS NOT a religious believer, but he was impressed with the role of religion in human psychologies and relationships. In his studies of religion, then, he was not interested in pursuing theology or philosophy, but in something quite different: "The influence of those psychological sanctions which, originating in religious belief, and the practice of religion, give a direction to practical conduct and hold the individual to it."[15]

"At a date when, in England, people gave up the practice of

[14] *Ibid.*
[15] *Ibid.*, p. 97.

burning witches," Marx had noted, "they began to hang forgers of bank notes."[16] To Marx this meant that the new class relationships brought by technology were no longer threatened by religious heresies: Capitalism was the new religion, and the dangerous heretics were those who violated the laws of property.

Weber saw that Marx had again accurately described the situation, yet had failed to see its causes. Technology had not simply caused the change in religious beliefs. If anything, it was the other way around: Religion, magic and witchcraft had grown irrelevant in the nineteenth century, helping stimulate the development of capitalist technology; and as technology grew, it helped make religion even more irrelevant.

To understand this line of argument—an argument of profound importance to our own times—it will help to move back with Weber to the ferment of ideas and activities known today as the Reformation.

> . . . if we look closely at Weber's Protestant Ethic thesis, we see that, whatever the correctness of its details, it is an attempt to explain the transformation of a whole social or cultural system through a change in the type of relations between personal and collective identities, on the one hand, and between them and various concrete institutional activities on the other. And it was this symbolic transformation which thus facilitated, even if it did not cause, the emergence of some new institutional developments.
>
> S. N. Eisenstadt, *Max Weber: On Charisma and Institution Building*

The Protestant Ethic

Sorcery and witchcraft had long since been banished from the Christian Church by the sixteenth century. Yet some vestiges of magic remained. Above all, many devout persons still believed that man's salvation after death required the work of a priestly "magician." To the layman, the ways of God were

[16] Marx, *Capital,* p. 837.

beyond man's control; it was priests who must act on behalf of others, who could dispense God's forgiveness, in accordance with the teachings he had left them. But the priests could be bribed; the church grew rich and powerful, as "sinners," unable to sacrifice directly to their god, readily offered not only their prayers and pleas, but their wealth as well, however meager it might be.

Whatever its excesses, this arrangement offered security and a relief from guilt to those who believed in it. "The normal medieval Catholic layman," Weber noted, "lived ethically, so to speak, from hand to mouth."[17] When they sinned, they could find forgiveness by turning to the priest in grief and penitence. Of course, the church expected them to attempt to change their ways, but for most men and women the requirement was weakened. Forgiveness, after all, came easily and could be gained from act to act. The priest was something of a magician, who held the key to eternal life, who dispensed forgiveness, and thereby granted release from the "tremendous tension" of sin.

This vestige of magic, then, gave the Catholic layman an inner security, whose moral conduct could be a planless and unsystematic cycle of sin, repentance, forgiveness, psychological release, and renewed sin. In his psychological security, the average man who lived within medieval Catholicism felt little impulse to question the general quality of his life; to examine his past, present, and future as some sort of comprehensive whole. His life, simply, required no further justification.

Then came Luther.

MARTIN LUTHER REJECTED the idea that priests or church possessed magical powers to save men's souls. Faith, and nothing else, would save man. Every person, not just priests, had a god-given job to do on earth, a "calling." With this message, Luther —intending something quite different—struck the first blow to release medieval believers from their psychological security and force them to question the meaning of their lives. Luther him-

[17] Weber, *Protestant Ethic,* p. 116.

self was fundamentally a conservative and embraced most of the doctrines of the Catholic church. Even after the church had driven him out—an excommunication he fervently resisted —he continued to support Catholic doctrines and thereby supported existing economic injustices and an authoritarian government.

For Luther, as Calvin after him, was less interested in social reform than in saving men's souls. Yet Luther had opened the doors of the church: The idea that all persons have a calling suggested that the devout could find their salvation not only in the cloisters, but on the streets.

Yet even Luther's image of human life retained an element of the magical that disturbed John Calvin. Whereas Luther's vision had derived from religious experience, Calvin's developed from logical rationality. Calvin could see no reason to believe that God dwelled in man. God does not exist for people; people exist for the sake of God. God and God alone is free, subject to no law, and hence beyond human understanding. Only as he has revealed himself to us can we know him.

What God has revealed is that only few persons are chosen for eternal grace, and the rest are damned. As God's decrees cannot change, each individual's fate is predetermined. Such was Calvin's stark and unforgiving image.

"In its extreme inhumanity," Weber wrote, "this doctrine must above all have had one consequence for the life of a generation which surrendered to its magificent consistency. That was the feeling of unprecedented inner loneliness of the single individual. . . . He was forced to follow his path alone to meet a destiny which had been decreed for him from eternity. No one could help him. No priest . . . no sacraments . . . no church . . . even no God. For even Christ had died only for the elect."[18]

Still, though people cannot be saved by their works, the success of their works can demonstrate that they are among God's chosen few. Burdened with the idea of predestination,

[18] *Ibid.*, p. 104.

the individual comes to ask, "Am I one of the elect? How can I know?" In this dark uncertainty, one idea offers hope: that the individual exists only to serve God. He who is elect will increase the glory of God through his worldly actions; and to do this he must not fail in his efforts. Thus, though there is no way out of the psychological uncertainty, it can be reduced. In success, people find evidence of their inner grace; in success, they are convinced of their salvation. But to succeed, a person must suppress his or her natural desires. Each must systematically plan and industriously pursue those goals that glorify God, which can be done only by enriching one's self.

Religious efforts, then, move into everyday life and work. The glorification of God is never-ending; it is a part of every waking and sleeping minute, of every action, every relationship. Each Christian has to be a monk all through life, forced to pursue his or her ideals within mundane, everyday occupations and activity. The Reformation thus brought the self-denial of the monastery into every sphere of life, affecting a believer's relations to all other persons, bringing pressures of change throughout society.

There was a struggle going on between the old order and the new. And it was the Calvinistic group which recognized the change as it was taking place and who came to regard the business process as one which was instituted by God. . . . Man was to be strenuous in business, serving the Lord. This was the motto of the Calvinist, and with it was carried over into business the discipline of religious life.

George Herbert Mead, *Movements of
Thought in the Nineteenth Century*

In these pressures of change, a strange thing happened. Calvin believed in an ethic of self-denial: but now, in the name of self-denial, wealth and possessions were glorified and exploiting one's neighbor was justified.

For the Puritan, self-denial "turned with all its force against one thing: a spontaneous enjoyment of life and all it had to offer." Sports were accepted only insofar as they helped one keep fit and efficient; if they were simply an impulsive enjoyment of life, they were as detested as the enjoyments of the dance hall or the public house. Science, art, and music were fully accepted, but only so long as they fulfilled religious value.

In literature and the fine arts, however, "asceticism descended like a frost." Nudity and the erotic were banned, and radical views became impossible. Idle talk, superfluities, vain ostentation, all showed irrational attitudes that lacked purpose, and were soberly denied. Thus, "that powerful tendency toward uniformity of life, which today so immensely aids the capitalistic interest in the standardization of production, had its ideal foundations in the repudiation of all idolatry of the flesh."[19]

Other religious and social ethics have urged self-denial. But in the Protestant Ethnic, the asceticism was linked with the individual's life in this world. Rather than abhorring all possessions, a person is seen as a trustee of those things that have come through God's graces. The good Christian then "subordinates himself as an obedient steward, or even as an acquisitive machine." This is a God-given duty; it "bears with chilling weight on his life." The greater the possessions, the greater the duty to hold them undiminished and to increase them by restless effort.[20]

Thus the link to the development of capitalism: The Protestant Ethic discouraged consumption, especially of luxuries; at the same time, it unloosed the impulse to acquire. The great campaigns of the devout against the temptations of the flesh and indulgence were struggles as well against irrational spending and for rational saving. Thus capital accumulates through a compulsion to save. And from accumulated capital and the impulse to accumulate more, production escalates higher and higher. Capitalism flourishes.

Weber is often criticized for exaggerating the importance of religious beliefs to the rise of capitalism. His argument is read

[19] *Ibid.*, pp. 166–169.
[20] *Ibid.*, p. 170.

to suggest that he thought that only Protestants brought about capitalism, that Catholics still live in the Dark Ages, or that all of England, even Europe, was suddenly taken over by the Protestants. Even sophisticated readers and critics have accused Weber of pretending that the seventeenth-century Puritans of England lived by the views of Calvin himself.

Weber warned against such interpretations. What he argued was that the Puritan outlook directly influenced the lives of some individuals in some communities to the extent that the lives of other people in those and other communities were indirectly affected. The general result of these changes in life was to favor the development of rational, middle-class ways of working and living. This was not the only influence on the rise of capitalism, but to Weber it was the most important and the most consistent influence. "It stood at the cradle of modern economic man," he wrote—but he did not write that it alone had given birth to the new man.[21]

IN THE PROTESTANT ETHIC, Weber tried to show that ideas, beliefs, and values do influence both the individual and society. Capitalism, then, did not simply grow out of the feudal system in the mechanistic and occasionally violent way described by Marx. Rather, the new institutions of capitalism were encouraged and supported by unusual complexes of values, most strikingly those of acquisitive self-denial. These in turn were related to the psychological qualities of men and women seeking to find order and security in private worlds that have suddenly ruptured from the established, traditional culture.

At most, the Protestant Ethic offered "a powerful ally" to the rise of capitalism. But once under way, the energetic economic system could do without its ally. Inevitably, the puritanical ideals fell away as people grew used to their riches. And so, ironically, the powerful and wealthy were the first to see through the ideals that justified their position; the disadvantaged, especially from a lower status, remained the most genuine believers in the godliness of frugal enterprise.

[21] *Ibid.*

The strength of their belief put the disadvantaged at a further disadvantage. For, once capitalism was under way, success was more likely for the person who could spring free from the ethical or religious ideals that justified sacrifice. Some persons, of course, desire not just riches but also the power and prestige that wealth might bring, especially "when the imagination of a whole people has once been turned toward purely quantitative bigness as in the United States." But it is only the poets among businessmen who are seduced by this romanticism of numbers. The real leaders, and especially the permanently successful entrepreneurs, are not taken in by it. Wealth is their success, and success is their ethic.[22]

The church and its religion had little attraction for these active men. If asked for the meaning of their restless activity, they had no good answer. But, to Weber, the answer was simple: "that business with its continuous work has become a necessary part of their lives. That is in fact the only possible motivation, but it at the same time expresses what is, seen from the view-point of personal happiness, so irrational about this sort of life, where a man exists for the sake of his business, instead of the reverse."[23]

The godly thought that possessions should lie on one's shoulders like a light coat, to be thrown aside at any moment. But in the spirit of capitalism, they form into an iron cage: We become slaves to our possessions and to the production that makes them possible. The religious spirit flees the cage, yet "the idea of duty to one's calling prowls about in our life like the ghost of dead religious beliefs." The cage has become something beyond justification related neither to spiritual nor to cultural values, nor to our economic needs. Thus, our jobs and our production become ends in themselves, and the pursuit of wealth turns into a simple sport.[24] In Marx's terms, we are alienated.

WEBER ARGUED that the ascetic religious ideas have helped

[22] *Ibid.*, p. 71.
[23] *Ibid.*, p. 70.
[24] *Ibid.*, pp. 181–182.

change the course of history, yet he denied that they were the sole cause. To do so would be to fall into the same error made by Marx. He did not intend to throw out Marx's one-sided emphasis on economies and technology and replace it with an "equally one-sided spiritualistic causal interpretation of culture and of history," he insisted. "Each is equally possible, but each, if it does not serve as the preparation but as the conclusion of an investigation, accomplishes equally little in the interest of historical truth."[25]

Weber pointed out that he had set out to study only a situation in which the influence of religious ideas was beyond doubt. This was enough to show Marx's deficiency. It would have been easy to take this demonstration further, pretending that everything characteristic of modern culture had grown from Protestant rationalism. But that would be nonsense. "That sort of thing," he noted in a scathing footnote, "may be left to the type of dilettante who believes in the unity of the group mind and its reducibility to a single formula."[26]

Thus Weber found Marx not wrong, but lacking. Man and society were influenced by their economic relations, but they were influenced by other things as well. Even human ideals and ideas could influence change; but they were not always important, and never the sole "cause" of change. They too were "caused" by a diversity of things. They did not simply emerge mechanically from earlier ideas, but from the interplay of other ideas and ideals with social and economic conditions.

Summary and Direction

Marx had railed against capitalism for alienating man. Weber saw that Marx had been both right and wrong: the worker is indeed separated from the means of production—he is alienated, as Marx had pointed out—but not simply because of capital-

[25] *Ibid.*, p. 183.
[26] *Ibid.*, pp. 283, 284, n. 118.

ism. Capitalism offered but one special case of an alienating process; socialism offered another. Together, they revealed a general phenomenon of modern times: Alienation is the result of the organizations that men form in response to new technologies. It was not capitalism, but the bureaucratic organizations it spawned that were the real threat.

> If, in Marx, the class struggle is at the centre of attention and defines all other problems, with Weber bureaucracy becomes the central concept. From this perspective . . . one begins to ask about the impact of this type of organization on the social structure and on the individual personality. What institutional forms are possible within a bureaucratic society? What are the chances of individual freedom in a society of giant bureaucracies interfering in the most intimate aspects of private life?
>
> Nicos P. Mouzelis, *Organisation and Bureaucracy*

Somehow, despite human ideals, organizations get out of hand. It is not necessary to believe that evil or selfish persons have seized power to serve their own ends. This does happen, of course, yet even given leaders of vision and good will, organizations have a way of taking on a life of their own. They grow beyond the abilities of even their leaders and operate contrary to their intentions.

Combined with "inanimate machinery" of technology, the "living machine" of bureaucracy would create a new bondage, "a framework into which people might be forced to fit as helplessly as the fellahin who had to accept the old Egyptian society. This may happen if a technically good, that means a rational, bureaucratic organization is the only ultimate value determining social organization."[27]

To Weber, rationality meant that the means men use are appropriate to the ends they have in mind. In a bureaucracy, those ends appear to be clear-cut: to effectively administer a legislative program, to increase productive output. What, then,

[27] Max Weber, *Gesammelte Politische Schriften* (Munich: Drie Masken Verlag, 1921), p. 298.

is most rational in a bureaucracy? Efficiency: an organization is most rational when the most efficient means are chosen to attain its goals. This means that rational bureaucracy is necessary to any complex economy, polity, and society. In fact, Weber argued, the capacity to operate in such efficient organizations was part of the vital genius behind the amazing success of industrial capitalism.

If an organization is seen as a tool of humanity, then one could only applaud those efforts that made the tool more efficient. But Weber was disturbed. Bureaucracies in Western society seemed to discourage what Karl Mannheim would later call "substantive rationality." Substantive rationality "reveals intelligent insight into the interrelation of events in a given situation"; the individual is the criterion; a person's actions are measured against his or her own goals and aspirations. In Marx's terms, it is the rationality of praxis; it is the rationality of what we have seen as "critical involvement."

But organizations encouraged a different kind of rationality, a "functional rationality," in which only the goals of the organization are truly important. In functional rationality, an individual's action has no intrinsic value; it gains value only by its contribution to the goals of the organization.[28]

Theoretically, a society could be rich in both types of rationality. Indeed, in Mead's and Marx's utopian dreams, functional rationality would have a place, but always in the service of substantive rationality. Such dreams are elusive, however. For in modern organizations, functional rationality drives out substantive rationality. The more functionally rational and bureaucratic the organization grows, the more are the purposes and meanings of the individuals' lives ignored. In the functional rationality of the bureaucratic organization, the individual becomes a simple cog.

Weber looked deeper into this "alienation" than had Marx and discovered that not only economic motives lay at the bot-

---

[28] Karl Mannheim, *Man and Society in an Age of Reconstruction* (Cambridge: Harvard University Press, 1948).

tom of the problem. Other goals and desires can also lead individuals to exploit one another, condemning their fellow beings to an alienated existence. For, as industrialism accelerated, organizations throughout society—not only in business, but in government, law, and education—developed in ways that were ever less responsive to the needs and lives of all the members involved.

No one knows who will live in this cage in the future, or whether at the end of tremendous development entirely new prophets will arise, or there will be a great rebirth of old ideas and ideals, or, if neither, mechanized petrification, embellished with a sort of convulsive self-importance. For the last stage of this cultural development it might well be truly said: "specialists without spirit, sensualists without heart; this nullity imagines that it has attained a level of civilization never before achieved."

Max Weber, *The Protestant Ethic*
and the Spirit of Capitalism

It was not only the laborer who was alienated from himself and his society by his work; an ever deeper and more complete alienation was being suffered by those who worked in the front offices, and even in the levels of top management. In modern times, Marx's alienation was moving from the factories into the front offices, where men and women were trapped in a cold cage of functional rationality.

Chapter Nine

The Technology of Organizations: Images of Control and Change

FOR A TIME, Weber's warnings were ignored. But fears of organization and technology were in the air, and others soon carried them to bizarre conclusions.

Aldous Huxley told of a society where development of human consciousness would be controlled from the very moment of conception, where feelings of unrest could be quickly ended with drugs, sex, and other sensual escape, where even the thought of disloyalty would be impossible.[1] Huxley had written in the thirties of life in a future century. But a few more years of life in this century convinced him that he had been wrong: This *Brave New World* was not a thing of a distant tomorrow. It was just around the corner.[2]

In ways, George Orwell's vision was even more disturbing. To Orwell, writing in the wake of the Second World War, Western culture was turning into a gigantic state-controlled organization. By *1984* the mega-organization would be supreme, all discontent would be brutally suppressed, loyalties and beliefs manipulated, history and languages manufactured at official

---

[1] Aldous Huxley, *Brave New World* (New York: Harper & Row, 1932).

[2] Aldous Huxley, *Brave New World Revisited* (New York: Harper & Row, 1958).

whim, and even the most private moments closely watched by "Big Brother."[3]

These visions, everyone knew, were fantasies. But what made them so fearsome was that the fantasies were extensions of the functionally rational organizations the authors saw around them in twentieth-century England. In the wake of the Second World War, the fears spread rapidly. The horror of Nazi extermination of six million Jews seemed to foretell the future of Western society. It would be an organizational nightmare: a mindless system of obedient managers and technicians who do their jobs without question, eager for the favor of their superiors, anxious to escape criticism. In 1948, *1984* seemed frighteningly near.

The theme found an American idiom in C. Wright Mills' chilling vision of "Cheerful Robots" who had lost their freedom through uncomprehending conformity. Other critics had said as much. The bureaucratic perspective was taking over American life. Every decade saw fewer possibilities to earn a living income or to find one's identity outside a large-scale organization. Never in history had the organizational mentality so dominated an entire society. Modern man was in the grip of his organizations, and they were emasculating him.

Mills gave the subject another twist. "The problem of freedom," he insisted, "is the problem of how decisions about the future of human affairs are to be made and who is to make them. . . ."[4] And here Mills turned from social criticism to exploration.

Under what conditions do men come to *want* to be free and capable of acting freely? Under what conditions are they willing and able to bear the burdens freedom does impose and to see these less as burdens than as gladly undertaken self-transformations? And on the negative side: Can men be made to want to become *cheerful* robots?

C. Wright Mills, *The Sociological Imagination*

---

[3] George Orwell, *1984* (New York: Harcourt, Brace, Jovanovich, 1963).
[4] Mills, *The Sociological Imagination,* p. 215.

Mills's critical questions can lead us in many compelling directions, which must be pursued if we are to understand ourselves and recognize our possibilities. Among the most compelling in our times, as Mills and Weber recognized, is an exploration of the thrusts of functional rationality in our large-scale organizations. For never before in the history of the world have leaders so fully rested their right to control other men and women on rules and laws. Never have authority and work been so highly rationalized.

Still, it is difficult to identify these trends. Marx might have seen them as a revolution, a massive mutation of our social order, in its very centers. Whatever the nature of the current transformations of our society, we are not yet at the end of them. Indeed, they have only begun, even for those who labor in the vital centers. Many persons living today may never recognize their effects to any great degree. For any changing society, especially one in the midst of massive transformation, never changes evenly.

Even those who suffer and enjoy its impacts may fail to recognize the transformation or succeed in ignoring it. Many persons will continue to live in the ways of yesterday; others are already caught in an exuberant rush to the future. Most, perhaps, will live in an unclear present, accepting changing opportunities and constraints with little regret for what is lost, little worry about what is to come.

The sketch that follows, then, is both speculative and interpretive. It draws sensitizing concepts and arguments from Weber's classic discussions of bureaucracy, from F. W. Howton's suggestive discussion of "Functionaries," and from Talcott Parsons' distinction between technical, managerial, and institutional processes of complex organizations.[5]

---

[5] Throughout the first half of this chapter, I have been stimulated especially by F. William Howton, *Functionaries* (Chicago: Quadrangle, 1969); see also Talcott Parsons, *Structure and Process in Modern Societies* (Glencoe: The Free Press, 1960), p. 65.

Organization and Functional Rationality

To sensitize his cultural and historical studies, Weber constructed an "ideal type" bureaucracy. His model was the ponderous, rigid organization of German government, heavy with
Prussian respect for hierarchy and authority—a striking contrast to modern industrial organization. Yet he cut so incisively
to the essentials of bureaucracy of his day that his images continue to stimulate and inform.

To Weber, these were the compelling features of bureaucracy:

A sharply defined hierarchy of authority.

A division of labor based on functional specialization.

Systems of rules and procedures identifying the rights and
duties of employees.

Impersonal relations, both between specializations and up and
down the ladder of authority.

Promotion based on competence and expertise.

The latter two items are familiar targets of contemporary
dissent and despair.[6] But it is the first three—hierarchy of authority, functional specialization, and rule by rules—that most
help us recognize the thrusts of our own times:

1. Functional rationality: Abstract rules are essential to a
complex organization. For abstract rules offer a "universal language" that can be understood even by those who are separated
from one another by geography, culture, and social distance.
These rules cover the rights and duties of employees, as well as
the procedures for dealing with work situations.

One advantage of these abstract rules is that they fit together
smoothly with other abstract rules. Ideally, all such rules can

---

[6] I have simplified Weber's arguments extremely. For a brief but more adequate treatment, see Hans Gerth and C. Wright Mills, *From Max Weber:
Essays in Sociology* (New York: Oxford, 1958), pp. 196–244. For a suggestive synthesis of thought on bureaucracy in political contexts, see Harvey
Wheeler, *Democracy in a Revolutionary Era* (New York: Praeger, 1968),
pp. 79–101.

be deduced from two general canons that lie at the heart of bureaucratic organization: efficiency and effectiveness.

2. Functionally rational authority: Abstract rules can be applied "vertically" in an organization, that is, authority can be rationalized. In an army, for a prime example, the hierarchy of authority is striking: From general on down through private, it is always easy to tell who outranks whom.

Rationalized authority has an important psychological effect: it promotes "impersonality." As the soldier learns to "salute the uniform, not the man," the new junior executive learns to relate to his or her superiors and subordinates as embodiments of roles, rather than as whole human beings. This stylized difference muffles the personality clashes that otherwise might occur, especially between individuals in differing specialties or bureaus.

3. Functionally rational specialization: Abstract rules can also be applied "horizontally" in the organization, that is, the division of labor can be rationalized. When it is, we speak of "specialization": the rational arrangements of jobs or functions that are not interchangeable.

Specialization usually escalates the problems of authority, encouraging "vertical" rationality, for each new specialized task increases the problems of coordination and control. In modern organizations, stimulated by capital and technology, there is a continual mushrooming of technicians and experts. This expands problems of coordination, calling out more elaborate structures of command; and it changes the hierarchy of authority in another way: As the importance of the specialist escalates, promotion and selection are increasingly based on technical competence or the merit of the individual.

Weber's model of rational bureaucracy, barely introduced here, is an "ideal type": although never existing in real life in its pure form, the model lets us ask a crucial question: How closely does this or that organization approximate the "ideal type" of rational bureaucracy?

Looking back through history and across cultures, Weber

found other bureaucracies, in ancient Egypt, in Confucian China, in the Roman Empire, in the Papal Church, and in the medieval state. But in the modern world, something new was happening.

In a way, Weber stood in awe of the bureaucratic invention. He recognized the need to organize in order to meet the great challenges and potentials of life in a complex society. He saw the organizations that surrounded him—in government, commerce, industry, and the military—as among the greatest accomplishments of mankind. True, they were marred by inefficiencies, incompetence, selfishness, and ignorance. But these flaws could be, perhaps would be, corrected in the future.

That prospect cast Weber into a profound despair, for all too likely they would be corrected not through the advance of human reasonableness, not to the betterment of man, but through the increase of a functional rationality that was blind to human values and the essentials of human life. The trend was unmistakable: Functional rationality was suffocating substantive rationality.

We are born in organizations, educated by organizations, and spend much of our lives working for organizations. We spend much of our leisure time paying, playing, and praying in organizations. Most of us will die in an organization, and when the time comes for burial, the largest organization of all—the state—must grant official permission.

Amatai Etzioni, *Modern Organizations*

As Weber feared, the trend has continued, even accelerated, in the years since his death. Not surprisingly, the acceleration can be seen most clearly in the development of industrial corporations in America. It first appeared in the application of functional rationality "horizontally" in the organization to the roles of the craftsmen and laborers—in a "technology of technology" that made its most dramatic appearance in Henry Ford's automobile production lines. In short order functional rationality made another leap, in the "vertical" rationalization of authority reflected by the rise of "scientific management" or, more accurately, a technology of management.

Today, functional rationality seems to be reaching to another level—to the relations of the "institutional agents" of our large-scale organizations: the presidents, boards of directors, and other men and women who manage the relations of their organizations with other organizations. This might be termed a technology of institutions, seen in developing capacities for planning—planning the operations not just of individual organizations but of entire societies.

To attempt to recognize these trends, we must again go back some distance, this time half a century or so, to pick up Weber's exploration of the centuries-long movement toward rationality in Western life.

Communication and Coordination: The Technology of Technicians

Until the First World War, most industries in America remained small by present-day standards—no more than a few thousand employees, usually only a few hundred—and their plans of organization remained simple and rather personalized.

Most jobs were repetitive and routine. To coordinate the various parts of an industry required little more than overt control: Keep a person in line and at his job, and all will be well. The important thing was that the individual be motivated to please his superiors, and the motivating force was ready at hand: scarcity. Men and women would work at their routine tasks to escape the desperation of unemployment and hunger; some would even redouble their efforts, hoping for a pay raise, perhaps a better job.

All that was needed to keep things going was some system whereby every employee, no matter how important his job, felt the critical eye of a superior on him. Thus, the early industries developed rigid hierarchies, sharply rising pyramids of authority, with a handful of men near the top of each pyramid.

These few men had all the knowledge and other resources necessary to control the entire enterprise. To be sure, there were problems of coordination, but they did not seem crucial. Great profits were being made, and the new technologies were being adequately utilized. The answers to problems of industrial coordination were emerging slowly, and that would do.

Then, in the early twentieth century, the very foundations of Western civilization were shaken by man's first war of large-scale technology. World War I stimulated industries in ways unimagined; the drive for production and profits was frantic, bringing new improvements aimed at efficiency and increased production. Perhaps even more important than the war was what followed. For financial crises and recessions of the early twenties forced American businessmen to look closely at their organizations, particularly at the technological problems of production.

In the booming war economy, automobile manufacturers were especially strained. They had grown rapidly, too rapidly. Now they found themselves burdened with heavy financial investment; they needed to reorganize, somehow, some way.

New technologies were at hand, and Henry Ford recognized what they meant to production: Each person on the production line needed to do only a certain specialized task, repeating it over and over again. Combined with the specialized efforts of hundreds of others, coordinated in a highly rational system, the result was an ever-quickening flow of cars through the doors of the factory, into the salesrooms and onto the highways. The modern production line had been born.

Ford did not discover the idea; he simply capitalized on it. It was the same principle that Jean Valjean, the hero-victim of *Les Miserables*,[7] used in the late eighteenth century to convert a traditional pottery works into a capitalist empire. The method was simple. Traditionally, each craftsman had worked at his own project from beginning to end. Valjean simply rearranged the production, having each man perform a special function.

[7] Victor Hugo, *Les Miserables* (New York: Dodd, 1925).

To make a cup, some molded the basic forms, others the handles, others the bases; while still others glazed and fired. The result was a tremendous increase in output and a lowering of prices that found willing buyers in the marketplace.[8]

Neither Jean Valjean nor Ford had the advantage of any special technology that was unavailable to their competitors. Nor did they enjoy great advantages of wealth. To be sure, money was required, but many others had as much or more capital as either Valjean or Ford in their times. Their success was due primarily to organization—to their ability to rationalize the division of labor. They capitalized on an invention of mechanization: the technology of technicians.

But Ford's America held some possibilities that Valjean, little more than a century earlier, could scarcely have believed. Not only were there new powers of production; now there were new capabilities of communication that made it possible to organize and coordinate a technology of technicians on a massive, complex scale.

Every year of the twentieth century seemed to bring new possibilities in communication. The telegraph had helped create a reasonably efficient railway system across the expansive continent, opening new markets and sources of raw materials to the industries of the urban centers. Improved and extending roads linked cities ever more closely, with the horse and buggy and even horseless carriages. Within the cities, public transportation and improved streets made commerce and business transactions easier and enabled workers to travel greater distances between factory and home.

Literacy spread, and advertising quickened. New ways were found to produce paper quickly and cheaply, and printing presses multiplied. As factories poured out more and more consumer goods, newspapers, magazines, and circulars reached an increasing variety of readers at ever more distant points. The new literacy, availability of paper, and inventions such as shorthand and the typewriter allowed new accuracy and complete-

---

[8] Harvey Wheeler, *The Politics of Revolution* (Berkeley: Glendessary, 1971), pp. 54–55.

ness of record-keeping. The flow and precision of information within the organization escalated.

Such developments in communication and transportation made it easier to coordinate activities in an increasingly diversified industry, within an increasingly complex society. And Ford had showed the way.

FORD'S SUCCESS CAPTURED the imagination of the industrial world. Other auto manufacturers began to copy his production-line techniques, and other businessmen dreamed of becoming the Henry Ford of their line of industry. The competition was dramatic and brutal. Again and again, what had been a small-scale handicraft type of industry was faced with the challenge of mass production, and the choice was to go big or to go under. In the automobile industry, especially, this was no real choice for most of the small manufacturers: To go big required not only imagination and courage, it also took capital, and with every year, ever more capital. In the early twenties there were some three hundred independent automobile manufacturers in America; by 1935, there were fifteen.[9]

For those who survived, new industrial empires emerged, with men like Ford reigning as the new princes of capitalism. Like Ford, many held tight personal control over their rapidly expanding organizations. Like Ford, also, they missed another lesson that quickly became essential to success in our technological society.

Ford had seen that technology opens new possibilities that can be exploited through rationalizing technical jobs. Machine technology made it profitable to turn workers into technicians, in effect by developing a technology of technicians. Ford had pioneered, brilliantly, in making the technology of industry functionally rational. He showed how the new potentials of communication made it possible to exploit the new machine technology to create a new organization in which each job on a production line could be highly specialized. Each laborer could,

[9] Howton, *Functionaries*, pp. 145–146.

indeed, function like a cog in a large productive machine. Competing with the small handicraft producers, the system worked brilliantly.

To Ford and the businessmen who followed his lead, the new communications were simply devices that made the new technology of technicians possible, inventions that helped them to more efficiently transmit orders and information and to coordinate the actions of their employees. For a time, those who simply used the new communications to help create and coordinate their new technology of technicians were in the driver's seat, far ahead of their less imaginative competitors. But Ford, as other captains of industry through the first two decades of the twentieth century, failed to recognize even greater potentials of the new communications for industrial organization.

Then, in the early thirties, those potentials were put to use by other giant producers, to create a new level of technical rationality—a technology of management. The new invention turned out to be the basic genius of American corporations through the mid-twentieth century.

Communication and Consensus: The Technology of Management

This time General Motors led the way. By the early thirties they had already developed a new kind of organization, strikingly different from those used by Ford and other old-style capitalists. Like Ford they developed an efficient technology of technicians, but to it they added a technology of management.

If the production lines could be rationalized, why not the lines of decision and control? Why not find the strengths and weaknesses in the systems of authority and then reorganize in ways more efficient and effective? If functional rationality works on the production lines it can work on management. In practice, that meant that the reins of rigid authority that had infuriated Marx and touched Weber's morbid fascination must be loosened.

Traditionally, as in Ford's company, it was the job of only a few top leaders to "think functionally." All basic decisions—on policies and on methods of operation—were made in the central offices of the owners and their top aides. Under some conditions, in the hands of bold and capable leaders, this can make an efficient and responsive organization. But in the dynamic economy of twentieth-century America, the rigid system quickly reached its limits, floundering in the face of everyday problems of operation and failing to respond to opening opportunities.

Men like Ford still lived with images of economics carried over from an era when "production" was the key problem of industry: Make an article well, price it low, and someone will buy it. The key to success, virtually the only key, was found in more efficient production. With innovations in communications and transportation, and continually spreading wealth, markets were no critical problem. More customers could always be found for cheaper products. Thus, to those seized by Ford's vision, the organization is a huge machine, mechanically coordinated from the top. It has virtually one job, to produce, and it must do that well.

In the twentieth century, that formula first worked, then failed. General Motors was first to recognize a profound implication of Ford's production lines: Production was no longer the key to success. Now markets were the thing. If there were buyers waiting, anyone with capital could follow Ford's lead in increasing production. The need was to discover and create new markets. The organization must be flexible; in all departments and functions, it must be able to recognize and respond to new opportunities.

It was not only the desire to respond to new opportunities that demanded flexibility, however. In an industry so complex and diverse as auto manufacturing, managers at all levels every day meet problems that no set of operating rules can handle. When this happens, authority grows sluggish and self-protective. Faced with unforeseen problems, middle managers without authority tend either to do nothing for fear of doing the wrong thing or to turn to their superiors for orders. Then the organization develops a chronic constipation, its channels stuffed with questions and orders, its managers often unable to move even when they feel the need.

The leaders of General Motors recognized that to keep a modern corporation functioning smoothly, it is not enough for only a handful of leaders at the top of an organization to make all decisions about what would best serve the organization. Managers at all levels must do so. Whatever his or her job, the employee must attempt to energetically innovate—in line with company goals, of course—to find labor-saving devices, to conserve materials and capital, thus helping to push down the cost of each unit produced. Up and down the lines of management, men and women must "think functionally" and act as if the success of the company is their own personal responsibility.[10]

> Like their not-so-distant ancestors in New England . . . [the new "engineers" of large-scale organizations] saw functional rationality as a new ethical system; the individual man must live totally for the Cause, he must not only accept but embrace the discipline demanded by the logic of the new industrial system. He must efface himself and ask others to do the same, all the way down the line.
>
> F. William Howton, *Functionaries*

The General Motors' invention was basically simple. Policy decisions remained in the hands of the central executives, and the operations of the entire organization—including the critical financial operations—continued to be coordinated by their central staff. But operating decisions were decentralized. More and then more discretion and responsibility for the administration of policies were given to the men and women of middle management. The reins of rigid authority were being loosened, or so it seemed. But to more cynical observers, the decentralization of authority was less reality than illusion.

WHATEVER ELSE WAS REQUIRED, the new technology of management was made possible by the ever-increasing capacities of

[10] *Ibid.*

communications to coordinate and control giant and far-flung enterprises. Now intercoms and telephones linked offices to one another, affiliates in other cities and countries. Postal services worked with a new speed and efficiency. Duplicating machines brought "instant printing" to secretarial offices. New methods of accounting and record-keeping developed, along with new ways to quickly send, store, and retrieve written reports and coded data. The auto industry's own contribution to twentieth-century communication—the cars and trucks that now streamed out of the factories—joined sleek new trains and even planes to deliver information, people, and products with ease and speed never before known.

The new systems of communication allowed quick and effective transmission of top-level decisions and concerns to those below. Equally important, the new methods of gathering, storing, and analyzing information allowed constant feedback from the lower ranks to the executives at the top. Inspectors from the central office could visit regional offices; branch managers could be called in for conferences and reports.

As in Ford's centralized system, the necessity to report and the knowledge that they would at all times be closely observed would hold branch managers of all levels in line, constraining their actions and encouraging their cooperation. "Authority" in administration could be decentralized, for the new means of communication would assure that the real decisions were kept where they belonged, in the offices of those at the top.

But the speed and scale of the new communications did not alone account for the success of the new systems of organization. Decentralization of authority promised to give the flexibility needed to meet the everyday challenges of large-scale, complex corporations. But why did decentralization seem to inspire such loyalty and effort?

In the conventional wisdom of industry in Ford's times, it was clear the employees best understood power, hunger, and money and that only these things would insure cooperation. But it is one thing to compel others to follow policies and procedures; it is far more difficult to win their loyalties and creative efforts. What was in the new system that accomplished what wages and fear could not?

An answer to this question was suggested centuries ago by Niccolò Machiavelli and was brought into the twentieth century by Robert Michels, as he labored to unite the perspectives of Weber and Marx. In a context of abundance, Michels saw, when there are wages enough for all to live in comfort, energies and loyalties are bought not simply with money, but also with rations of prestige and influence.

When men and women no longer fear hunger, it is one's status in the organization and other "symbolic" rewards that make the motivational difference. To be sure, salaries remain important, but even their importance is ever more found in the status they symbolize. Often, it is not the actual authority that the individual exercises, but the appearance of authority that matters, for that appearance, too, is a symbol of his importance and value.[11]

Thus, when the leaders of General Motors decentralized administrative authority, they hit on a powerful motivator. Not only did the delegated authority provide the middle manager the feelings of leadership and give him or her influence or its appearance in corporate decisions. It was also a powerful symbol of organizational trust and responsibility. Delegated authority told everyone in the organization how important and valuable a person was thought to be.

The ability to ration authority and other important forms of influence and prestige is a powerful means of control. However strong the lure of salaries, men and women will give their energies more eagerly to their superiors and to their corporation, in return for rations of prestige and influence. The organized use of this "status rationing" in the modern corporation joined the more traditional advantages that, as Michels argued, organizational leaders enjoy. Controlling the flow of information within the organization, they are able to encourage the idea that such organizational status, and even the symbols of status, are in fact

[11] Michels, *Political Parties.*

valuable; that "success" in the organization is indeed success in life; that organizational success requires both harmony and effort.

Further, through secrecy and the careful use of information about their subordinates, as well as through their specialized knowledge, they are able to maintain the belief that they deserve their special rank and that the decisions to promote one person rather than another are rational and fair results of organizational deliberation, with the best interests of the organization in mind.

Thus the powerful maintain their position in modern organizations, with the new media providing the means of exercising their influence and control on a large scale.

When American industry had grown so large that it had become necessary to decentralize marketing and production functions, this move was followed by much nonsense talk about the democratization of industry. . . .

What is generally overlooked in studies of decentralization is that no successful firm ever decentralized the financial function. There was never more than one treasurer to a firm and the centralized control of finances exercised the ultimate power over all members of the decentralized facility.

William Gomberg, "The Trouble with
Democratic Management"

Communication and Control: The Technology of Institutions

In the wake of the Second World War, capacities to store and manipulate information increased by a quantum leap. Consequently, so too did the ability to organize on an ever-larger scale, while retaining power in the central offices. Again, technology made the leap possible; first in the form of massive and awkward "first generation" computers that worked on vacuum tubes and mechanical relay switches, then—as computers were turned to problems of redesigning themselves—in ever more compact and powerful solid-state instruments, operating with "subminiaturized" components at speeds that again and again eclipsed those of earlier years.

The computer made dramatic changes in industrial organization, even in the entire society, possible. The war had aggrandized automation, which in turn injected the already accelerating trends toward functional specialization. Then computers joined automation, and from this union emerged cybernetics—automated systems controlled by computers, able to correct their own errors and even to detect them before they occurred.

When applied to human organization, the idea of cybernetics —popularly defined as "communication and control"—was in many ways exhilarating. Through the miracles of cybernetics, we were told, we would be freed from the drudgery of repetitive tasks that, as Marx saw, alienated us from our very selves; human rationality could be extended in scope and power; errors and irrationality could be eliminated; the human capacity to plan the future would leap forward, ending the uncertainties of life that have plagued every nation and tribe through history. At last we would gain control over our destiny; we would be able to discover the flaws in our schemes in time to avoid them; we would be able to predict the behavior of millions of others and coordinate our own actions with theirs. Now Mead's dream might be realized: With the help of cybernetics, leaders would be able to take the attitudes of those whose lives they influenced.

But other possibilities of cybernetics were chilling. "Communication and control" suggested powerful manipulation and coercion, an end to human choice and freedom, the coming of Orwell's *1984* or Huxley's *Brave New World;* at its most extreme, it raised the possibility of a society governed not by humans but by machines.

As the years went by, it seemed that both the hopes and fears of cybernetics were exaggerated, at least for the near future. The ability of the computers to store and process information were quickly applied by corporations to both the technology of technicians and the technology of management. Cybernated machines replaced routine and repetitive tasks of production, though always at the risk of strong union resistance. Among management, the informational powers of the new electronics escalated abilities to coordinate and manipulate the operations of large-scale organizations.

But the social potentials of a technology of institutions remained virtually untouched. For the capabilities of new technologies are not always easy to seize or even easy to recognize. Usually each application is far more complex than it at first seems; usually, too, when some possibilities of a new technology are exploited, others must be neglected. Always, time is needed, not only to develop the new technology more fully but also for the society to accommodate itself to its possibilities and demands.

In part, those transformations can be seen as economic: The press of changing competition and internal organization brought new problems to industry, new strains to management, encouraging them to seek more effective ways of organizing. But, as always, managers' responses were influenced by their definitions of the stresses and strains, by the potentials that they and others saw in the new technologies, by the processes they used to search and sort out the potentials, by the goals that influenced their search and their efforts to innovate—and all were influenced by their basic assumptions and value commitments about the individual and society. Technologies, troubles, ideas, and ideals interplayed to bring still another mutation to twentieth-century organizations.

THE NEW TROUBLES WERE REAL ENOUGH. Without great distortion they could be reduced to one word: unpredictability. Problems of predictability have always plagued business ventures, but now they grew massive. In large part, the new problems were brought by the very success of the industries themselves.

After Ford, as we have seen, the old formula—produce well and cheaply, and it will sell—no longer worked. Now a new formula took shape: If buyers can be found, production can meet their demands. In a way the new formula was like the old, for both rested on the conventional wisdom that, to succeed, an industry must "find a need and fill it." But the new formula reflected a new key uncertainty: the uncertainty of reaching new markets.

The markets were there. The population was growing, and with each year—except in the most desperate years of depression in the thirties—the mean income of American families left more money to buy cars, radios, washing machines, refrigerators, and other everyday luxuries. But could an organization reach these new potential buyers?

The new technology of management in large part answered that uncertainty: as organizations grew more flexible and vibrant, they reached out ever more eagerly for the new markets. New organizations, geared to advertising and sales promotions, mushroomed. Production boomed, and organizations grew rapidly in size and in the amount of capital invested in them. Big business was becoming gigantic, and as it did the need for planning escalated. So too did the tendencies for industry and government to interfuse with one another.

The need for planning . . . arises from the long period of time that elapses during the production process, the high investment that is involved and the inflexible commitment of that investment. . . .

Technology, under all circumstances, leads to planning; in its higher manifestations it may put the problems of planning beyond the reach of the industrial firm. Technological compulsions, and not ideology or political wile, will require the firm to seek the help and protection of the state.

John Kenneth Galbraith, *The New Industrial State*

The rapid rise of the advertising industry in the past three decades reflects a striking change in managerial thinking. A new key to success had been discovered: It lay not only in reaching out to new markets, but in creating them; not only in responding to the needs of the public but in molding public response to the needs of industry. But even this key was not enough to assure the predictability of markets that modern industry seemed to need. Even if the efforts to bend tastes and attitudes had neared perfect control of market behavior, basic economic uncertainties would have remained to plague industries.[12]

These uncertainties seemed to make government controls and inducements necessary to a predictable economy. Labor demands for higher wages, for example, result in higher prices of products and services; these push up the cost of living, increasing demands for higher wages. Uncontrolled, this "wage-price" escalation readily brings inflation. Rather than too little money in circulation, there is too much, so much it loses its buying power. Those who have things to sell decide to hold onto them, rather than take dollars today that may be worthless tomorrow. When this happens, production falls off, unemployment mounts, and the dark shadows of depression creep across the land.

An economy based on consumption also depends on stable rates of employment, for, simply, unemployed men and women cannot buy their share of products and services. This means that if one sector of the economy—say, the auto or steel industries—is to remain healthy, so must all other sectors. If a major airline or aerospace industry suddenly fails, if electronics industries begin to collapse, the entire economy suffers. Again, auto sales fall off, production lags, along with demands for steel and other materials and components, resulting in further unemployment. Again, an economic spiral downward begins.

These and many other uncertainties could be seen even in nineteenth-century economies. But over the past half-century, with each decade, they became more threatening. With rising wages and prices and with corporations ever more dependent on one another for products and services, the degree of economic uncertainty increased—ironically, just at the time when capital investments and product planning escalated the need for predictability.

As the uncertainty and need for predictability rose, the government took an increasingly active role in the corporate

---

[12] In the following sections, I am especially indebted to John Kenneth Galbraith, *The New Industrial State* (Boston: Houghton Mifflin, 1967).

economy. For those who saw what was happening, the new relationship shattered traditional beliefs in the separation of economy and politics.

LIKE ALL POLITICAL BODIES, our government has been closely attuned to the needs of the economy, from colonial times on. But, guided by the ideologies of laissez-faire economics, for almost a century and a half it took a "hands-off" policy, allowing businessmen and corporations to act with only minimal restraints. Then, especially in Franklin D. Roosevelt's "New Deal" in the thirties, those policies changed. The government was becoming an increasingly active partner in a new political economy.

It is widely believed, even today, that the new activism of the government was resisted by big business. But John Kenneth Galbraith argues that the appearances were misleading.[13] True, angry opposition met the New Deal and continued through the following decades. But the dissent came from a dying breed: the individual "captains of industry" like Henry Ford.

To the new men of management at General Motors, General Electric, and U.S. Steel, the advantages of governmental controls and regulations far outweighed the disadvantages. Controls reduced the uncertainties of the markets and made it possible to plan on a larger scale, to embark on major projects that would not bear fruit until sometime in an increasingly predictable future.

In short, the government did not simply muscle in on the interests of big business. It was accommodating to the needs of the new corporate economy and, above all, to the needs for long-range predictability. Tax cuts, government spending, and programs of wage and price controls helped bring new, almost unexpected predictability to the American economy. Uncertainties remained, recessions and inflation still nagged, but all were far from the extremes known in earlier decades.

As government interlinkings with the new corporate econ-

---

[13] *Ibid.*, pp. 302–306.

omy grew closer and more intense, other parts of society were influenced. As planning came to dominate corporate thinking, the need for highly trained specialists in all phases of management grew crucial. Specialization meant schooling, and men and women were ready to respond to opening opportunities.

Here again government programs made a telling difference. Monies were channelled to colleges through tax breaks for contributions. Direct spending of government funds brought research contracts, training programs for critical specialties, scholarships and loans to colleges and individual students. Funding for primary and secondary schools also grew abundant, stimulated in large part by concerns over inequality and other social injustices but also by the search for functional "talent" that might be lost through ineffective schooling.

Rarely does a single social force have a controlling influence in changing, swiftly, the character of life in a large and complex society. The expansion of the Pentagon and its state-management is such a force. Failing decisive action to reverse the economic and other growth of these institutions, then the parent state, if it is saved from nuclear war, will surely become the guardian of a garrison-like society dominated by the Pentagon and its state management.

What greater threat—present and potential—is there to the security of Americans, to their life and liberty?

Seymour Melman, *Pentagon Capitalism:*
The Political Economy of War

A two-way interlinking of governmental and industrial planning was clearly seen in government programs and contracts that supported the basic and applied research so necessary to long-range industrial development. Even more clear was the increasing willingness of government to underwrite industrial projects, providing a risk-free market for new industrial developments by contracting far in advance for government purchases, even guaranteeing to absorb the costs of projects that failed. Nowhere was this more clear than in the continuing research, development, and production of the war industries.[14]

The interlinkings of industry and government on military operations were so striking that even General Eisenhower, at the end of his term as President in 1960, warned of the new "military-industrial complex" that was gaining control over critical decisions in American life. Others, trying to see farther, viewed the military-industrial linkings as but the current center of a more general movement. Some spoke of a "government-military-industrial-educational complex"; others added unions to the list. And good arguments could be found for each claim.

The new interlinkings of the central institutions, as well as the very real dangers to economic predictability, pointed toward a new formula for corporate and national success. The key was in planning and control, but not just in the planning of individual corporations fighting for the largest possible share of the markets. The key was in the large-scale, long-range planning and control of the entire economy.

Just as the industrial warfare between unions and management gave way in the thirties to systems of controlled conflict and negotiation, so the unbridled competition between corporations now seems to be giving way to controlled, collaborative competition. Corporate and government leaders meet to discuss long-range trends, to search for plans that are mutually beneficial, that will allow each corporate interest a predictable growth with a minimal risk.

To date, the planning is done primarily in the name of the economy. But that does not mean that the emerging "technology of institutions" interlinks only our large-scale business corporations to one another. As Weber saw, functional rationality creates in its own image; just as rules create more rules, so plans create more plans. Long-range planning also dominates the thinking in the other vital centers of our society—governmental, military, and scientific centers—as well as those

---

[14] *Ibid.*, pp. 296–342.

more clearly dedicated to economic profit. As planning in these centers of our society grows more massive and ranges farther into the future, it is ever more clear that the plans of one part of the centers depend on the plans of the rest, that the predictability required by each depends on coordinating the plans of all.

The decisive social change taking place in our time . . . is the subordination of the economic function to the political order. . . . The autonomy of the economic order (and the power of the men who run it) is coming to an end, and new and varied, but different, control systems are emerging. In sum, the control of society is no longer primarily economic but political.

Daniel Bell, *The Coming of Post-Industrial Society*

Summary and Direction

I don't pretend to know where this transformation will end. But clearly, something enormous is decaying in the fields of American life that even a few decades ago made up the centers of our society. And something enormous is emerging. New centers are developing to vie with the old and with one another for dominance, ever more intertwining with one another in intricacies of planning and coordination.

Other changes can also be seen, even today; but it is certain they are slight compared with what will come. For we are still a long way from the "fully planned" society. The technology of institutions is in its infancy, plagued with problems, resisted and ignored even by many persons in key positions in the centers of society. But already the new emphasis on information and communication is bringing changes in power and leadership of the centers. As the twenties and thirties saw the rise of the managerial elite, now new elites are emerging, to serve and challenge managerial leadership. These are the experts, "diploma" elites of scientists and other specialized professionals whose expertise is indispensable in the control and direction of a planned society.

The new experts, by creating and manipulating the new, scarce "capital"—the information and expertise so vital to planning and control—are today acquiring a power of their own. Some observers believe that the new experts will steadily gain power, until they virtually control the emerging society. The rise to controlling power of the experts is seen as man's hope by a few; by others as the coming of a new decadence, of an era of social control by those whose special talent is to manipulate symbols, and hence to manipulate the actions, even the thoughts, of those whose lives they plan.[15]

But it may be that these fears and hopes about experts are misplaced. As Weber suggested, although the indispensable technician is rewarded by an organization, he is not given its control.[16] Almost certainly, experts are even now becoming a new elite, but—unless there is a dramatic change in the current thrusts of our transforming society—I suspect that they will remain an elite in the service of tomorrow's new "Princes" of the corporate state.[17]

The new Princes, those who sit at the pinnacles of the emerging political economy, will be those who master the "technology of institutions," much as Alfred Sloan and his successors in the management of General Motors mastered the "technology of management." They will be the new men and women of power, who are able to manage and manipulate information and planning in ways that effectively control massive organizations and massive collectivities of persons in the new "planned society."

The promise of a planned society is awesome. It makes old

[15] A cogent and readable summary of these and other positions is found in Victor Ferkiss, *Technological Man: The Myth and the Reality* (New York: Braziller, 1969).

[16] Max Weber, "Bureaucracy," in Hans Gerth and C. Wright Mills, eds., *From Max Weber: Essays in Sociology* (New York: Oxford, 1958), p. 232.

[17] For a stimulating discussion of the emerging relationships of "experts" to "Princes," see Guy Benveniste, *The Politics of Expertise* (Berkeley: Glendessary Press, 1972).

dreams new again. Through massive planning, we can avoid the relentless tides of economic inflation and depression that Marx predicted; we can end poverty, deprivation, and other social inequities; we can free men and women from the drudgery of meaningless work; we can move from a society constrained by power to one that is open and permissive of individual expression.

But the dangers are equally awesome, for planning could mean the end of human freedom and, even more dispiriting, an end to joy and creative effort. In a planned society, human alienation could be lessened. But in it, too, alienation could grow even deeper.

The key question can be put simply: Will the planning be concerned, before all else, with the quality of individual life that is open to all who live in the planned society? In practical terms, the question is finally one of control. To some critics, this simply means that leaders must be made more responsible and human. If leaders act in their own special interests, then the control of our society must be so organized that the special interests of leaders are to plan and to act with primary concern for the quality of life throughout their society.

With corporate managers holding the reins of widely diversified, global firms, but conceiving of themselves essentially as professionals, what are the rules—the standards—with which these men are to be governed in their use of the immense power they possess? As well, how are those *within* the corporation—especially its multitudinous family of technocrats and middle-level executives—to be protected from encroachment on their legitimate interests? Given the big corporation's central role in the economy, these questions are of crucial public importance.

Richard J. Barber, *The American Corporation:*
Its Power, Its Money, Its Politics

Even in this limited view of control the human prospect is filled with doubt. Are there any indications that responsible and aware leadership is developing today? Massive planning is spreading, but to date it is dominated by functional rationality, and more than anything else it is used for the benefit of corporations and government agencies in the names of profit, production, growth, and the continued well-being of the individual administrators. To be sure, other individuals and organizations also benefit, but their gains—as their losses—are of only secondary importance. When times are easy, it may appear otherwise, but when real decisions must be made, is there reason to believe the actions and feelings of others will be noted by the functional planners for anything more than their possible effects on functional operations?

ONCE—even short years ago in the rise of the technology of technicians—techniques fairly well determined the symbols that leaders used to run their organizations. If a technique worked, it was retained and written into the organizational plan. But today, the relation is being reversed. In the technology of institutions, the plans are the thing; the technologies, the organizations, even social institutions are manipulated to meet the symbolized requirements of an anticipated future.

This suggests the possibility that symbols—and the ideas and ideals they represent—are gaining a social and political potential unknown before in modern history. But what kinds of symbols are being used and likely will be used in planning? What ideas, goals and ideals do they represent? What symbols should be used, what images of the individual and society should they represent?

The problem of uninvolved and irresponsible leadership is profound. But the human possibility may be even more deeply threatened, for it may be that organizational thrusts of functional rationality will themselves virtually escape human control, that even the power of the new Princes of the corporate state will become an illusion. Once Aldous Huxley could fear that it is the ape in man—the irrational, selfish passions—that determines the goals of humans and their organizations.[18] Now

---

[18] Aldous Huxley, *Ape and Essence* (New York: Harper, 1948).

we suffer the fear anew: in a technology of institutions, large-scale organizations—the tools man has created to meet his collective problems—may take control of man himself.

To explore and debate this and the many other possibilities of our times, we must, among other things, attempt to recognize more clearly how in a technology of institutions political power and position interlink with the ability to create and manipulate symbols. To be sure, force remains a basic tool of power in our times; the tension between responsible freedom and coercive law remains real. But if we fix our attention only on the possibilities of either authority or overt coercion, we risk falling into new, subtle cages of manipulation.

For the aged arts of political fraud that Hobbes so feared have found new devices. Even today communications and information are being used consciously not just as the crude propaganda devices so familiar in warfare and advertising but as the vital nerves of systematic planning and control. We must explore the lesson of cybernetics: Communication and concession can create control.

We must also explore the relation of ideas and ideals to social change. For, as Weber tells us, inspiration and knowledge alone will not influence the directions of our transforming society. Ideas and ideals do not in themselves change history; at most they move men and women to attempt to change their relationships, organizations, and institutions. Indeed, without continuing critical exploration of our possibilities we remain the dupes of history that Marx described.

Critical exploration, then, can inform our actions, but it is our actions that change things, and perpetuate them. If Weber is right, the question of which symbols and whose goals shall be utilized in a planned society will be answered, in large part, in the conflict, compromise, coordination, and constraint of competing status-interest groups. Let us follow him in the explorations that led to this critical perspective on the individual and social change.

Chapter Ten

The Invitation in Weber: II

WISDOM CAN BE DECEPTIVE. To the modern ear, "May you live in interesting times" may sound like a quaint version of "Have fun." But to the ancient Chinese, it was no blessing to invoke "interesting times." It was a curse.

The wise Confucian knew that some novelty in life, even if it brings hardship, is stimulating. But every person can tolerate only so much change; when that point is reached, more novelty brings confusion, desperation, even terror. If all is in flux, meanings and goals that once seemed reasonable grow strange, and our view of the world and our place in it clouds over.

Today, we seem to be so cursed. Things are happening in the centers of our society, thrusting us into a future that is unknown, promising, threatening. There is an excitement and pleasure to life in this transforming society; there is vibrancy, hope, and possibility. There is also something tragic, and something trivial. And we don't quite know what to make of it all.

"ONE CAN ONLY SPEAK of what is in front of him, and that is now simply the mess."[1] Samuel Beckett seemed to be reaching

---

[1] Quoted by Tom F. Driver, "Beckett by the Madeleine," *Columbia University Forum* (Summer, 1961). Reprinted in Samuel A. Weiss, ed., *Drama in the Modern World* (New York: Heath, 1964), pp. 505–506.

for a way to express the "tragic vision" of modern man, the dim, nagging awareness of the irrationality of human life, of the ever-present, unspoken reality of death, of the inhumanity of social organizations. It is an ancient vision, and in the confusion and turmoil of modern times that ancient vision is again emerging as a day-to-day fact of individual life.

At heart, the reemergence reflects a failing of the social bond, an erosion of the cultural order. Through the twentieth century, the certainties that gave form to our thoughts, to our sense of self, and to our awareness of others have dissipated. Those certainties had made it possible to neglect the tragic strains and the triviality of social life. But with each decade, the tragic and the trivial have grown more difficult to ignore.

Still, we hope. Surely, we believe, there must be some pattern, some rules that we can agree on in our contemporary culture, there must be a discernible character to the social order that makes it worth fighting for, even worth living for. But when we look closely, it is difficult to see more than a scattering of organizational and cultural bits and pieces that refuse to form a believable whole. The easiest answer is to not look closely, but when we forget that answer, or when it no longer seems adequate, we face that special curse of contemporary life: Coherence is in question, all seems to be relative, little or nothing is certain.

In the confusion, it is difficult to resist the despair that leads to defeat. It is tempting to settle into a troubled sleep, accepting, as the final word, Beckett's conclusion that "this dust will not settle in our time. And when it does some great roaring machine will come and whirl it all sky high again." But perhaps we can follow Camus, accepting a "tragic vision," yet holding to a faith in man as well, in an effort to live and create, "dangerously."

This is what Max Weber struggled to do in his monumental efforts to embrace the tragic nature of life that so limits the human possibility and to overcome the triviality that puts the individual's freedom and responsibility so much in doubt. He questioned almost everything he encountered, holding only to what he saw as the individual's remaining hope—the ability to reason. The task, his biographers tell us, proved exhausting. He saw reason grow irrational in human affairs, and even in his own inner life.

To Weber this irrationality is humanity's crowning tragedy. It is also the deepest challenge to freedom and human possibilities.

In Weber's thought, the whole vast ambiguity of our century was held for one brief moment in a desperate synthesis. As his widow put it, he took it upon himself "to bear" without flinching "the *antinomies* [contradictions] of existence"—to live without illusions and at the same time in accordance with his personal ideals. When he was asked once what his learning meant to him, he answered quite simply: "I want to see how much I can endure."

H. Stuart Hughes, *Consciousness and Society*

Individual, Conflict, and Community

If any one proposition is basic to Weber's work, it is this: The way a person acts cannot be understood without understanding what he or she intends to do. In this, Marx's perspective on the relation of being and consciousness again is seen; the split of being and consciousness is seen as our own creation, a fiction that we have convinced ourselves is real.

What does make up human life, Weber saw, is subjectively meaningful action. Marx had said as much, but Weber emphasized what Marx had neglected: that we act knowingly. To be sure, some behavior is simply responsive, even a reflex; but often individuals seek goals, and there is a relationship between those goals and the ways people act. We have seen this insight, even more clearly argued, in Mead. But Weber tackled a problem that Mead had all but ignored: that the meaningful action of rational individuals creates collective irrationality.

In his study of the Protestant Ethic, Weber discovered a

curious irony. Religious zeal generates worldly striving. To Weber this was one more evidence of the problem. Often, in the affairs of human beings, rationality breeds irrationality. In part, this is due to a conflict of values, to an "ethical irrationality." For unless people agree on absolutes—say, in an all-powerful god—their value conflicts are irreconcilable. The reason is simple: they share no criteria to finally agree that one set of values is better than another.

Luther's conflict with Catholicism might be seen as the rational efforts of an individual to come to terms with his world, but it should also be recognized as the rational efforts of other individuals to defend their church. In the same way, the struggle of Calvin with Lutherans was a conflict of rational individuals; so, too, were the struggles of later Calvinists with early Calvinists. In such conflicts, each individual or group may act rationally within its own sphere, but they differ in the ways they view themselves and their worlds. They clash, and there is no possibility of a rational solution of their differences. Thus, the rationality within individuals gives birth to irrationality between them. Reason breeds unreason.

Thus Weber found a source of irrationality in our world that Mead overlooked. For some of the conflicts of individuals and of groups arise from an opposition of values that no debate or argument can end. It is not only in questions of morality, religion, or art that such irreconcilable conflict can be seen. Indeed, it can be seen in all forms of human activity, and even between spheres of activity—between economics, politics, religion, and science—and the attempt to harmonize one with another will almost certainly fail. For in a world of relativity there is no necessary harmony in power, morality and knowledge.

In every action is a choice, and every choice requires rejection.[2] And the choice, often, is not between "good" and "bad."

---

[2] This aspect of Weber's thought is examined by Julien Freund, *The Sociology of Max Weber* (New York: Pantheon, 1968), pp. 25–29.

Life is not so simple. As Western democracies have clearly demonstrated, for example, to pursue the idea of freedom for all is to create inequality; to pursue the ideal of equality for all is to restrict freedom.

In the irony of Protestantism, Weber saw another way that reason gives birth to unreason. The consequences of man's rational actions are often unintended, unexpected, and even contradictory to the goals that were sought. History is heavy with this "paradox of consequences": it is a history of contradictions in "the relation of man and fate, of what he intended by his acts and what actually came of them."[3] Luther did not intend to pave the way for a heretic like Calvin; Calvin would have despaired at his part in the rise of men such as Ben Franklin. And, when the Puritans rejected wealth as a goal, they unintentionally helped create an economic mentality and a dogged pursuit of success that endangered true religion.

Perhaps there is little reason for most of us to be interested in such subjects for themselves. But in the context of Weber's critical explorations, they speak directly to the troubles of our times. For in the Protestant Ethic and the rise of capitalism, Weber saw a striking expression of an "unintended consequence" of individual rationality, a problem that plagues Western culture—the spread of "functional" rationality. And he saw signs that the problem could threaten the very humanity of twentieth-century man.

In the course of the development of functional rationality, Western society suffered the "loss of community" that is so troublesome today. For most men and women, it is not only God who has died; it is also a part of the individual himself— that part which is the mystique of others in us. To put it more bluntly: not only religion, but our relationships to one another have been "demystified." The price of rationalization is an emotional detachment of each of us from one another.

[3] Max Weber, *The Religion of China,* Hans Gerth, trans. (New York: The Free Press, 1951), p. 238.

Viewed optimistically, this centuries-long development has reduced the social distance that Mead saw between "them" and "us," at least to the point that we are able to trade goods and even ideas. But viewed negatively, it has been bought at a high price: a loss of brotherhood, a damping of love as well as hate, a loss of firmly anchored reference points for living.

This loss is not something totally new to our times. Nor did it begin only in medieval times. Rather, it developed over centuries of increasing functional rationality that Weber traced all the way back to the beginnings of Western history. But before we follow him back to those times, let us look briefly at the image of the individual and society that emerged from his restless quest.

IN WEBER, a less sensitive and less complete version of Mead's social psychology is joined to a more sensitive and complete version of Marx's sociology. Like Marx and Mead, Weber begins with the social action of the individual—action, that is, in which the actor takes into account the past, present, or future behavior of others. Actions, then, involve the ideas that people have of one another, their abilities to take the role of the other, their definitions of the situations in which they see themselves.

Clearly, there is a possible infinity of such meanings, ideas, or definitions. How, then, does order come about? The affairs of humans are confused and filled with conflict, some of it blind and selfish, but also other conflict that emerges from rational, even well-meaning actions of individuals who differ in values or fail to see the "unanticipated consequences" of their actions. But if men and women give their actions their own meanings, why isn't there total chaos?

. . . multiplicity is the truth of human experience. In fact, even as the Greeks had sacrificed in turn to Aphrodite, Apollo, and the gods of the city, we attempt to serve peace, justice, love, truth, and equality; were we to select any one of these values even temporarily, we might offend and vex the rest.

Julien Freund, *The Sociology of Max Weber*

Faced with this basic problem, it is tempting to conclude that social order depends on the control of conflict, that the key to understanding order is the explanation of deviance. But to Weber conflict is expected. What others call "deviance" is no more deviant than order is. Conflict is a natural state of human life, and the social bond depends on the expression of conflict. Order—the orderliness of a society, or the psychological order we call "personality" or "self"—is a more difficult thing to explain.

Weber's explanation encompasses the existential but, as those of Mead and Marx, it is an existentialism grown socially aware. A "meaning" is the relationship we see between our act and its goal. Because we recognize this relationship from past experience, the meaning gives our action some coherence and links it to other actions. Each new situation may be unique, but as we give meaning to it, our acts take on some regularity, some pattern. Seeking coherence in continually changing situations, we create and impose order on ourselves. At the same time, we create and renew the possibilities of social order, by acting in ways that allow others to predict the course of our action.

This is the foundation of the "social relation"—the actions of two or more individuals in which the meanings of each are oriented to the actions of others. The actions may be highly varied, each actor may have a different meaning, and their relationship may be fleeting, but while it lasts there must be a minimum of agreement. The moment individuals are no longer able to predict the behavior of others, there is no longer a "relationship."

When we talk about "American society," the "University of California," or "Dow Chemical," we simply mean that some people in certain situations will act more or less in predictable ways and know that others will. The "social relationship," then, describes recurrent social action: "governments," "organizations," "institutions," and "social classes" are not "real things" in themselves but only terms we use to describe complex webs of human action.

Yet we usually act toward those complex webs as if they were real. Most dangerously, we fall into a belief in the existence of a "legitimate order." What is done out of habit, for emotional reasons, out of self-interest, or because we think that order is related to ultimate or religious values comes to be seen as the ongoing "system of order"—an order that is somehow real and superhuman.

This view, stated so baldly, seems to treat every social form as a "whole cloth." Rather, Weber argued, society is a dynamic tension of individuals in communal relationships. The conflict between these individuals and groups varies from fairly peaceful competition for opportunities to bloody violence. Some of these conflicts, as Marx had pointed out, are fundamentally over possessions. But the fact that people fight for wealth was to Weber only one part of the story. They fight as well for prestige and for power over one another, for these too are basic to their styles of life. And, at times, they even fight for ideals, for these offer coherence and meaning to their lives.

But, as Mead saw so clearly, if men and women find meaning in conflict, they also find it in community—a subjective feeling that they somehow belong together. Conflict and resolution, and the moving together of individuals and groups, has led through the course of history to contemporary patterns of dominance and compliance, arrangements of "status groups," in what Talcott Parsons has called "a relatively delicate balance between . . . forces working in radically opposed directions."[4]

Society, then, is viewed as a tension of status groups, which differ from one another in the prestige they enjoy, in their style of life, in the social and economic power they wield, and in a more or less clear view of themselves in relation to others. Thus, according to Weber, Marx's view of social stratification and change is useful, but it is not adequate to our contemporary problems. Individuals and groups compete, even violently, for wealth and economic power, but they also compete to maintain

[4] Talcott Parsons, "Max Weber and the Contemporary Political Crisis," *The Review of Politics* (1942), pp. 168–169.

their status and social power. And, most importantly, the two forms of conflict—over material interests and over ideal interests—aim for ends that are often incompatible.

This suggests, for example, that it is misleading to see modern collective rebellions—antiwar movements, youth movements, black, Chicano, and Native American movements—as expressions of Marxian class interest. It is true, for example, that a heavy proportion of blacks are poverty-stricken and that many of the stated goals of black leaders point toward a more equal distribution of opportunities. These goals are oriented toward what Weber called a "rationally motivated adjustment of interests"; they aim to slice the economic pie more equally. But, especially in the abundance of today's America, to gain that goal could aggravate even more basic problems in ethnic relations, for it would point out the poverty of wealth that fails to bring esteem.

In fact, today's ethnic demands are not simply class demands —the demands of groups that see themselves as related by economic interests. Rather, they are the demands of self-aware status groups, seeking to increase not only income and opportunity but also dignity and power. In the sixties, cries of "give us jobs" modulated into "Black is beautiful," and "Black Power." The series of slogans reflected the emergence of a self-conscious competitive status group, seeking alternative ways of life to those of the dominant, middle-class white status groups.

In this light, the emergence of the many ethnic status groups active today offers a challenge not only to American social order but also to American ways of thinking and valuing. And it offers hope. For, as Weber argued again and again, self-aware status groups are frequently the sources of moral ideas that shape not only the conduct and ideas of the individuals who belong to them but also the self-interested actions of many others.

As had Mead, Weber emphasized the impact of the status group on the individual. Not only does it constrain and direct his everyday actions, it presents a complete "society" in which the individual matures and from which a world view emerges. Though individual actions are the stuff of social life, only rarely can it be said that the individual acts with some effective autonomy. Indeed, as Marx had seen, most of the time most men and women act dumbly, in unreflective imitation.

Despite human potentials, the liberty of the individual is sharply defined at birth, by social relations and institutions. Under some conditions, an individual may struggle to at least partial freedom from their domination; but in other conditions the traditions seem to be crushing. In twentieth-century Western society, Weber worried, their weight had grown oppressive and was rapidly increasing.

That meant we must try to see more clearly how social institutions change. Can individuals or even groups influence them?

Weber was not content to see any accepted belief or convention or institution as something given: he sought to demonstrate that the dominant beliefs and institutions of today are the relics of past struggles among "suffering, striving, doing" men. Perhaps this explains why a man who was passionately involved in the events of his day nevertheless spent a major portion of his scholarly career on an investigation of social changes that had occurred some twenty-five hundred years ago.

Reinhard Bendix, *Max Weber:*
An Intellectual Portrait

Ancient Judaism: Lessons of Social Order and Social Change

If Weber is right—that moral ideals helped kindle the spirit of capitalism and helped shape industrial societies—the sociological questions grow insistent. Why here and now? Why not in other times and places? Why didn't capitalism emerge in the richness of sixteenth-century Florence; why not in Imperial China?

Was something unusual happening in early Western societies

that might help us understand the rise of capitalism? Perhaps if we knew the answer to that question, we would be better able to recognize the possibilities of our own lives in our own times; perhaps we would more clearly recognize the parts we play in the stability and change of our society.

This line of thinking led Weber into his monumental studies of the religions of India and of China, and to their contrasts with Ancient Judaism. And it turned his attention to the development of the city in medieval Europe. For in that history of social and economic changes, he saw the centuries-long growth of functional rationality that laid the foundations for the rise of the Protestant Ethic and the rise of capitalism.

ATTEMPTING TO UNDERSTAND his own time, Weber looked back over the centuries. Some three thousand years ago, in the misery of a tiny nation torn by civil dissent and threatened by powerful enemies, a new image of human life began to take form. In it were early traces of the demystification and the rationalization so important to our own time. And in it was a profound turn from the world views that have dominated the cultures of the East, opening possibilities of freedom and equality that are still being explored today.

Until the appearance of the Old Testament prophets, the countries of the Near East were developing along the same lines as the despotism of the Orient, that so well served the elite at the expense of the masses. But somehow, out of a history of misfortune and military disaster, a prophecy of salvation emerged in Israel to give meaning to the lives of both the educated and the uneducated. Magic, which so tightly locked the status communities of the East off from one another, clearly separating "them" from "us," began to lose its meanings for the Hebrew.

In India, for example, the pariah castes attempted to be ritually correct in their conduct, in hopes of being reborn higher in the caste-structured world which was eternal and unchangeable. But for the Jew the religious promise was just the opposite: "The world was conceived as neither eternal nor unchangeable, but rather as having been created. Its present structures were a product of man's activities, above all those of the Jews, and of God's reaction to them. Hence the world was an historic product designed to give way again to the truly God-ordained order. The whole attitude toward life of ancient Jewry was determined by this conception of a future God-guided political and social revolution."[5]

Weber traced the evolution of Jewry through the history of conflict, war, and misery of a people fighting against a hostile environment and larger, aggressive neighbors. Through centuries of internal and external strife, the basic tenets of Jewry had emerged, but often in some competition with the magic of idol worship and the mysticism of religious ecstasy.

The idea of a God who guards the social order and rewards those who serve him is found throughout the world and throughout history. But the Israelites' image had a novel twist. It was based on a two-way contract: the Israelites had chosen Yahweh as their God and entered into an agreement with him. Thus, though Yahweh protected the laws and customs of Israel, his protection did not mean that they were unchangeable, as in India. As the law rested on an agreement, it could be changed with a new agreement, or by revelation.

Under the covenant, too, magic, sorcery, and sacrifices lost their meaning. Yahweh's favor was not so easily or mystically gained. Rather, men and women must strive to live up to their side of the bargain, which in turn increased the importance of priests who could rationally and intellectually discover what Yahweh's will was.

But not everyone interpreted the covenant in this way, or took it so seriously. The history of ancient Israel is a continuing battle between priests of a rational religion and those who held to old practices of sorcery, ecstasy, and idol worship. Their conflict continued through the one brief moment of their na-

---

[5] Max Weber, *Ancient Judaism* (Glencoe, Ill.: The Free Press, 1952), p. 4.

tion's splendor. The Jews had fought a great war of liberation from the Philistines, and the city-kingdom established by David led to the glory of Solomon's reign. For the first time in its history, the small state enjoyed wealth and power and a role in world politics. Solomon's glory lasted only some forty years, and the country was soon divided within itself. Yet the grandeur was remembered, and Yahweh was seen as an all-powerful god.

Ironically, the moment of glory had been an illusion: the great nations that surrounded the little monarchy were simply taking a breather in their wars of conquest. Now, they again threatened. As an "impending gloom beclouded the political horizon," a religious innovation occurred in Palestine. In it, Weber saw the turning point of Western civilization.

Rarely have entirely new religious conceptions originated in the . . . centers of rational cultures. . . . The reason for this is always the same: prerequisite to new religious conceptions is that man must not yet have unlearned how to face the course of the world with questions of his own. . . . Man living in the midst of the culturally satiated areas and enmeshed in their technique addresses such questions just as little to the environment as, for instance, the child used to daily tramway rides would chance to ask how the tramway actually manages to start moving.

The possibility of questioning the meaning of the world presupposes the capacity to be astonished about the course of events.

Max Weber, *Ancient Judaism*

THE SEEDS OF THE INNOVATION were sown in the ancient Palestine of David and Solomon. There they took root, as political conditions worsened, in the fertile discontent of the intellectuals and the recently urbanized public. The development illustrated again what Weber had seen elsewhere: Innovations in human ideals and images of human life develop not in the great centers of civilization, but on their peripheries. The same theme is seen in the willingness of people on the peripheries of major societies to exploit new technologies. As Marx also noted, for example, the seeds of capitalism arose not in the great centers of feudalism, but on the peripheries of their influence.

But there was more to it than that. Palestine was on the periphery of the major nations of the Middle East, yet close enough to be stimulated by their commerce and vital cultures. But the new image of human life that took form in Palestine was at first the vision of only a few. Other persons, other groups, held to old images and other ways of life.

The nation of ancient Israel—as our nation today—can be seen as a tension of status groups, each competing for its own special interests, not only in wealth and possessions (material interests) but also for their ways of life and world views (ideal interests). How, from this conflict and confusion, did an entire nation come to accept the idea that the basic duty of everyone is to act morally in his daily life? How, that is, did the inspirations of a few become the belief of an entire nation, and eventually the dominant image of the Western world?

The transition was far from abrupt; it took centuries. Yet, Weber saw, the pivotal steps in this history of change were taken in only a few years, as the glorious monarchy of Solomon began to fall apart. There, in ancient Palestine, the discontent of the general public fused with the inspiration of the "charismatic" prophets. The story is one that even today, perhaps especially today, gives pause.

The peoples of ancient Palestine were cursed with "interesting times." In a generation or two they had struggled through a disruptive transition. Once a nomadic, militarized people, they knew strong ties of kinship, and the status and power of each clan were clearly recognized. Now they were declassed, more or less economically autonomous, and demilitarized; they lived in a city where the old status hierarchies of the clans were of little note; and their economic interests were closely tied to those of strangers.

In the glory of the monarchy, as long as the authority of the king remained strong, their lives held a semblance of order, despite the abrupt changes they endured. But the traditional authority began to crumble, and their rulers fell to squabbling as rumblings of war threatened from powerful neighbors who had often before overwhelmed them. Men and women grew restless, and began to question the traditional views of the individual and the world.

In their confusion and discontent they turned to the prophets of doom, who had been little heeded in happier days. Not long before, as the monarchy was emerging, these prophets had resisted the idea of kingly power, and in the midst of the glories of the monarchy had predicted impending doom. When times were good, these lonely demagogues, the "titans of the holy curse," found little sympathy with the royal court, with the powerful families, the established priests, or even the general public. Yet, when times grew difficult, people turned to them for inspiration and leadership.[6] But why?

WE WILLINGLY FOLLOW OTHERS—whether leaders in a movement or authorities in government—usually for one or more of three reasons: tradition, rational laws, and personal inspiration, or what Weber called "charisma." Almost all leaders base their claims to leadership—their claims of being legitimate authorities —on more than one of these. But usually, at any time, in any society, one type of claim outweighs the others.

In the history of the Western world, Weber saw, traditional authority has been gradually replaced by rational authority. In traditional modes of power, the "right to rule" is based on long-accepted understanding. So too are the rules for conduct, of both the leader and the led. Those who are powerful are held together by personal loyalties that have developed through their common education and shared ways of life. "Political" authority and "moral" authority are one and the same.

In sharp contrast, rational authority rests on a belief that the rules are *legal*. Thus, the rational mode of power is a product of human deliberation, a kind of "agreement to agree." Per-

[6] *Ibid.*, Chapter XI.

sonal relationships, then, are rationalized, as the individual's conduct is governed by a system of rules that is applied rationally to all members of the corporate group.[7] Rules are emphasized rather than persons or traditions. And the "rationality" of actions is measured by their influence on the organization. Hence, once members accept the organization as supreme, the rationalization increases, and other factors that are so important to the traditional authority—kinship, friendship, and even money—decline in importance.

In the history of Western society, traditional authority shows amazing endurance, but the overwhelming trend is toward its replacement by rational, legal order. Any existing nation, community, or long-lived movement rests on a mixture of traditional and rational authority; one is not all of a sudden fully replaced by the other. But the ratios change.

Intermixed with tradition and law is the appeal of individual leaders and systems of leadership based on "charisma." Indeed, at times, the charismatic appeal of an individual or group grows so powerful that the existing demands of both tradition and law are for a time ignored. This is a moment of social innovation, for better or worse. And this is what happened in ancient Palestine—and has happened again and again through the history of Western society.

The charismatic leader is "set apart from ordinary men and treated as endowed with supernatural, superhuman, or at least specifically exceptional powers or qualities. These are . . . not accessible to the ordinary person, but are regarded as of divine origin or as exemplary, and on the basis of them the individual concerned is treated as a leader."[8]

The "magic" of the charismatic is not something God-given. It lies in the minds of men and women. Charisma, that is, is only in part a quality of the leader; more fully it is also a quality of the group in which the leader has become a focal point. Charis-

[7] Max Weber, *The Theory of Social and Economic Organization* (New York: Oxford, 1947), p. 333.
[8] *Ibid.*, pp. 358–359.

matic leadership and charismatic authority are based on the meanings ascribed to the individual; somehow, as a person, he or she is able to make sense of the emotional discontent of others. The charismatic leader's influence depends on the ability to connect the energies of popular discontent to goals that are meaningful to others.

This is what the "charismatic" prophets of doom were able to do in the context of the discontent of the intellectuals and the common people of Palestine. In those disturbed times, a yearning for the charismatic found meaningful focus in the messages of the prophets.

The concept of charisma serves to underline Weber's view that all men everywhere are not to be comprehended merely as social products.

Just as for George H. Mead the "I" is ordinarily in tension with the social roles derived from the expectations of others, so for Weber the potentially charismatic quality of man stands in tension with the external demands of institutional life.

Hans Gerth and C. Wright Mills,
From Max Weber: Essays in Sociology

To ENDURE FOR ANY TIME, the charismatic leader's vision must be validated. But, here again, in the desire to hold to the meaningfulness brought to their lives by the charismatic leader, men and women seek signs of the "truth" of his messages, rather than signs that might prove them false. This is what happened in ancient Palestine: the people found the "truth" of the new prophecies in the integrity and courage of the prophets.

Had not these prophets foretold doom even in good times? Had they not been willing to face dangerous hostility, in order to preach their message? No one, except a madman, would act that way unless he was compelled by a power greater than himself. The prophets must have been inspired. Their prophecies of doom had come to pass; surely so would their new prophecies of salvation, offered in the despair of their exile.

The discontent of an oppressed people who had briefly enjoyed better things resonated in the inspired prophets. Their concern turned on a perennial dilemma: How is it possible to believe in one's God when misfortune strikes at every turn? The answer emerged as the Jewish nation fell victim to Babylonian conquest and was forced into its centuries of exile. That answer, a turning point in Western views of individual life, is subtle in its logic.

Whatever happens in this world is not due to chance, or magic, but is a result of God's will. Thus, even misfortune is his doing. Because of their special covenant with him, he is especially hard on his chosen people and punishes them for their sins. In this way, their misfortune becomes a special sign of their grace; it not only comes to be seen as a punishment for sins but gains a positive meaning. Through it, men and women know that God is not aloof, but actually is influenced by their conduct. Their suffering is the path to salvation, for all of their people. Thus, political activity is of no avail—salvation will come when God wills it, and until then men and women can simply strive to do his will. It is a person's duty to act morally in daily life, to accept what must be accepted, and to trust in God.

In this great religious innovation—the emergence of a religion of the "here and now"—lay the foundations of the distinctive ethic that would play such an important part in the history of Western politics, in the rise of capitalism, and in the discontent of our times. In Ancient Judaism, the individual's view of himself in the world began to be stripped of its ties to magic and mystical speculation. The person, it came to be believed, must simply strive to do God's will. Morality, then, is neither mystical nor magical, but rational.[9]

The seeds of the demystification of the world and of our rational ways of life, then, were sown in ancient prophecies and took root in the discontent of a persecuted people. A new image

[9] Weber, *Ancient Judaism,* Chapters XI–XIV.

of the individual was emerging, a less mystical, more rational image. In it, rampant magic was banned from the world. True, men and women still believed that Moses could turn a scepter into a serpent and part the Red Sea with his faith, that Lot's wife could be turned into a pillar of salt, that the walls of Jericho could be felled by trumpets, and that an occasional little boy could actually hear the voice of God. But these and other miracles were the works of a God who otherwise tampered little with everyday affairs. Nor could that God be moved by incantations or sacrifice. Through worship men and women could show their faith, in sacrifice they could seek signs of God's favor, through living as he had taught them they could hope to prove themselves worthy of the redemption only he could give. But he was beyond the reach of the religious magician.

The first steps had been taken; countless others followed, leading to the decline of kinship in the merchant life of medieval cities, to the Reformation and the Protestant Ethic, to the "death" of God and the glorification of functional rationality in the modern world.

WEBER, THEN, EMPHASIZED three general processes of social change. First, forms of social life can mutate in the interplay of tensely balanced status groups, in the more or less controlled competition over ideal interests and material interests. Most often, the change evolves slowly. But in extreme times, the competition might erupt into open conflict and violence, bringing an abrupt reform or even the pervasive change of a "Marxian" revolution.

A second source of change—"charisma"—often appears in the more open conflict of status groups. Dramatic eruptions of charismatic infection are recurrent in human history, as in the roles of the prophets in ancient Palestine, and in the lives of Christ, Mohammed, and Gandhi, of Charlemagne, Napoleon, Hitler, and Castro. And it is recurrent in less inspired power, even within the rationalized and specialized bureaucracy of our government, in the appeal of a Kennedy or Reagan. It is seen in a Cesar Chavez or Huey Newton and less dramatically in the popular boss, community leader, or shop steward.

Occasionally a dramatic change occurs that seems traceable to the infectious efforts of such charisma. With a focus on the inspiration of the leader, movements grow potentially more eruptive and revolutionary than they might be when controlled by more rationally organized groups. But the inspiration and contagion of even a lone charismatic leader depends usually on the ideals and interests of the status groups he leads. And the success of the inspired movement depends on the nature of the tensions and balances of the energies that bind the opposed forces of society.

In stable times, when most persons are content with their lives or when the power of the law or a special status group is overwhelming, there is little hope of successful revolution, or even reform. But at times, even a handful of men or a single individual can have profound political impact. For the balance between radically opposed forces in a society can become so delicate that the difference made by a war or a political movement may have far-reaching consequences.[10] Thus, too, can the grand idea of a single man or of a small group of "visionaries" or "madmen" bring change. It is not that the idea, the war, or the movement causes the change; rather, it is that it simply adds enough weight to throw the balance toward one end rather than another.

[Communities] are not organisms. They are not born, and they do not die like living things. They are strategies of collective life which are formed and destroyed by men. They are primary examples of the ancient truth that "man cannot have his cake and eat it too." To form new communities men must transform their old ones. Revolutionary upheavals are discernible in the formative periods of all of the historically significant communities.

Don Martindale,
"Community Formation and Destruction"

---

[10] Parsons, "Max Weber and the Contemporary Political Crisis."

Those who seek widespread changes in our society today may take heart from this perspective, for in many ways our society appears to be delicately balanced, even precariously off balance. But they should not miss the further lesson in the "paradox of unanticipated consequences" that Weber offers: the new world which the "successful" revolutionary or even the reformers help build may not be the one they aim toward. And, unless the tensions of opposing forces within a society have already brought it to the point of change, the more violent the efforts of a small minority, the more they serve to increase the weight of law and regulation. Thus, as Marx also noted, premature "revolution" can create the conditions that make a true revolution difficult, if not impossible in the future.

For, as we have seen, there is a third way of change in the societies of man: the regimented march of organized rationality. Critical to the development of both democracy and capitalism, it is at once the genius and the nemesis of Western society.

AS THE INSPIRATION of the Jewish prophets became part of the everyday lives of their people, their charisma was "depersonalized"; now it was not a special man who inspired followers, but a more organized group that demanded the people's loyalties. There was, in Weber's words, a "routinization of charisma." "It is the fate of charisma," he wrote, "whenever it comes into the permanent institutions of the community, to give way to powers of tradition and of rational socialization. This waning of charisma generally indicates the diminishing importance of individual action. . . ."[11]

It is a mistake to think that only the open violence of competing status groups or the contagion of charisma bring innovative change, while routinization and rationality bring only stability. For the "decline of charisma" can give way to the creation of the new legal norms. Then it is not charisma, but routinization—the vehicle of functional rationality—that is the instrument of change. So, too, the destruction of old forms of

---

[11] Max Weber, "The Meaning of Discipline," in Hans Gerth and C. Wright Mills, eds., *From Max Weber: Essays in Sociology*, p. 253.

rationality goes hand in hand with the creation of new forms.

But if functional rationality is a creative force, its genius is always to create in its own image. Rules create rules. Ironically, this happens in part because rational rules create new irrationalities. Each rule is originally designed to accomplish certain tasks; yet when the rule controls an individual those tasks are neglected. When this happens, about the only way the individual's behavior can be changed is through more rules. Thus an organizational dialectic can be seen: controls (functional rules) → unanticipated consequences → increased controls (functional rules).[12]

It is not only the "underling" who falls victim to advancing rules. There is a striking difference, for example, in the results of power struggles among the top leaders in rational organization, compared to those under charismatic and traditional authority. The charismatic or traditional leader who successfully meets the challenge of an opponent thereby gains in personal influence over loyal followers.

But in a rational system a struggle for power increases bureaucratic control, over all participants including the leader. For the holder of a bureaucratic office must hide personal ambitions and drives for power by appealing to impersonal regulations that appear to impose on all persons involved. When challenged, the leader is forced to seek new rules that will frustrate the challenge. But the rules in turn limit the leader's own actions, as well as the challenger's. In this way, rational control by rules advances. And Weber warned, after centuries of advancing rationality in Western society, the weight of rules and rational organization threatens to crush the social inspiration and creativity out of human life.

Thus, for Weber, the important conflicts of our time, those from which new forms of human life may emerge, will be missed if one simply looks at the struggle of social classes, as

---

[12] Nicos E. Mouzelis, *Organisation and Bureaucracy: An Analysis of Modern Times* (Chicago: Aldine, 1968), p. 60.

Marx tended to do, or at the social relations of individuals, as had Mead. For the critical struggles of our time are at once institutional and at the same time ethical and ideal; they are seen in the conflicts of politics, economics, and science and the competing ideals and ideas about the individual and society that interplay with them.

The Challenge to Critical Sociology

Weber had set out to resolve the same basic problem that had driven Marx: How can the humanness and freedom of men and women survive under the inescapable progress of capitalism? But the capitalism that Weber lived in was a half-century more advanced than that of Marx, allowing him to discern the complexities of administration and the intricacies of its influence on life even beyond the corporation. It is not capitalism, in itself, that the individual must fear most, Weber argued; it is the organization that capitalism encourages. Marx had failed to see the "organizational revolution" that had already begun in his time. But Weber could not predict, either, what the half-century following his death would bring.

He had foreseen the rise of a technology of technicians and even a technology of management. But his world did not allow him to more than suspect that the trend might continue to even another level, to a "technology of institutions." This new technology is seen in the rationalization of even the "institutional agents" of organizations—the presidents, boards of directors, and other men and women whose job is to manage the relations of their organization with other organizations. As this technology of institutions grows, the centers of society interlink ever more closely; systematic planning is applied to ever larger parts of the economy, government, and community life. As control and planning concentrate, the coordination and control of society grows ever more like a massive, integrated "social system."

Our social order is transforming, but in Michael Harrington's words, the transformation is an "accidental" revolution.[13] Blinded by the myths of private property and the necessity of consensus, blinded as well by fears of socialism and communism, the overwhelming majority of Americans fail to see the powerful thrusts of functional organization in the twentieth century. The transformation is taking place virtually unnoticed, even by those most closely a part of it. It is proceeding haphazardly, yet always in the direction of functional rationality.

If Weber was right, the choice is not between bureaucracy and no bureaucracy: Large-scale rational organization is the fate and genius of modern life. Nor does there seem to be a choice between planning and no planning. The promises of planning are too great, too seductive, to be ignored. Nor does there seem to be doubt that the large-scale, rational organizations emerging today are creating new potentials for control.

There seem to be no easy options. As Weber, we can attempt to recognize the massive transformations of our times and struggle to control them. Or we can ignore them, and let them control us.

THE KEY QUESTIONS WERE POSED in the last chapter: Will tomorrow's planning be concerned, before all else, with the quality of individual life? Will control rest in the hands of a self-serving few? Will it be turned to the service of all? Or will it perhaps rest in a functional system of rules and regulations, controlled by no human purpose at all?

These, and countless other possibilities, seem to be before us today. Indeed, even these possibilities are far more complex than has been even roughly hinted at here, for the transformations of our social order are taking place in larger contexts that also seem to be in troubled change. In recent years, fears of ecological disaster have grown heated. In the most feverish projections, our entire society is headed for disaster. Population

---

[13] Michael Harrington, *The Accidental Century* (New York: Penguin, 1965); see also his *Socialism* (New York: Saturday Review Press, 1972).

is mushrooming, creating new pressures in our cities. Combined with affluence and technology, the new populations create new appetites, new demands that destroy one natural resource after another. The environment is being turned into a huge garbage dump, and our air and water polluted, threatening "ecocide"—the destruction of the very ecology of which we are a part. Thus, as we destroy our environment, we seal our own fate.

Perhaps, as most new social fears, these are overdrawn. Population growth can be controlled, pollution can be monitored, antipollution laws can be passed and enforced, habits of consumption can be modified. But even the most optimistic views demand new attention to ecological problems and bring home a profound lesson of human life: Our world is not only social, political, and economic—it is ecological, and every action is somehow related to every other. And that means the effort to gain control over our transforming society—control either by an elite few or by the many—must consider ecological conditions and relationships. These conditions and relationships have escaped attention in our traditional politics and our traditional images of ourselves and our society.

Nor do the challenges and complexities stop at the borders of our nation. For American society is transforming in a world of transforming societies. To be sure, some are in strikingly different transformations from those of the West, and that is a fundamental problem. For, just as in early stages of capitalism, as Marx saw, the rich get richer and the poor get poorer, today the gap between the "have" and the "have not" nations is widening. To some observers, this "relative deprivation" on an international scale suggests a coming revolution, an international, violent revolution of the exploited. To others it is a demand for world-wide planning, for a politics that goes beyond the traditional boundaries of nationalism, to a view of the world as an economic system, even as an ecological unity.

If these possibilities have been neglected in this book, it is not because they are unimportant to an understanding of our times, our troubles, and our prospects. Indeed, they are critical. But the themes of this book have already grown so complex that they threaten to crowd out the invitation they were meant to illustrate—the invitation to critical sociology.

WE DO NOT YET KNOW the answers to the countless questions that challenge us today; indeed, we do not even know how to ask them adequately. Perhaps we never will. But it is too early to retreat to such a pessimistic conclusion, for we have not yet marshaled the energies and capabilities that are available to us. We have not explored and debated the human possibilities of our emerging organizations and institutions.

Nor have we openly criticized and explored the various images of individual consciousness and social order that conflict among us today. We have not looked as deeply as we are able beneath the surfaces of our arguments about freedom and responsibility, law and order, reason and relativity, planning and control. To attempt to do so, I believe, is to accept the challenge of critical sociology that we find in Max Weber, in Karl Marx, and in George Herbert Mead.

It is difficult to hold this challenge in mind. It takes us into the seemingly contradictory possibilities that individuals and their organizations emerge, endure, and change in tensions of both consensus and conflict, that each of us is rational and irrational, creative and conforming, dependent and autonomous, mysterious and open, and far more. When we do grasp such perspectives, we risk the discovery of things hidden and mysterious. We risk a growing awareness that, in human affairs, things are not always what they seem, no matter what depths of penetration we reach.

To accept the challenge, then, is to risk confusion, uncertainty, and the creation of new blindnesses. For, Weber tells us, to understand social and cultural order and change, we must understand ourselves. But to understand ourselves, we must attempt to do no less than understand the emergence, stability, and change of our social and cultural order. That is a large order. It requires that we consider, all at once, virtually the entirety of human experience, in its individual and societal forms, in its present forms and past, even in its anticipated future.

We are far from such capabilities. For now, we can only struggle for insights into what seem the most critical limits and potentials open to us. In this, we can follow Weber, looking back to earlier times of massive transformation and beyond, yet always looking at ourselves, our times, and our possibilities.

For even our visions of the future—the images of the individual and society that help limit and direct our attentions, attitudes, and actions—are rooted in our histories and cannot be understood apart from those histories. Yet our visions can be changed only in the social present. That social present is at once also both past and future, fused in the commonplace art of our lives—in Marx's "praxis," in Mead's "self-and-other awareness," in Weber's "suffering, striving and doing."

Chapter Eleven

On an Invitation to Critical Sociology

SOCIOLOGY ITSELF IS CAUGHT in the dilemma of modern times: Life is rational, but it is also irrational, emotional, and mysterious. As few other human efforts, sociology is torn between the apparent contradictions represented in romantic images of emotional man and enlightenment images of rational man. In large part the history of sociology is a history of attempts to resolve those contradictions in favor of one or the other or by discovering their compatibility.

In these attempts, sociologists have struggled to find anchoring points around which knowledge of human experience might be coherently organized. Faced with evidences of massive transformations in our central institutions and with evidences of personal suffering and confusion, most writers tend to emphasize one of two general stances. To some, the sources of personal troubles are found, finally, in institutional changes. The structural changes of a society—the mutations of economic organizations, the spread of new technologies, the shifts in occupational structures, the emergence of a technology of institutions—transmit change through the rest of society, altering ways of schooling, of family life, of leisure, creating confusion in our individual lives and altering the ways we think and feel. Thus, this line of argument suggests, institutional change shapes individual consciousness.

To others, in sharp contrast, institutional changes result, in large part, from individual efforts to resolve personal troubles and to realize personal possibilities. This line of argument celebrates the individual's capabilities to act creatively, to innovate, to introduce novelty into relationships, and thus to introduce change into the institutions of society. Transformation of a society, this line of argument suggests, is possible only if individual consciousness has first been transformed. New technologies, economic problems, and political programs can erode the old institutions of a society; but they cannot create new ways of thinking and living, and so they cannot truly transform a society. Societal transformation can occur only in response to a widespread change in individual consciousness—a new awareness of possibilities, perhaps a new blindness to possibilities once valued.

So stated, the argument seems simple: Either social structures transform consciousness, or consciousness transforms social structures. Which perspective is right; which wrong? Perhaps both.

Each, that is, might be right and at the same time wrong. We miss this possibility as we pose questions as "either/or" alternatives. Which is true, we ask, this idea or that, neglecting to consider whether both might be true, both false, or that each might be more true than false, more false than true—neglecting, as well, the possibility that each might be more or less valid in one time and place and more or less invalid in another.

Rarely in the affairs of individuals and societies are we faced with simple "either/or" choices. More often we confront some sort of "both/and" situations: an action is both creative and destructive; a project is both successful and a failure; an argument is both partially right and partially wrong.

The problem, then, may not be so much in what the "social structure" argument or the "individual consciousness" argument pays attention to. The problem may be in the possibilities they ignore.

[When a man] disregards the systemic nature of the world with which he must deal . . . he finds himself in a mess. He does not quite know what caused the mess and he feels that what has happened is somehow unfair. He still does not see himself as part of the system in which the mess exists, and he either blames the rest of the system or he blames himself.

Gregory Bateson, "Conscious Purpose versus Nature"

If we are to understand ourselves and our society, we must also look beyond the individual and his immediate surrounds. Mead's social psychology shows how critical this is. Yet it also reveals how impotent even the powerful perspectives of social psychology can be when they fail to recognize that economics, organization, and power must also be studied, in their own terms.

As focus moves from the individual to the group, to the organization, and to the society, new phenomena appear that cannot be explained by attention only to the more basic parts. In the same way, as we move in the other direction, from organization to individual, much cannot be explained by attention only to the larger group. There is a relative interdependence of individuals in groups, of groups in organizations, of organizations in society. But there also seems to be a relative autonomy, and the greater that autonomy, the greater the likelihood that something crucial will be missed if we look only at the lives of individuals or only at the larger organizations.

Just as Marx saw that the individual's alienation cannot be understood or combatted unless its social rootedness is recognized, we must look at individuals and at the same time beyond them, to the social forms that compel, constrain, and enable. If we are to understand those forms, we must discover their relation to the other parts of our society. As did Weber, we can strive to see the ways our institutions relate to one another and to technological and ideological change. And we can attempt to recognize how those ever-changing institutions relate to the suffering, striving, doing—to the private meanings, intentions, mysteries, and efforts—of men and women as individuals and as members of groups.

In this, we might again follow Mead, attempting to see more clearly how institutions and individuals interpenetrate, how the parts and the whole are each distinct and yet interfuse with one another in an interplay of tension and change. We have seen this creative dialectic of individual and society also in Marx and Weber. It emphasizes that human choice is not between simple alternatives, that seemingly contradictory things can coexist and even fuse into one another, that in the interplay of existing institutions, emerging technologies, and human action and thought, both individual consciousness and social relationships are recreated.

In the work of these classical sociologists—Mead, Marx, and Weber—can be seen a fundamental effort of critical sociology: an effort to come to grips with the nature of individual consciousness and its relation to social order and change. Each of these three men firmly grounded his theories of society in the actions and perspectives of the individual. To be sure, each fell short of a perspective on consciousness and society that might be fully adequate to our times. The outlines of Weber's social psychology are incomplete; Mead's images of society, built on his sensitive social psychology, are structurally naive; Marx's social psychology and his sociology remain ill-joined. Each can also be criticized on many other points, yet together, I believe, the three offer an invitation to a perspective on the individual and society that can be profoundly sensitizing to our times.

The productive point of their unity is found in the creative interplay of the individual and society. Though they used differing terms, each saw this dialectic rooted in praxis, in action, in man's suffering, striving, and doing. But each developed this basic proposition in his own way.

From Relativity to Involvement

The young Marx set out to solve the "riddle of history," the relation of subjective consciousness to objective being. He thought he had solved the riddle and at the same time discovered how social order develops. Our consciousness arises as we meet and solve our problems. In praxis, *we act in response to our surrounds;* and as we do, our subjective self is both created and expressed in the objective world. In this interplay, the social form also arises and changes. The individual and society develop in some sort of creative waltz: Changes in one call out changes in the other, and neither can change without the other changing as well.

Neither Weber nor Mead adopted Marx's terminology, yet both extended the idea of praxis. Weber emphasized something that Marx had disregarded. As we act in response to our surrounds, we act toward goals. *We act intentionally.* In the creative interplay of individual and society, the individual's purposes and goals play an important part. In our striving, suffering, and doing, we alter our own consciousness; and as we do, our society changes as well.

Mead wrote before the youthful writings of Marx were rediscovered and seems to have taken little note of Weber's work. Yet he shared many of their basic perspectives on the individual and society and extended them in his images of social psychology. Consciousness, he in essence agreed, emerges as the individual meets and solves his problems. But the most important thing is not that we are conscious and act intentionally. What really matters is that *we know that we act intentionally.* The individual is self-aware. Praxis, in this fuller sense, is the individual acting toward goals and watching himself as he acts.

It is not simply that we are aware that makes us so important to social order and change; it is that we are self-aware. It is not simply that as we seek goals, we support or change the society we live in. It is that we are able to see ourselves in action, to question what we are doing, to look at our selves and the world around us, to evaluate our goals and our actions, to criticize what others are doing and expect us to do. We can, to some degree, step outside of our selves and our surrounds and ask "Why?"

With that question, critical sociology begins.

We locate ourselves in society and thus recognize our own position as we hang from its subtle strings. For a moment we see ourselves as puppets indeed. But then we grasp a decisive difference between the puppet theater and our own drama. Unlike the puppets, we have the possibility of stopping in our movements, looking up and perceiving the machinery by which we have been moved. In this act lies the first step toward freedom.

Peter Berger, *Invitation to Sociology*

This means, as Weber insisted, that even those who are distant—geographically, socially, and historically—can be critically involved in our self-awareness. While learning to take the role of distant others, we learn to see our selves as they might see us, and thus we gain a more complete perspective on our selves. We also discover possibilities that might be open to us, by viewing the world in the ways we imagine others would view it. Seeing our selves through the eyes of distant others, we are liberated to some degree from the prescriptions of our own milieu and involved to some degree with the distant others. Our freedom, then, rests not simply in self-awareness but in self-and-other awareness.

Something else might also happen as self-and-other awareness expands to include more distant others: we may come to realize that our own personal troubles relate to the personal troubles of others. We may also begin to recognize how the conditions and the possibilities, as well as the actions, of other living persons relate to our own possibilities. As our self-and-other awareness grows, we may even recognize that our own actions may influence the lives of others and the ways that they view the world—and that when we influence others to change, our own lives and possibilities also change.

As we come to recognize how our awareness, intentions, and actions relate to those of diverse others, we may also discover a sense of responsibility emerging—a responsibility quite different from the kind discussed in high school civics classes and even more different from the "responsibility" demanded by those who cry for "law and order." It is not a responsibility to a given order, but rather a responsibility to ourselves that cannot be untangled from a responsibility to others. It is a recognition that the qualities of our own lives, of our own self-awareness, depend on the qualities and awarenesses of others' lives.

[Personal knowledge] commits us, passionately and far beyond our comprehension, to a vision of reality. Of this responsibility we cannot divest ourselves. . . . For we live in it as in the garment of our own skin. Like love, to which it is akin, the commitment is a "shirt of flame," blazing with passion. . . .

Intellectual commitment is a responsible decision, in submission to the compelling claims of what in good conscience I conceive to be true. It is an act of hope, striving to fulfill an obligation within a personal situation for which I am not responsible. . . .

Michael Polanyi, *Personal Knowledge*

From Involvement to Social Criticism and Exploration

Involved responsibility, then, is not a responsibility to a given social order or to given ways of life. To be sure, in our self-and-other responsibility, we may support the given order—perhaps because we have concluded that any possible change at a certain time may bring more losses than gains to self-and-others. But if we are critically involved, this conclusion is always tentative.

For as self-and-other involvement grows, we lose our reverence for authority and established institutions. This is not to say that we necessarily become the enemies of the established order, but only that we lose our ability to blindly worship it. As the webs of self-and-other involvement widen and deepen, we come to take a critical stance toward our society. We begin to look more closely at our social institutions, searching for their self-and-other meanings. We grow suspicious of surface appearances, recognizing how readily we create masks to hide ourselves from others, how cleverly we erect facades to cover our true relationships to one another.

Thus, self-and-other involvement gives rise to social criticism. Social criticism, then, is a search for the human meanings of the inequalities, the deficiencies, and the imperfections of society. But it is a criticism that arises from the responsibility of involvement, and—at its best—it proceeds with that same responsibility. This kind of social criticism, then, is not an indulgence or a negativity; it is an essential and an inevitable part of the fundamental processes of self-and-other involvement.

It recognizes that if we are to understand personal troubles we must also look to the structures, processes, and contradictions of the larger society in which we live, not only in its present form, but also in its history of change. We learned the lesson from Marx and Weber, but they were not alone in their vision; it is seen in others who, as C. Wright Mills put it, are imaginatively aware of the human promise of their work.[1] Such men and women, Mills saw, persistently ask three sorts of questions:

1. *"What is the structure of this particular society as a whole?"*
   This is the sort of question we have identified in the Beats, and in recent radicalism, a questioning of the organizational, institutional, and cultural processes of society and of the ways they relate to one another.

---

[1] C. Wright Mills, *The Sociological Imagination* (New York: Oxford University Press, 1959).

2. *"Where does this society stand in human history?"* What are its forces of change and stability? How do they relate to one another? How does our society relate to the historical period in which it is moving? How does this period differ from other periods; what are its essential features? Why this special character; why here, why now—why not that, why not there, why not then?

3. *"What varieties of men and women now prevail in this society and in this period?* And what varieties are coming to prevail? In what ways are they selected and formed, liberated and repressed, made sensitive and blunted?"[2]

Mills has thus raised three great questions of structure, history, and personality. To answer them requires the use of a sociological imagination able to see wholes when only pieces appear, the meaning of little acts for big events and processes, and the force of social structure upon the individual. . . . The sociological imagination is not some esoteric or secret weapon to be used only by properly initiated members of a profession. With determination and a persistent style of work, student or layman can address themselves to these questions, and in the process develop the sociological imagination.

C. H. Anderson, *Toward a New
Sociology: A Critical View*

Moving back and forth through these questions, Mills wrote, your capacity for astonishment grows lively. You discover that ideas and decisions that once seemed sound now seem shallow. You realize that you are living in a world of relativity; you realize, too, that history and society have a transforming power that seems beyond your influence. But you also realize that you are part of that society, a part of that history.

You realize, then, that the question is not whether or not you will be involved in the society and era you live in. "No one," Mills urged, "is 'outside society'; the question is where each

[2] *Ibid.*

stands within it."[3] As you come to live this recognition, it is as if you awaken in a house you have been sleepwalking in.

Pursuing the question, you grow critical of your surrounds and of your relationships and those of others. You become a social critic; the criticism increases your awareness, and as awareness grows new questions, new possibilities arise. Thus the critic turns explorer.

But the explorer must also remain a critic.

SOCIAL CRITICISM SEEKS to identify those values, ideas, and social forms that should be, even must be, changed in the name of self-and-other involvement. Social exploration extends the effort, seeking the possibilities, limitations, and probabilities of human life. Thus, there is a creative interplay between criticism and exploration, in which human possibilities are the locus. It is an interplay of uncovery and discovery; an uncovery of contradictions and deficiencies in our society and our lives, a discovery of what is likely to happen, what is unlikely, what is possible, what probably can be done and what cannot.

In this interplay of criticism and exploration, the meanings of history grow personally vivid. So, too, do the comparative studies of other societies and of the histories of other societies. We have already seen the basic reason why this is so: we grow self-aware as we see ourselves through the eyes of others. We learn to recognize our possibilities by relating and comparing our capabilities and conditions with those of others.

In the same way, the imperfections and the possibilities of our society can be more clearly recognized by contrasting it with its earlier forms and by comparing its history and its present conditions with those of other societies, in other conditions.

Here, the interplay of exploration and criticism with self-and-other involvement is seen more fully. For when we forget our origins we lose a part of ourselves. Yet, as we grow in self-and-other awareness, our remembrance and understanding of

[3] *Ibid.,* pp. 174–175.

our origins change. Seeing ourselves through the eyes of diverse others, seeing the possibilities and conditions of our lives, we come to better recognize the meanings of our own individual history.

We come to recognize that the biography of our own life cannot be understood until the many relationships it involves are understood, until the economic and social conditions in which we grew are fathomed. Growing aware of the lives and biographies of others, we come to recognize that they, too, cannot be understood apart from the various surrounds they have lived and grown in; we come to realize that those surrounds cannot be understood apart from larger, societal conditions.

Recognizing this, we come to realize that other men and women who have lived in other historical times—such as Ben Franklin, or the Wobblies, or the ancient Israelites, or even the Beats and the campus radicals of the sixties—cannot be understood apart from the groups and societies that they lived in. As we learn to recognize this, we may discover another compelling thing: that when the lives of men and women in other times are understood, they return the effort. Seeing ourselves "through their eyes," we see ourselves-and-others more clearly.

THUS CRITICAL SOCIOLOGY IS intensely personal and humanistic; the questions of critical sociology, finally, turn on their meanings for individual human life. This points to an unavoidable assumption: that an individual is capable of thinking, choosing, and acting, to some degree independently of his social and ecological surround and to some degree independently of his bodily demands.

The assumption goes even further: Critical sociology asserts that our reason—at least to some degree, under some conditions—can influence our intentions; that our intentions can influence our choice of acts; that our actions can influence our relationships to others and perhaps even influence our society.

Still, there is also a recognition in critical sociology that the individual, to a large and varying degree, is not free, that often our actions have little influence on others, that we can be unable to creatively determine our goals, that we can be unaware. For human "purposes" are often blind. Just as it is inadequate to embrace images of the individual and society that do not allow for the play of human purpose, so it would be inadequate to assume that conscious purpose is always the fundamental determinant of human and social life.

Freudians are not alone in suggesting the inadequacy of a sociology based only on "intention" or purpose. Conceptions of the "unconscious" are joined by emerging concerns for "extrasensory perception," parapsychology, and the transcendental experience of Eastern religions. Possibilities that ten years ago appeared ridiculous to most sociologists and psychologists are today open to consideration. At the very least, it is difficult to avoid the evidence that some individuals often act in ways beyond our rigid and limited ideas of what "rationality" is—indeed, that all of us may be influenced in our behavior at least to some degree by our "intuitions," "peak experiences," even by mystical awareness or transcendent consciousness.

Physiology offers further evidence on the inadequacy of a sociology based only on rational purpose. Research in recent years has emphasized the importance of chemical balances and imbalances, suggesting that "experience" may be strikingly different from person to person. This is not to belittle the effects of perceptions, memories, anticipations, and definitions on human actions. It is to emphasize, however, that sociological questions are closely interlinked not only with the questions of psychology but also with those of biochemistry.

So, too, perspectives on social structures and processes suggest that more than rationality must be considered. We have seen this awareness in Marx and Weber. Over a half-century ago, Robert Park proposed that sociologists look at two types of organization. One is those that are more or less "intentional" creations: a social class, family groups, or corporate bureaucracies, for example. The other type is the "ecological organization," based on a kind of competitive cooperation, a "symbiosis" that links humans together in impersonal, unintended patterns, that cannot be explained by any rules or rational purposes.[4]

It may be, as Harvey Wheeler argues, that as we become increasingly aware of ecological, psychological, and biological influences, we are entering a "new age of reason." [5] Even if this is so, we should take a lesson from the "old" age of reason: "Enlightenment" alone will not take us to a glorious future. We must allow for another possibility: Just as individuals are capable of acting with responsible intention, they are also capable of blind ignorance, of selfishness, of indifference.

This means that critical sociology cannot promise potence. Critical sociology itself teaches that knowledge alone does not bring change; that at most it influences attitudes, ideals, and intentions in ways that may eventually help create the conditions that are necessary for change. Thus, critical sociology at its best offers not a promising route to salvation, but a hopeful search for human possibilities.

From Criticism and Exploration to Involvement

A message of profound importance plays through all of this: finally, all sociological understanding is also self-understanding. This means, among many other things, that the critical sociologist is part of what he or she is studying. Critical sociologists, then, must also turn their critical gaze upon themselves. They must search for the limitations in their perspectives, they must attempt to identify possibilities they have missed, in the arena they are exploring and in themselves.

[4] Robert E. Park, "The City: Suggestions for the Investigation of Human Behavior in the Urban Environment," *American Journal of Sociology* (1916), pp. 577–612. See also Warren Peterson and George K. Zollschan, "Social Processes in the Metropolitan Community," in Arnold Rose, ed., *Human Behavior and Social Process* (Boston: Houghton Mifflin, 1962).

[5] Harvey Wheeler, *The Politics of Revolution* (Berkeley: Glendessary Press, 1970).

To be a critical sociologist, then, is to be continually concerned not only with your own potentials and actions but also with your own biases, blindnesses, and deficiencies. It is not only that these will limit your search. Certainly they will, which is reason enough for concern. But there is another possibility as well: As you grow aware of your own errors and limitations, you may come to better recognize the society you live in. For even our shortcomings are usually not ours alone but are linked to the biases, blindnesses, and deficiencies of our society and our historical times.

In knowing conceived as awareness, the concern is not with "discovering" the truth about a social world regarded as external to the knower, but with seeing truth as growing out of the knower's encounter with the world and his effort to order his experience with it. . . .

To know others he cannot simply study *them*, but must also listen to and confront *himself*. . . . In the last analysis, if a man wants to change what he knows he must change how he lives; he must change his *praxis* in the world.

Alvin Gouldner, *The Coming
Crisis of Western Sociology*

The invitation to critical sociology, then, is not an invitation to embrace a particular theory of the individual and society. More accurately, it is an invitation to an attitude. It is characterized not by explanations and conclusions; it is characterized, instead, by efforts to ask questions—irreverent, explorative questions that interplay with your own self-and-other involvement.

To be sure, the questions are not ends in themselves. The critical sociologist does try to describe and explain, but always tentatively, always with knowledge that the statement is inadequate, perhaps even that it will prove false in the light of greater knowledge. For the answers that we pose, the propositions and explanations that we tentatively offer, give rise to new questions. Those questions lead us on, and as they do the answers we have struggled to gain are challenged by new propositions that lead in turn to further question and search.

BUT THERE IS a limit to all of this. The reason is by now familiar: Critical sociology is rooted in an emerging self-and-other involvement. Each new question and each new insight upsets the coherence of what we previously knew, not only about the world we live in, but also about ourselves. With each new awareness, then, we must pause to find a new coherence. This takes time and emotional effort, and each person does it his own way.

This means that critical sociology cannot, in fact, be "taught" to someone else. We can provide the occasions for other persons to discover; we can provide examples to excite their appetites for exploration. We can support them, encourage their efforts, and challenge their arguments. But we cannot lead another person to new self-and-other awareness, for this must be gained in one's own private realms that are largely unknown to outsiders. We can only urge explorers on somewhat, encouraging them to ask "Why?" and cheering their efforts.

The invitation to critical sociology, then, is not easy to accept. Each of us, at any point in our lives, can take only so much novelty and uncertainty. We can expend only so much energy and endure only so much of the anxiety that critical sociology involves. At times—as even Weber discovered—any effort may be too much. But at other times, under some conditions, we may be able to endure a struggle that once seemed impossible.

Definitions of Selected Terms

Alienation: An ambiguous concept that refers to the inability to feel one's self a "whole" person. Marx (Chapter Five) saw alienation arising from the threefold interaction (see "dialectic") of the individual, nature, and industry. In the modern world, this dialectic encourages actions that are not in "good faith" (see definition), thereby separating individuals from the objects of their production, from their labors, from their own needs, and from other persons.

Anti-culture: A "subculture" (see definition) that achieves its internal coherence and sense of unity in its opposition to the meanings and values of the dominant, surrounding "culture" (see definition).

Authority: The ability to influence another person or group, without necessarily having the physical power to enforce compliance. Weber (Chapter Ten) traced the roots of authority to tradition, to rational law, and to "charisma" (see definition).

Bad faith, acting in: Action that fails to express the individual's own will and subjective life, and is thereby "alienating" (see preceding and also "good faith" and "praxis").

Capitalism: An economic theory in which economic production and distribution are based on private ownership, individual profit, and competition. By contrast, in mercantilism, a politico-economic theory that preceded capitalism in Europe and America, the distribution and imports of business are carefully controlled by governments; in socialism both production and distribution are functions of the state, wielded in the interests of all the people.

Caste: A grouping of people, whose ways of life differ from other groupings, and from whom they may differ in appearance (in biology, dress, and so on). Castes differ in status, prestige, and power, and movement from one caste to another is virtually impossible. Caste structures are enforced by taboo, marriage sanction, and occupational segregation.

Charisma: A special quality of leadership, based in the attribution of exceptional powers to the leader, who is able to link the emotional unrests and energies of others to goals that are meaningful to them.

Class, social: An abstraction referring to aggregates of individuals in similar economic positions, having similar ways of life and similar opportunities and life chances. Note that classes are not "groups" (see definition); members of a class may or may not be aware of their shared situations or class interests. (See also "group, status-interest.")

Community: A "group" (see definition) living in a given area, marked by a feeling of common identity and unique social and cultural meanings and values.

Conflict, social: Rivalry or opposition between individuals or groups, each seeking to gain or protect valued objects, territories, ways of life, prestige, or power; thus conflict may involve religious or idealistic conceptions, as well as more materialistic matters.

Control, social: The processes in which a group coerces, constrains, influences, and/or directs the behavior of its members.

Culture: The meanings and values held in common by the persons in a group or community; in this book, analytically distinguished from "institution" and "organization" (see definitions), even though the three terms refer to qualities of the same, indivisible whole.

Dialectic: In Hegel, the creative interplay of ideas: a thesis is met with an antithesis and the tension between the two gives way to a synthesis, which both contains the thesis and antithesis and transcends them. Marx and Mead both turned Hegel's dialectic to the relations of consciousness and society.

Enlightenment: An eighteenth-century movement toward rationalism, skepticism, and empiricism.

Ethical irrationality: Weber's term (Chapter Ten) for the irreconcilable conflict of values between even rational persons who do not agree on absolutes.

Existentialism: A broad philosophical movement that addresses Marx's riddle of history (Chapter Five): the divorce between thought and action, being and consciousness, existence and essence. Existentialists, in general, share Marx's conclusion: the divorce is a false one; humans must act in "good faith" to their own subjective lives, which cannot be separated from so-called objective facts of life. (See "praxis.")

Extrasensory perception (*ESP*): Awareness or experience received by other than those senses normally accepted as valid perceptors, i.e., other than sight, smell, hearing, and touch.

Feudalism: An economic-political-social system in the Middle Ages, in which serfs worked land owned by vassals, who in turn payed allegiance to and provided military service to an overlord.

Generalized others: Mead's concept (Chapter Two) of the individual's abstract conception of the organized attitudes and expectations of others. There is no single generalized other; an individual may conceive of and act with reference to many generalized others, as well as many specific significant others.

Good faith, acting in: Sartre's concept (Chapter Five) of action that is a specific expression of one's will and subjectivity; i.e., "true praxis" (see definition).

Group, social: A number of persons who share meanings and/or values that other persons do not share, and who are to some degree aware of their commonalities.

Group, status-interest: In Weber's usage (Chapter Ten), a "group" (see preceding) that is to some degree aware not only of shared meanings and values, but also of shared situations or shared self-interests in matters of wealth, prestige, power, and/or valued ways of life.

I: Mead's concept (Chapter Two) of that aspect of the self identified with impulse, creativity and freedom, expressed in the individual's response to the attitudes of others. (See "me.")

Ideal type: Weber's methodology for attempting to verify the subjective interpretations gained through "verstehen" (see definition). Ideal types are constructed through: (1) careful observations of acts and their apparent goals; (2) construction of *tentative* typologies to *orient* (not determine) comparison of social actions, relationships and structures in various places and times. Through the interplay of verstehen, type construction, and interpretive-comparative inquiry, Weber was able to generalize, yet maintain a focus on conscious, intentional behavior in both individual and institutional forms.

Ideology: Generally accepted ideas and beliefs that are harmoniously integrated into extant world views, serving to make the existing order, including its injustices and inequalities, appear reasonable. (See "utopia.")

Institution, central: A "social institution" (see definition) that strongly influences or controls behavior related to other institutions of a society, usually in interaction with other central institutions; from another perspective, an institution organized around the most powerful values of the social order (see definition). In contemporary America, for example, the political and economic institutions are clearly "central." (See related terms, following.)

Institution, peripheral: A "social institution" (see definition) that has little influence on the "central institutions" (see preceding) of a society. In contemporary America, for example, religion appears to be becoming increasingly "peripheral."

Institution, secondary: A "social institution" (see following definition) that has some influence on the "central institutions" (see preceding) of a society, and/or on which the central institutions are to some degree dependent. In contemporary America, for example, the family and education appear to be secondary institutions, though the family may be "moving" toward the peripheral and education toward the central.

Institution, social: Complex arrays of shared expectations for behavior, that emerge in the self-involved struggles, negotiations, and accommodations of interacting individuals and groups; essentially meanings, values, and goals that overlap from person to person with adequate compatability to provide a relatively coherent "blueprint" for individual, group, and societal activity. Thus sociologists speak, analytically, of institutions of the family, political institutions, economic institutions, religious institutions, and so on. In the term "institution," then, emphasis is on patterns of *expectations;* in "culture" it is on patterns of *meanings and values;* in "organizations" it is on patterns of *activity*. It should be noted that sociologists differ markedly on their usage of all three terms.

Me: Mead's concept (Chapter Two) of the conventional, habitual aspect of the self; the organized set of attitudes of others the individual assumes to be his or her own attitudes. (See "I.")

Order, social: The complete array of persisting patterns of interaction, expectations, meanings, and values in a community or society. (See "culture," "institution," and "organization," which emphasize various qualities of social order.)

Organization, social: Arrays of patterned interactions of two or more individuals or groups, usually characterized by role differentiation and structures of authority. Analytically distinguished from "culture" and "institution" (see definitions).

Paradox of consequences: Weber's concept (Chapter Ten) derived from observing that the consequences of intentional actions may be not only unintended, but also unexpected and even contradictory to the goals that were sought. This paradox, Weber believed, deeply challenged not only social inquiry, but human society.

Parapsychology: The study of supposedly "supernatural" phenomena, such as extrasensory perception (see preceding), telepathy, peak experiences, mind-reading, clairvoyance, futuristic visions, and so on.

Praxis (roughly, "human practice"): Subjectively meaningful action of the individual in response to his or her surrounds (Marx's term); akin to Weber's concept of "social action."

Rationality: In Weber's usage (Chapter Eight), the choice of actions or selection of means that are appropriate to desired or designated ends. (See "functional rationality" and "substantive rationality.")

Rationality, functional: The choice of actions or selection of means that are appropriate to the goals of an organization and/or determined by the abstract rules or goals of an organization. (See "substantive rationality.")

Rationality, substantive: The choice of actions or selection of means that are appropriate to an individual's, or interacting individuals' own goals or needs; akin to "praxis" (see definition and see also "functional rationality").

Relativity of human experience: The idea that there can be no certainty of "reality," since each individual's consciousness is a unique and continually reorganizing assemblage of perceptions, memories, intuitions, ideas, and extrasensory awareness that cluster and merge with little regard for time and place.

Revolution: Generally, an overthrow of a government or form of government or social order. In Marx's usage (Chapter Seven), a mutation of a society in its very centers; thus revolution is evolutionary and may or may not be marked by violent overthrow or violent conflict.

Role, social: A set of expectations for the behavior of an individual in a given group and situation.

Role of the other, taking: Mead's term (Chapter Two) for the process of recognizing how other individuals define the situations they are in, the expectations they believe constrain and direct them, and the opportunities they see open to them. (See "verstehen.")

Socialization: A process in which the individual comes to adopt the general attitudes, meanings, and values of his parent or chosen "culture" (see definition) or "subculture" (see definition). The process is neither fully conscious or intended by the individual or by the parent or other agent of socialization, but emerges in a complex "dialectic" (see definition) of mind, self, and society (Mead, Chapter Two).

Society, functional: Mead's concept of an intentional, humanistic community of perfected social intelligence, in which each individual is able to "take the roles" (see definition) of all other individuals who perform the many varied roles or functions of the community.

Stratification, social: The processes of hierarchical division of a society, especially along lines of wealth, prestige, and power.

Subculture: A subgroup in a society sharing distinctive meanings and values that differ to some important degree from the meanings and values held by other groups in the society. (See "culture" and "anticulture.")

Symbolic interaction: In Mead's usage (Chapter Two) the presentation of gestures and the responses to the meaning of the gestures. The term is also used as a label, applied by Herbert Blumer, for a sociological perspective that emphasizes the centrality of meaning in social processes and organization.

Technology of institutions: The application of "functional rationality" (see definition) to rules, regulations, and social roles (see definition) involving *transactions* of organizations with one another. (See related terms, immediately following.)

Technology of management: The application of "functional rationality" (see preceding) to rules, regulations, and social roles (see preceding) *vertically* in an organization, with special concern for organizational coordination and control. (See related terms, immediately preceding and following.)

Technology of technicians: The application of "functional rationality" (see preceding) to rules, regulations, and social roles (see preceding) *horizontally* in an organization; characterized by specialization, a rational arrangement of roles that are not interchangeable. (See related terms, immediately preceding.)

Utopia: Generally, a vision of an ideal or perfect society. As used by Mannheim (Chapter Six), "ideologies" (see preceding) become utopian when the visions of improvement are embodied in action.

Verstehen: Weber's methodology of sympathetic empathy, an effort to understand another's behavior by, essentially, "taking the role of the other" (Mead's concept, see preceding). By itself, however, the method of verstehen is inadequate, as meaningful behavior blurs off into unmeaningful, and as actions give rise to the "paradox of consequences" (see preceding). To cope with these problems, Weber developed his method of "ideal types" (see preceding).

Bibliography of Major Quotations

The quotations that are included in this bibliography were selected to provide a listing of further readings, as well as to illustrate the themes of the text. The date following the author's name indicates year of first publication; date of present edition, if different, follows publisher's name.

Anderson, C. H. *Toward a New Sociology: A Critical View*. Homewood, Ill.: Dorsey, 1971, pp. 348–349.

Barber, Richard J. 1970. *The American Corporation: Its Power, Its Money, Its Politics*. New York: Dutton, p. 98.

Bateson, Gregory. 1968. "Conscious Purpose versus Nature." In David Cooper, ed., *To Free a Generation*. New York: Collier, pp. 44–46.

Bell, Daniel. 1973. *The Coming of Post-Industrial Society*. New York: Basic Books, pp. 366–367.

Bendix, Reinhard. 1960. *Max Weber: An Intellectual Portrait*. Garden City: Doubleday, p. 273.

Berger, Peter. 1963. *Invitation to Sociology*. Garden City: Anchor, p. 21, p. 176.

Birnbaum, Norman. *Toward a Critical Sociology*. New York: Oxford, 1971, p. 205.

Boulding, Kenneth E. 1964. "The Place of the Image in the Dynamics of Society." In George K. Zollschan and Walter Hirsch, eds., *Explorations in Social Change*. Boston: Houghton Mifflin, 1964, p. 16.

COSER, LEWIS A. 1967. *Continuities in the Study of Social Conflict.* New York: The Free Press, pp. 109–110.

COSER, LEWIS A. 1971. *Masters of Sociological Thought.* New York: Harcourt, Brace, Jovanovich, p. 347.

DUNCAN, HUGH DALZIEL. 1962. *Communication and Social Order.* New York: Aldine, p. 90.

EISENSTADT, S. N. 1968. *Max Weber: On Charisma and Institution Building.* Chicago: University of Chicago, pp. xlvii–xlix.

FREUND, JULIEN. 1968. *The Sociology of Max Weber.* New York: Pantheon, p. 27.

FROMM, ERICH. 1962. *Beyond the Chains of Illusion.* New York: Simon & Schuster, p. 113.

GALBRAITH, JOHN KENNETH. 1967. *The New Industrial State.* Boston: Houghton-Mifflin, pp. 20–21.

GERTH, HANS, and MILLS, C. WRIGHT. 1958. *From Max Weber: Essays in Sociology.* New York: Oxford, p. 73.

GOMBERG, WILLIAM. 1970. "The Trouble with Democratic Management." In Warren G. Bennis, ed., *American Bureaucracy.* Chicago: Aldine, pp. 44–45.

GOODMAN, PAUL. 1970. *New Reformation: Notes of a Neolithic Conservative.* New York: Random House, p. 164.

GOULDNER, ALVIN. 1970. *The Coming Crisis of Western Sociology.* New York: Basic Books, p. 493.

HARRINGTON, MICHAEL. 1965. *The Accidental Century.* New York: Penguin, p. 145.

HOROWITZ, DAVID. 1971. *Radical Sociology, An Introduction.* San Francisco: Canfield, p. 9.

HOWTON, F. WILLIAM. 1969. *Functionaries.* Chicago: Quadrangle, pp. 146–147.

HUGHES, H. STUART. 1958. *Consciousness and Society.* New York: Vintage, p. 290.

LAING, R. D. 1967. *The Politics of Experience.* New York: Ballantine, pp. 54–55.

LASCH, CHRISTOPHER. 1965. *The New Radicalism in America: 1889–1963.* New York: Knopf, pp. 145–146.

LEWIS, JOHN. 1965. *The Life and Teaching of Karl Marx.* New York: International, p. 10.

LORWIN, LEWIS. 1933. *The American Federation of Labor*. Washington, D.C.: The Brookings Institution, p. 355.

MANNHEIM, KARL. 1929. *Ideology and Utopia*. London: Routledge and Kegan Paul, p. 173.

MARTINDALE, DON. 1964. "Community Formation and Destruction." In G. Zollschan and Walter Hirsch, eds., *Explorations in Social Change*. Boston: Houghton Mifflin, p. 86.

MARX, KARL. 1867. *Capital*. Vol. I. New York: International, 1967, p. 645.

MARX, KARL. 1853. *Enthullungen über den Kommunisten-prozess zu Köln* (Basel and Boston). Cited in Henri Lefebvre, *The Sociology of Marx*, translated by Norbert Guterman. New York: Pantheon, 1968, p. 160.

MEAD, GEORGE HERBERT. 1924. "The Genesis of Self and Social Control." Reprinted in Andrew Reck, *Mead: Selected Writings*. Indianapolis: Bobbs-Merrill, 1964, p. 280.

MEAD, GEORGE HERBERT. 1936. *Movements of Thought in the Nineteenth Century*. Chicago: University of Chicago Press, pp. 182–183, pp. 361–362.

MEAD, GEORGE HERBERT. 1929. "National Mindedness and International Mindedness." Reprinted in Andrew Reck, *Mead: Selected Writings*. Indianapolis: Bobbs-Merrill, 1964, p. 360, pp. 364–365.

MEAD, GEORGE HERBERT. 1932. *Philosophy of the Present*. Chicago: University of Chicago Press, p. 89.

MEAD, GEORGE HERBERT. 1917. "The Psychology of Punitive Justice." *American Journal of Sociology* (1917–1918), p. 578.

MELMAN, SEYMOUR. 1970. *Pentagon Capitalism: The Political Economy of War*. New York: McGraw-Hill, p. 227.

MERLEAU-PONTY, MAURICE. 1964. *Sense and Non-sense*. Evanston: Northwestern University Press, p. 45.

MESZAROS, ISTVAN. 1972. *Marx's Theory of Alienation*. New York: Harper & Row, pp. 103–104.

MICHELS, ROBERT. 1915. *Political Parties: A Sociological Study of Oligarchical Tendencies of Modern Democracy*. New York: Dover, 1959, pp. 372–373.

MILLS, C. WRIGHT. 1959. *The Sociological Imagination*. New York: Oxford, pp. 174–175.

MILLS, C. WRIGHT. 1951. *White Collar: The American Middle Classes.* New York: Oxford, p. 215.

MOUZELIS, NICOS P. 1969. *Organisation and Bureaucracy.* Chicago: Aldine, pp. 33–34.

ORWELL, GEORGE. 1948. *1984.* New York: Anchor, p. 62.

PFUETZ, PAUL E. 1954. *The Social Self.* New York: Bookman, p. 91.

PIRANDELLO, LUIGI. 1919. "The Rules of the Game." In *To Clothe the Naked.* New York: Dutton, 1962, p. 92 (Originally titled "The Game of Roles.").

POLANYI, MICHAEL. 1964. *Personal Knowledge: Towards a Post-Critical Philosophy.* New York: Harper, p. 236, pp. 64–65.

POWELL, ELWIN H. 1962. "Beyond Utopia." In Arnold Rose, *Human Behavior and Social Interaction.* Boston: Houghton Mifflin, p. 372.

PRESCOTT, PETER. 1973. *A Darkening Green: Notes from the Silent Generation.* New York: Coward, McCarn & Geoghegam, p. 169.

ROSE, ARNOLD. 1954. *Theory and Method in the Social Sciences.* Minneapolis: University of Minnesota, p. 23.

ROSENBERG, BERNARD, and FLIEGEL, NORRIS. 1965. *The Vanguard Artist.* Chicago: Quadrangle, p. 30.

RUSTIN, BAYARD. 1966. "The Watts 'Manifesto' and the McCone Report." *Commentary*, p. 30.

SCRANTON, WILLIAM, et al. 1970. *The Report of the President's Commission on Campus Unrest.* Washington, D.C.: Government Printing Office, pp. 71–73.

SHAW, GEORGE BERNARD. 1889. Reprinted in R. W. Ellis, *Bernard Shaw and Karl Marx: A Symposium.* New York: Random House, 1930, pp. 109–110.

SHIBUTANI, TAMOTSU. 1961. *Society and Personality.* Englewood Cliffs: Prentice-Hall, p. 90.

TAWNEY, R. H. 1930. "Foreword" to Max Weber, *The Protestant Ethic and the Spirit of Capitalism.* Translated by Talcott Parsons. New York: Scribner's, 1958, p. 1 (c).

WEBER, MAX. 1917–1919. *Ancient Judaism.* New York: The Free Press, 1952, p. 207.

WEBER, MAX. 1904–1905. *The Protestant Ethic and the Spirit of Capitalism.* New York: Scribner's, 1958, p. 182.

Name Index

Subject Index